TRENDS IN HIGHER EDUCATION

Editor
Prof. Ramesh Chandra

Publications
KALPAZ PUBLICATIONS
DELHI-110052

TRENDS IN HIGHER EDUCATION

Trends in Higher Education

Rs. 890

ISBN: 81-7835-237-0

This book is Vol. No. 9 of Universal Education and Technology in 21st Century (Set)

Published in 2005 in India by
Kalpaz Publications,
C-30, Satyawati Nagar, Delhi-110052
E-mail : Kalpaz@hotmail.com

Laser Typesetting at : Master Computers, Delhi
Printed at : Ajit Printers, Delhi

Contents

Preface

Higher education has immense potential to contribute to the consolidation of democracy and social justice, and the growth and development of the economy. The enhancement of democracy lays the basis for greater participation in economic and social life. Higher levels of employment and work contribute to political and social stability and the capacity of citizens to exercise and enforce democratic rights and participate effectively in decision-making. The overall well-being of nations is vitally dependent on the contribution of higher education to the social, cultural, political, and economic development of its citizens.

Higher education must help erode the inherited socially structural inequities and provide opportunities for social advancement through equity of access and opportunity. It must produce, through research, teaching and learning and community service programmes, the knowledge and personpower for national reconstruction and economic and social development to enable countries to engage proactively with and participate in a highly competitive global economy. The problems and weaknesses of the higher education system are extensive and varied. They will not disappear on their own or be overcome by institutions on their own. They must be confronted at a national level and addressed with vigour. This will require extensive, integrated, iterative national planning as well as multiple co-ordinated interventions and initiatives. The proposals will, however, provide a more rational, focused, effective and efficient framework and basis for overcoming the problems over a period of time.

Although the costs of higher education are relatively higher than that of school or other levels of education, continued expenditure in higher education is important. Schooling and other levels of education cannot produce the kinds of knowledge or the highly skilled professionals that are necessary for successful entry into the arena of globalisation.

This book discusses the effects of new technologies in the system of higher education. It also highlights the major problems and weaknesses of the present system and indicates the principal outcomes that must be achieved through the reconfiguration of the higher education system.

Editor

1

Open Learning in Higher Education

Traditionally, the system of higher education has been largely course-based, and as a result most educational activities have centred on the course. However, the past decades, has seen the introduction of a number of educational initiatives designed to enhance the accessibility and flexibility of higher education, bringing with them a number of significant benefits for both students and employers. For many students, traditional and methods of teaching raise enormous difficulties. Taken together, the above developments lead to an increase in accessibility an flexibility. They open up higher education opportunities to a wider section of society including part-time and mature students, and remove many of the barriers of inflexible structures previously encountered by many students. As a corollary, increasing numbers of institutions are realizing the need to explore new approaches to teaching and learning, and are beginning to explore how open learning materials might be incorporated into new and existing modules to enhance the flexibility.

The educational philosophy behind open learning is entirely in accordance with a number of educational practices which many higher education lecturers would wish to support. The open learning approach, brings together sound educational principles and an organizational framework which is practical and suited to the needs of our times. Its success depends on the provision of effective learning materials which have been specifically designed to enable students to take responsibility for their learning. It is characterized by the flexibility, adaptability and responsiveness of organizational structures and not least by the reduced reliance on teacher availability at specific times and places. In all these respects, open learning provides a significant alternative to conventionally taught courses within traditional higher education structures. Within a programme that uses open learning materials, there can, of course, be substantial differences in the amount of openness and control offered to students. At one extreme, students may, with guidance, be allowed to make important decisions about many aspects of their learning, including: what to study; how to study; where to study; when to study, etc. In addition, students may be involved in decisions such as the kind and amount of support needed and who might provide it and whether the learning will be assessed and, if it is, how it will be assessed and when. At the other extreme, lecturers may wish to exert far more control over the learning process, determining what is studied, broadly when it is studied, and how and when learning will be assessed.

However, even when such parameters are defined at the outset, the use of learning materials which encourage active learner involvement and which can be studied away from an educational establishment may still allow students greater flexibility and control over learning than is usually possible in conventionally taught courses offered within traditional educational structures. Finally, the middle course between teacher control and student autonomy is readily achieved by the inherent flexibility of an approach in which open learning is given a significant role.

At present, despite the success of local schemes, the use of open learning still appears to be somewhat marginal. It is largely confined to areas where access to conventional education provision is problematic, or where a student population tends to be scattered over a fairly wide geographical area. Confusion is still exististing in the terms we use to describe the situation in which students are seen as active agents in their own learning. Four phrases which hit the ears regularly, and which are frequently used in a way which suggests an easy interchangeability, are 'independent learning', 'distance learning', 'open learning' and 'flexible learning'. Independent learning simply implies that the learning can be done largely by learners on their own, in any way that fits their own personal style. Thus, any book is a vehicle for independent learning and all students study independently for projects, working in libraries or workshops and frequently setting their own agendas. This sort of independent learning is a widespread phenomenon and has been a feature of 'real education' ever since individuals began to study, research and seek to understand on their own account. It is at the heart of learning, for, in the final analysis, all education is self-education. Consequently, whatever educational structures we set up, this sort of learning is bound to go on spontaneously and productively. In the other hand, it is perfectly possible for colleges, schools and other educational establishments to build on what comes naturally, and enhance the independent learning capacities of their students.

A systematic distance learning appeared on the scene a long time ago. At first, it consisted simply of correspondence between experts and their distant admirers as acts of friendship. Then, as the efficacy of the approach was realized, it developed more normally into a relationship between a tutor and a student. Many teachers enhancing their qualifications forty years ago will remember presenting themselves at the examination rooms of the University of London, clasping their distinctively coloured Wolsey Hall course notes to their bosoms. Since then, Woisey Hall has identified more lucrative markets, and distance learning has achieved its greatest expansion ever through the development in the early 1970s of the Open University. This massive investment of public resources moved distance learning into a new era of sophistication, using tutor support and multimedia approaches like radio, television and interactive computer programs. It tackled several problems which had long bedevilled higher education. Britain's female population, discriminated against for generations, represented an untapped pooi of talent.

With the advent of the open university, the opportunity was opened up for women of all ages to engage in university study. This could be done conveniently at a distance, with support and in a way which made it possible to overcome financial constraints, and match the demands of academic work with other family and occupational responsibilities. However, the open university—in order to remain credible and maintain the structure necessary to accomplish its mission—was forced to erect some barriers to access. In particular, courses generated at Level Two and above had to operate at a level which was demonstrably equivalent to what other universities were providing. Consequently, some of the possible concessions which might have helped students could have been interpreted as intellectual dilution, and had to be avoided. Despite this, the message of 'openness' was taken on with enthusiasm, and the notion of more comprehensive, adventurous and welcoming educational programmes was pursued with vigour. By the mid-1970s, the use of the term 'open learning' was beginning to emerge. Open learning was concerned with equal opportunity, and preached the message that whatever training and education individuals required and wished for should be accessible to them. In other words, education should be designed to match more closely the aspirations of learners. Education was to become 'learner-centred'.

Open learning came to imply any situation in which all those features and characteristics of learning programmes and systems which reduce opportunity and access are identified and modified to avoid closure. Adopting the flexible and open approach to teaching and learning can offer real rewards to any college brave enough to install the necessary management and develop or buy in the support required. Open learning and flexible learning, by eliminating barriers to access and applying the principles of open learning provision, can:

— extend the geographical reach of courses in terms of the hinterland for recruitment

— increase the penetration and take-up rates within the local market area

— ensure higher success and retention rates among students once enrolled

— maximize the use of existing physical and human resources

— enable tutors to handle more students without appreciably increasing their workload

— improve the quality of the student learning experience, and thereby the reputation of the providing institution

— enrich and enhance the nature of the tutor's job through variation, open procedures and more creative approaches to assessment.

However, there are certainly problems to overcome. Institutions consist of an uncomfortable truce between people and structures. Those who already occupy powerful or personally satisfying roles within the existing structure will undoubtedly wish to preserve the status quo. Radical change always tends to increase workload before it eventually rationalizes and controls it. Individuals at all levels are made uncertain as time honoured skills and procedures are called into question. In addition, even those who support the changes know that it is always the new departures which receive the sharpest critical analysis, and they worry about the consequences of failure.

Many teachers in higher education fear that the new methodologies being advanced will replace them and make them redundant. Such doubts and reservations cannot be ignored. It is a fact that relatively few manage to set then sights on the beneficial consequences of a shift towards more open approaches a different kind of job, more rewarding, more creative and more supportive of students. Open learning is designed to improve the quality of learning and access to it, not to dehumanize it or to shake out dedicated staff.

The continuing move for providers of higher education to widen access faces teachers with the challenge of meeting the learning needs of increasingly large, heterogeneous groups of students who may also be at different starting points in terms of background knowledge, needs and academic ability. The use of learning materials can help cope with larger student numbers while still maintaining the quality of educational provision. Since teacher contact time tends to be a relatively small proportion of total study hours, the use of open learning materials to cover much of the core 'information giving' can free lecturers from that role, enabling them to focus more on facilitating the learning process and providing guidance and support to individual students and small groups of students.

In this way, available contact time may be used to ensure that individual learning needs are met, and to focus on learning activities that cannot be achieved by materials-based learning. Indeed, by combining the advantages of materials-based learning and face-to-face contact in mixed-mode modules/programmes, it is possible to capitalize on the advantages of each. Published learning materials have usually been written by experts in their field, and during the developmental process are reviewed by further subject experts and groups of students who work through the materials, providing detailed feedback regarding their relevance an usefulness from a user's perspective. With such systems in place to ensure quality, a programme that incorporates effective learning materials may offer better experience than an equivalent taught course, particularly when teacher contact hours are limited.

If one is prepared to accept these arguments, the use of such learning materials can save education institutions considerable development and course planning time, although any learning materials that are used do, of course, need to be fully and carefully integrated into the overall educational philosophy and structure of the programme in which they are used. Meanwhile, the shift of emphasis for the lecturer from primarily a teaching/ lecturing role to one of facilitating learning can be enormously rewarding, reminding one perhaps of halcyon days when considerable periods of time were spent with students on an individual basis or in small groups. In addition to the use of open learning materials to meet the needs of large numbers of students. open learning can also enable lecturers to offer options to small groups that might otherwise not be regarded as economically viable when face-to-face teaching costs are calculated. There is also evidence, which may surprise some educationalists, suggesting that open learning materials can provide an effective means of changing attitudes.

For those higher education lecturers involved in delivering programmes of professional education, this is an important consideration. The benefits of open learning do not, therefore, appear to be restricted solely to the cognitive domain. The application of theoretical and conceptual issues to work experiences is also of central importance for teaching groups such as social workers, nurses and midwives, teachers and managers. The use of carefully designed activities, open learning materials can provide an effective means of helping students to relate theory to practive, thereby bridging the theory-practice gap that dominates much of the literature on professional education. Perhaps not surprisingly, there are also some potential disadvantages.

The cost of the learning materials can be high, whether they are developed in-house or bought in from an external producer. This may require pump-priming funds, or some form of loan, since in higher education fees follow student enrolments, and this can make it more difficult to fund any new development that is front-loaded in terms of costs. If money is borrowed to purchase learning materials or to develop them in-house, and has to be repaid from income derived from running the programme, a sound business-planning approach is vital. There may also be additional costs incurred in adapting or augmenting the materials so that they can be used within a particular programme to ensure that learning outcomes are full addressed. An even greater disadvantage in some areas is that suitable learning materials simply do not exist, forcing lecturers to consider whether they should become involved in developing them in-house.

The use of open learning may involve a period of considerable uncertainty for some lecturers while they adjust to the shift in emphasis from the role of teacher to that of facilitator of learning and to a perceived loss of control over the learning process. To address this issue, some producers offer their learning materials on a computer disk to enable teachers to select particular sections, adapt the text and add local examples, case material, etc., prior to reproducing the material for use with their own students, the rationale being to increase the sense of ownership. Some teaching staff will, therefore, need additional preparation to develop the skills, attitudes and confidence required to facilitate learning and to encourage students to become more self-directed. They may initially require considerable help and support from more experienced open learning tutors.

Initial staff development and institutional development needs can incur high start-up costs which need to be regarded as a long-term investment. Although, in the long run, effective, supported use of open learning materials within an educational programme can enable students to become more self-directed, this can take time to develop.

Teaching staff must realize that, initially, some students may need considerable time and support during their early exposure to open learning until they have developed sufficient confidence to work with reduced teacher input, direction and control, and patterns of independent learning have been established. In addition, lecturers may need to adopt more flexible working hours to meet student' needs, particularly those of students studying part time.

Open learning can allow students to shape their own learning programme by defining their own learning outcomes and working through learning materials at their own pace. The use of individually negotiated learning contracts can help ensure that learning meets the specific needs of individual students, although this is essentially a two-way process. It aims to help students avoid repetitious learniing and build on existing knowledge and skills. A further benefit is that students can study in ways that are best suited to their individual circumstances, and make optimum use of available time to meet their own particular learning needs.

As a practical consequences, opportunities may be increased for those who, due to unsocial working hours and personal commitments, might otherwise be unable to attend a more traditional programme. In addition, there is also the important educational gain in the understanding of, and commitment to, the learning process. We have seen that open learning offers flexibility and the scope for individuals to study different topics at different depths and different speeds according to specific interests and needs. The use of learning materials can allow learners to exert greater control over the pace, place and time of learning. These benefits are nicely summarized for us by the Open Tech slogan of the mid-1980s: 'open learning enables people to learn at the time, place and pace which suits them best.'Given the stages through which quality learning materials must pass during development, they can offer students exposure to the ideas and teaching of nationally recognized experts who might not otherwise be available to lecture in their local institutions. The use of good learning materials can help to ensure quality education provision that is not dependent on who is teaching, how the teacher is feeling and other factors that can affect the quality of face-to-face provision, such as unsuitable teaching accommodation and the like.

If the quality and suitability of learning materials are carefully evaluated prior to their use, an open learning programme can be of a very high quality. Not only may the use of such learning materials raise the morale of hard-pressed lecturers who are committed to the delivery of quality learning opportunities for their students, but they can also help to engage the understanding of students and thus motivate the learner. Among the advantages perceived by students is also the choice of working either alone or in small groups, depending on preference and on individual learning styles. The use of learning materials need not, therefore, necessarily imply isolation. Moreover, learning materials are always available to the student for reference in a way that a teacher cannot be. As a further benefit, it can be easier to make up for lost study time if a student is absent due to illness or some other reason. Students can also become more self-directed and begin to acquire the habit of lifelong learning that is all-important when working in environments that may constantly be changing. As noted above, it can help to empower students to take charge of their own learning through greater control and ownership of the learning will process. Students who are able to organize and structure their own learning will have developed the key skills of self-motivation, self-discipline and self-management that are now required in so many work contexts. Turning now to the major potential disadvantages, some students may experience isolation if they are not able to attend regular, scheduled face-to-face sessions during which ideas can be exchanged and the enthusiasms of others shared.

Student support by teacher's is the key to motivating students to ensure that they successfully complete a programme of learning. Negotiated access to tutorial support at specified times/places is crucial, as is the installation of direct telephone lines with answerphones. A student whose interest and motivation may be failing is unlikely to persist in trying to get in touch with his or her totor if the swichboard is always slow to answer a call, or if an individual is constantly unavilable. Due to the problems associated with isolation, students will often welcome a mixed mode of delivery, whereby open learning materials are integrated within a module that includes some scheduled face-to-face sessions that allow students to benefit from the advantages of both modes of delivery. The creation to self-help groups can also provide a valuable source of peer support that can help to reduce the sense of isolation. Students need to feel a high level of commitment and internal motivation to succeed, since much more is left up to the learner. It has to be acknowledged, therefore, that open learning may not suit all individuals at the outset: some students may need considerable support initially before they begin to feel comfortable and confident with a more self-directed mode of learning.

Industrial and commercial organizations are looking to open learning to help meet the education and training needs of the workforce Those higher education teachers who are offering education and training programmes for either the public or private sectors should be aware of the reasons why an increasing number of employers are finding that the use of open learning materials can help meet their needs.

Cost effectiveness is often assumed to be one of the main benefits of open/distance learning and, indeed, it may turn out to be highly cost effective. At present, however, there is insufficient evidence either to support or to challenge this assumption. It can be difficult to measure in any meaningful way the full costs of providing an open learning programme and compare these with the full costs of an equivalent conventionally taught course. When costing any education programme, it is necessary to calculate both the fixed costs and the variable costs, which will vary depending on the number of students. Fixed costs for open learning include items such as the cost of accommodation, publicity material, scheme managers and administrators, institutional overheads, and developing or purchasing the learning materials.

If open learning is to become more widely used within higher education, and if it is to offer a good educational experience for every open learner, we need to consider a number of key issues in relation to staff and institutional development. Lecturers will need to develop the skills required to evaluate published learning materials prior to their use within specific education programmes. They will need to distinguish between 'experienced and competent providers of open learning and those whose enthusiasm outruns their competence and whose ignorant or exploitative approach to open learning might bring the whole idea into disrepute'.

Any systematic evaluation of learning materials will need to assess the extent to which they meet an agreed set of criteria, including the learning outcomes for a particular education programme. A minimum of 10 per cent of the total study hours may be required to evaluate a set of materials. If the evaluation suggests that the materials are not entirely appropriate either to student needs or to the desired learning outcomes, then additional time and resources will be required to adapt or supplement the materials. In addition, as we have seen, some teachers may need considerable support while adjusting to a shift in their role from teacher to facilitator of learning, as well as help in encouraging students to become more self-directed. Some may also want to acquire further skills in guidance and counselling in order to provide better student support, and to help students to formulate their own objectives and plan how these might best be met. Some teachers will also need specific preparation on the use of the learning materials, telephone tutorials and the management and administration of an open learning system.

A programme of staff development will usually be required to develop a critical mass within the overall population of teaching staff with the necessary attitudes and commitment to implement open learning successfully. And, even if there are already significant numbers of teaching staff who are experienced in using open learning. They will need time to become thoroughly familiar with the learning materials that form the basis of a specific module or programme.Once successful open learning schemes have been established both within and beyond mainstream undergraduate provision, they can be set up as demonstration projects within an institution, or even within the higher education sector as a whole, to help raise the level of awareness among colleagues.

Internal debates may be needed within an institution about the proportion of the total number of study hours that can be dedicated to open learning and still contribute towards an award previously based on fixed number of hours of classroom teaching. The concept of minimum course attendance requirements would obviously need to be reassessed. This in turn raises the question of whether it is necessary to specify minimum time periods for the achievement of particular learning outcomes. Some students may be capable of achieving specific learning outcomes in a considerably shorter time than other students and should perhaps be allowed to complete summative assessments whenever they are ready, rather than at fixed points in a module or programme. The emphasis needs, therefore, to be shifted away from specifying numbers of study hours, module/ programme duration and/or minimum attendance, and towards the development of more flexible means and timescales for students to demonstrate the achievement of specific learning outcomes at predefined academic levels.

Open learning students may be weighted differenly in statistical returns, making it less beneficial for staff members wishing to incorporate open learning materials into their programmes for sound educational reasons. They can be recognized in the same way as, and given the equivalent weighting to, any other student in the institution. Student support is recognized to be crucial to the success of any programme incorporating open learning materials. Students need to be provided with clear information about the availability of tutorial support when undertaking any programme of self-directed learning: the use of open learning should not be viewed simply as a means of reducing the amount of teacher contact or teaching hours. As already suggested, students should also be encouraged to set up self-help groups or study pairs to help reduce the sense of isolation that some may feel. In the first instance, students may also require special preparation to help them to appreciate and take full advantage of the flexibility afforded by open learning and to seek tutorial or peer support when needed.

Conventional teaching requires relatively little administrative support and, as a consequence, there is a tendency to underestimate the amount of administration time needed to establish and manage an effective open learning system, and the cost of providing that support. Administrative support is needed to deal with enquiries, and to ensure the avialability of learning materials which need to be ordered, checked, logged in, stored and issued. If a loan scheme is in operation for the learning materials, returned items also need to be checked, and non-returned items need to be chased to ensure their availability for future students. The establishment and maintenance of accurate and up-to-date records is also essential, particularly if assessment does not occur at fixed points in the programme or at fixed points in the year, and if a large number of students have enrolled. A crucial aspect of any open learning system is, therefore, an efficient administrative system. As open learning operations develop within a school, department or faculty, it may become necessary to appoint an administrator with special responsibility for open learning.

Existing institutional validation procedures may not readily accommodate the special needs of a programme with a substantial open learning component, and may need to be adapted. Members of a validation panel for an open learning programme must be familiar with the specific issues that would need to be addressed in both the supporting documentation and during the validation event, to ensure that sufficient attention is paid to all aspects to the open learning system that could affect the overall quality of the student learning experience. This should include the provision of flexible student support and also adequate administrative support for both students and teachers. Whenever published learning materials are to be used, evidence would be required that a systematic evaluation of the materials has been undertaken to establish their suitability for the proposed use. In a mixed-mode module/programme, validators must ensure that the various components are well integrated, and that a consistent educational philosophy is maintained throughout and is clearly understood by all members of the course planning team. Where learning materials are being developed in-house, it should be noted that it would be entirely inappropriate for validators to require to see all the learning materials prior to validating the course. They should, however, reassure themselves that sound procedures have been implemented, by requesting a clear description of the stages of materials development and the steps that have been taken to assure quality, together with a sample of the learning materials that have been developed. Following validation, it would be necessary to ensure that the course/programme/module evaluation tool was suitable and catered for specific issues relating to the open learning system that could affect the overall quality of the learning experience.

Distance higher education: Advantages

Growing numbers of students are utilising the internet to enrol in distance programmes offered by institutions outside of their countries, often with little knowledge of the nature of the programme or of the reputation of the school offering the programme. They are in general providing off the shelf programmes which are simply used overseas. The decisions about the curriculum, standards, faculty, and requirements are all made by the sponsoring institution. The motive for establishing multinational higher-education enterprises is almost always to make money. This is of course the aim of the growing number of for-profit institutions, but it is also the case for most traditional non-profit universities. British and Australian institutions have been especially active internationally as a way of making up for budget cuts at home. The multinational and distance movement does not really contribute to the internationalisation of higher education worldwide. Knowledge products are being sold across borders, but there is little mutual exchange of ideas, long-term scientific collaboration, exchange of students or faculty, and the like. Multinational and distance institutions operate in a largely unregulated environment. Accrediting systems are trying to catch up with new developments, and government agencies, both in the sponsoring and in the receiving countries, are concerned and sometimes critical.

It is easy for governments to permit these new institutions to enrol students —every person in a multinational or distance institution will not be attending a traditional university where the costs are higher, government often foot much more of the bill. While the trends discussed here constitute some of the major trends, there are many truly collaborative academic arrangements aimed at fostering international research, teaching, and enhancing academic programmes. Information technology has the potential to benefit large numbers of ordinary people, including those in rural areas, provided it is applied in the relevant sectors domestically.

All over the world access to the internet is viewed as empowering people by giving them access to information. A major constraint on internet usage is the degree of literacy of the population but this will be less of a problem in future as literacy improves especially in the younger generation. Equally important is the availability of relevant content in Indian languages. Government departments responsible for disseminating information to the rural population have a major responsibility to ensure that such information is available in a convenient fashion.

Internet access in rural areas could in principle serve as a vehicle for providing information that may be of use to the rural population, including information on prevailing prices in different markets, recommended agricultural practices, etc. The ability to access information from all over the world will lead to substantial improvements in the quality of education. Of course the financial resources required to equip all our schools and colleges with internet access is a major problem but we should aim to universalise availability at least from second-ary school onwards.

Universalisation is important because otherwise we will build permanent stratification into the system, with a sharp distinction between those who are IT familiar and those who are not. Fortunately, costs are coming down rapidly which should make it easier to achieve this objective. Distance learning could prove to be an extremely cost-effective way of providing high quality teaching in the public school system. Similarly, tele-medicine enables specialists located in hospitals in urban areas to assist local doctors in outlying areas with both diagnosis and prescription. Needless to say these advantages will not flow automatically.

A great deal needs to be done if we want to exploit the potential benefit from the IT revolution fully; the most important in this context is the need to upgrade our telecommunication infrastructure, not only in the metropolitan centres but all over the country. Large investments are needed in this area to create a high capacity backbone which can ensure good quality connectivity with adequate bandwidth available in all parts of the country. We also need a competitive telecommunication industry, with private sector suppliers competing with the public sector to improve service. Transforming a sector from a public sector monopoly to competitively structured industry is not an easy proposition and many problems of implementation have arisen. Another important prerequisite is the level of education and skills of the labour force. The telecommunications in the past two decades with digital switching and modern transmission technology has led to a massive expansion in capacity, at continuously falling costs.

The convergence of these developments produced information technology with computers, located all over the world, being able to communicate with each other through telecommunication networks. It is now possible to access, transmit and process large amounts of data from and to anywhere in the world at great speed and at very low cost opening up entirely new types of economic activity. The idea of linking computers to each other goes back to the early 1960s when the US Defence Department's Advanced Research Project Agency (ARPA) funded a research project to link computers in universities and research lab. More and more computers were linked to the network which ultimately grew into the internet.

Up to the early 1990s the internet remained the preserve of universities and businesses and that too almost entirely in the United States. Its conversion into a truly global phenomenon, with access open to millions all over the world, is very recent and begins with the development of the World Wide Web as recently as 1993. The web transformed the internet by introducing graphics, multi media and hypertext all of which opened up the possibility of multiple commercial uses, while the introduction of 'user friendly' browsers enabled individual users to surf the net with ease. The world has barely had time to catch its breath since then. The web has proved to be an extraordinarily popular interactive medium for communication potentially accessible by anyone anywhere in the world. The number of websites has increased from 30 when the web was introduced in 1993 to 3,25,000 in 1996 and an estimated 12 million today. The growing awareness that learning, not teaching, is the decisive factor in education, has brought support to distance education along with other methods of independent study. It can be equated with the combined, systematic and flexible use of at least three major elements: (i) print-based communication; (ii) broadcasting and face-to-face contact in support of an independent learner; (iii) out of these elements, face-to-face communication is transacted for a very short duration. There are no learning benefits to be gained from employing different media in instruction, regardless of their obviously attractive features or advertised superiority. "The best current evidence is that media are mere vehicles that deliver instruction but do not influence student achievement any more than the truck that delivers our groceries causes change in our nutrition. The ability of various media to increase learning is advertised by the multi-million dollar industry to push the sale of these machines for instruction. Therefore, the text material still remains a powerful and popular mode of presenting and transmitting a large amount of knowledge in a well organised and psychologised way to the learners.

By far the most important medium in distance education is the printed word. This applies to conventional correspondence study as well as to highly sophisticated multimedia presentations like courses of an open university. Although the choice of media depends on the nature of subject-matter, print media has been found largely effective in each of the cognitive, affective and connotive domains. In fact, a medium is just a support for course material in the form of print. Care must always be taken that this existing and fundamental medium should not be overlooked. Researches done in the area of 'learning from text' reveal that the written word is more effective in certain domains than the other. Cognitive psychologists and educators have designed certain instructional strategies to help teachers convey a large amount of information as meaningfully and efficiently as possible in the conventional formal group situation as well as in 'learning at home' individual setting. Although there is considerable variation in opinions as to how one can use cognitive learning research and theory in the formulation of instructional principles, yet agreement on certain points can be discerned. All cognitive theorists emphasise the importance of cognitive processes in the planning of instruction.

The major function of the instructor is to provide whatever guidance seems necessary to help the learner to organise new information in a meaningful way. There is a distinct preference for featuring situations which stimulate inquiry search pattern and for avoiding those situations which make the student a passive recipient of facts to be memorised by rote practices. Any instructional material designed to improve 'learning to learn' should explicitly describe the main points of the learning, how they are related, and how they might be interrelated with what the learner already knows. Advance organisers facilitate learning in almost all content areas, and with individuals of all grade and ability levels. The higher educational institutions of the century is being visualised as a place where knowledge will be generated, where knowledge will also be refined and reinvented, where knowledge will be examined, explored and restated, where knowledge will be acquired by both teachers and students, where knowledge will be shared by the community, and where knowledge will be transformed into experience, into action, into wisdom, into vision and in one form or another.

2

Information Technology in Higher Education

As far back as the 1970s, the predictions of the future role of computers in taking over the job of the teacher were common. Both information technology and the process of teaching and learning involve the storage, retrieval and manipulation of information, so it seems natural that the former can contribute to the latter, especially as more powerful computers are able to handle the type of information relevant to the more general education arena. In 1986, as part of a crystal ball-gazing exercise on the future school curriculum, Saunders felt that 'information technology is revolutionary in that it puts learning into the hands and control of the learner'.

It is worth looking at the reality of this vision, and at the contributions towards achieving it throughout the education system. There is little doubt that information technology is of growing importance within the education sector. Throughout Britain there is an entitlement to IT for all pupils in the 5-16 range due to the National Curriculum. It is expected that the programmes of study and attainment targets, which are specifically defined, should be delivered and tested within the context of a wide range of subjects. There are many more developments in IT within this age range which will contribute to the readiness of higher education students to use IT supported flexible learning. The government-funded CD-ROM in Schools Scheme has given a high profile to this technology as a support to more flexible learning styles. A recent survey of all secondary schools in three East Midlands local education authorities showed that 81 per cent have at least one CD-ROM system, usually based in the library resource area, and 95 per cent of these have a CD-ROM based encyclopaedia. If pupils are to use such resources effectively then they will need to be trained in enhanced information retrieval and schools are starting to put such training in place. There is a growing number of reports of networked CD-ROM systems throughout schools to further encourage pupils and teachers towards more flexible approaches to the flow of information for learning. In some schools CD-ROM is becoming part of the much wider multimedia environment.

UK's National Council for Educational Technology (NCET) has recently been gathering together the wide-ranging evidence of the benefits of IT to learning. The developments in schools have been possible because of the increased power of the technology available to them. In the higher education sector, they have been many developments reported by the Computers in Teaching Initiative. CTI was established in 1986 to:

- encourage the development of computer-assisted teaching and learning in UK universities;
- evaluate the educational potential of information technology at UK universities;

– promote an awareness of the potential of information technology among lecturers and students in all disciplines.

The Joint Academic Network (JANET) will be the backbone of increased flexibility in national and international communications, allowing students greater access to a wider range of information sources in a range of formats, such as text, images and video. There is also the potential to link into the cable television infrastructure which uses optical-fibre technology like SuperJANET, providing such communication facilities directly to the homes of both students and academics. The improved user interfaces will provide improved access to the technology for academics. However, if flexibility rather than constraint is inherent in the learning pathways, then the complexity of computer programming can be immense. Newer authoring programs are certainly improving access, but users still require a 'considerable time and effort to acquaint themselves with the more complex aspects of the package'. A lot of this software is used in industry for training purposes - but this encroaches on the perennial discussion on training and education. Most authoring packages were designed for industry where they are used in narrowly defined tasks. This provides flexibility of access, but constraints the learning, and in that way cannot really be considered to have a realistic future in higher education.

If the flow of information is too constrained then the learning experience will be a poor second to the more conventional learning methodology. We have to be sure that the technology can do what we are asking of it. To do all this we have to think about our pedagogy as a whole; the total art and practice of teaching needs to come under scrutinyPerhaps we exaggerate abóut the current level of interest in computer based teaching and learning (CBT/L) in higher education, but our real point is that we are on the verge of a major upsurge in CBT/L materials development and an increasing number of our colleagues are beginning to search around for guidance and leadership as they take their first steps in the process. Reacting to the twin imperatives of falling staffs and ever-increasing student numbers we are all finding CBT/L is fast becoming an attractive option.

Obviously there are other reasons for the likely increase in CBT/L development, not least the enhancement and extension of student learning, but let us stick for the moment with the need to free up staff time from the more humdrum and repetitive aspects of their teaching activities. If the students can study at their own pace in front of a computer, and perhaps in their own time, then the lecturers will be that little bit more able to provide prime-time contact in addition to being able to engage in research. In managing student/teacher partnerships, IT could be used for the mutual benefit of both parties. There is no doubt that much of this is best done by taking together, as only in this way can students and teachers get to know each other to enable the rapport normally associated with good teaching. There are, however, ways of enhancing communications to the benefit of both. The use of electronic mail systems means that students can be sure of getting questions to a tutor and the tutor can manage his/her time in handling student questions, rather than having to cope with the continual stream of interruptions when trying to concentrate on other work. This also allows student queries to be answered remotely, from home for example through the use of modems. In this way, much of the communications between student and tutor could be at least maintained, and perhaps enhanced, without necessarily impinging on more tutor time when faced with a deteriorating staff/student ratio. If the student query needs a face-to-face discussion, then a time can be arranged via e-mail when the tutor will be available. This does, of course, assume that the tutor is able to manage the e-mail system effectively and efficiently, with a certain amount of self-discipline. It is now possible to send and receive complete documents via e-mail, and as this technology spreads, the handling in of assignments on paper might have to be reviewed, especially within the distance learning mode of flexible learning. The present technology already provides facilities for tutor-student conferencing, and the growing network infrastructure will add video to such systems.

Information technology is well suited to managing student use of resources. A look through the aims of the teacher and the outcomes for the student shows many areas of match to the current and developing technologies outlined above. It is all about finding, using, manipulating and managing information and information sources. New forms of interpersonal skills will need to be developed to use electronic communication systems to exchange information. Managing student learning pathways is largely associated with the individualized mode of flexible learning, and again this could be considerably extended and enhanced through IT-supported systems.

Digital Technology and its Impact on Education

Today, many people thought that computers would revolutionize education, that computer-based teaching and learning would become the savior of education and the solution to falling test scores. This has never really happened. Over the past two decades, many teachers have successfully prepared students, some with computers in the classroom and some without. Teachers could avoid computers, either because they chose not to learn how to use them or because they had none in their classroom or college to use. Teachers entering the profession have not been required to understand computational technology in order to graduate from college.

In US, the Internet has been in existence for almost two decades and began to extend into colleges about 15 years ago. It did provide an opportunity to expand learning options for teachers and students who were fortunate enough to have Internet access, a few computers, and appropriate guidance on usage. Often this took place in only one classroom and only one school within a system and did not become systemic throughout the school.

There are many factors affecting this slow implementation of computing and communication technology in colleges, including administrations with no knowledge of its value or no willingness to realign school budgets to include computational technology; insufficient in-service professional development programs for teachers; a lack of specific curriculum benefits or of resources for teachers to use in their courses; and deficient preservice preparation of teachers in technology or computation.

In 1993, United States' National Center for Supercomputing Applications (NCSA) released Mosaic, the first World Wide Web browser for all three computing platforms. The Internet had become the World

Wide Web, and now Mosaic allowed anyone who knew the basics about using a computer and a mouse to go out onto the Web and easily and quickly locate multimedia information. Files rapidly became hypermedia text pages, and nascent searching and information integration tools became easily accessible. So what is the difference between the past two decades of computers and Internet access and the present, since even now WWW access requires computers and an Internet connection? The difference is that the Web represents Information, and information cannot be disregarded the way that computers can be ignored. Teachers cannot choose to ignore or have their students omit available information on any subject when the goal is for them to learn.

Colleges were connect to the Web has been simply to access information and this incentive has made a great deal possible collaboration around numerous kinds of educational activities will become a primary motivation for connectivity among colleges, teachers, parents, and students. When students, teachers, parents, administrators, and even legislators can communicate via the Internet and begin to collaborate electronically on issues, the traditional educational process may see a fundamental transformation, with decisions about a student's learning being resolved in new and hopefully better ways. Traditionally, colleges and classrooms have tended to discourage many forms of collaboration.

In the archetypical system, decisions related to course content and delivery arrive top down from the administration, teachers spend all but a small portion of their day confined to a room, telephones are not easily available to teachers in most situations, students are rewarded for not talking and for working independently, and communication between teacher and parents is scheduled once or twice a year at most. Teachers who value communication with parents and students generally must do it on their own time from home.

The traditional education system, being more evolutionary than revolutionary, is unlikely to transform itself any time soon into an environment that teaches and encourages collaboration as a part of learning; emerging technologies, however, can catalyze this change much sooner than it would happen otherwise. Using electronic mail and "surfing" for information with a browser, such as Mosaic, involve communicating with others and locating information, but the real power of the Web will come from people being better able to accomplish their "work," regardless of its focus.

Communication via e-mail is a form of asynchronous collaboration. People enter messages that are sent to other people who read them, and perhaps respond, at a later point in time. Bulletin boards, such as the nearly ubiquitous Usenet newsgroups, are another form of asynchronous communication, to an open audience. Listserves based on e-mail are a very similar form of asynchronous, group communication.

Desktop video teleconferencing, on the other hand, allows real-time, synchronous collaboration, although bandwidth is consumed quickly with this technology. Chat sessions are a text-based version of synchronous collaboration, as are Multi-User Dungeons (MUDs), Object-Oriented MUDs (MOOs), or Multi-User Shared Hallucinations (MUSHes), where a number of people participate simultaneously in a shared conversation or activity. The real power of digital technologies is not yet tapped; other applications on the desktop for doing exciting and robust synchronous and asynchronous collaboration are just now emerging.

A few years ago, NCSA developed a system called NCSA Collage intended to help computational researchers share data from simulations, images generated from that data, text, drawings, diagrams, animation sequences, and screen shots from other analysis software with remotely located colleagues in a real-time, synchronous session. This software addressed a continuing need of research teams scattered across the globe.

The development of NCSA Mosaic caused a 100,000-fold increase in WWW NSFnet backbone traffic and brought in millions of users, thus creating a market for the dozens of commercial browsers that subsequently have been introduced. Since then, the commercial market has taken off phenomenally. Spyglass, Netscape, and Microsoft all have produced widely used browsers and Web technology, and scores of companies have jumped into the Web market.

Spyglass alone has created a licensing family of 36 companies with over 80 products. Netscape was created by a half dozen NCSA-trained programmers and is currently a market leader. The Microsoft Internet Explorer is a licensed derivative product from the University of Illinois Urbana-Champaign and Spyglass that is available to anyone with a Windows 95 interface a potential market projected to number in the millions within one year.

At last count, there were over 40 different browsers available on the Web. On the server side, NCSA WWW server software is used on roughly 50 percent of the installed base of WWW servers on the open Internet and about 70 percent of those in the EDU domain. In addition, commercialization of server software is proceeding at an astounding rate. With the explosion of commercial effort in Web-based technologies, it is clear that the Web is here to stay. In one form or another (and the exact form is both extremely important and virtually impossible to predict), the growth of access to TCP/IP-based networks the Internet as we generally know it and the availability of Web-based software and services, will only increase, driven by a vision of huge market potential. At the same time, the cost of access and services in this extraordinarily competitive sector will only decrease.

The rise of new technologies and the constantly decreasing cost of network bandwidth and processor power will help to insure that the Web is more than just a short-term trend. The next generation of collaborative tools needs to be Web-based. It is also important to recognize that the unique culture of the Internet, based historically in the cooperative environments of the academic and research communities, will not disappear in a more commercialized Internet.

While there is a continuing desire on the part of companies to lock users and developers into proprietary formats and programming interfaces, there is also a need for open systems that can be extended and modified in various ways and that can cross the boundaries of different operating systems and applications. This quality of interoperability has been one of the fundamental advantages of Web-based applications. The research and education communities also have established a tradition of placing their software in the public domain or, alternately, making it "free with copyright" along the model of the NCSA Mosaic software. Under this approach, individuals can use software for free, while the authors still retain the rights for commercialization.

The dynamics of the Web have transported this idea into an increasing number of commercial software sectors, from browsers to programming languages. This makes new technology widely available almost instantaneously and gives users and developers a rapidly expanding spectrum of possibilities for tool development. On the other hand, some have dubbed this the "heroin approach" to software adoption: users get "hooked" on free tools, then later pay to get the latest versions, full support, or software that is no longer available for free.

NCSA is now working to bring to the Web the kind of technology developed in Collage and to integrate synchronous collaboration with asynchronous methods. The Web provides a set of standards for handling a wide variety of media types and an installed base of browser software and server environments that can be integrated fruitfully into a framework for using collaboration methods in education.

The Web has become a condensation point for virtually every advanced technology developed over the last two decades by the computational science and computer science communities. All of these technologies are streaming onto the Web at fantastic rates, each bringing its own revolution in how we conceptualize the future digital communication infrastructure.

Many advanced and disparate technologies are being integrated into the global system, including object-oriented frameworks for application environments and databases; state-of-the-art security methods implemented at the connection, document, compiler, and interpreter levels; efficient distributed three-dimensional modeling and scientific visualization schemes; robust and truly persistent global naming and location methods; semantic-based object description and search techniques. The following examples show what these technological advancements can mean for learning environments.

Remotely controlled Mosaics represent a collaborative capability that could make distance teaching a much easier and more meaningful way to learn. An instructor who knew the Internet Protocol address of each student's machine and had control privileges could regulate the presentation being delivered to the students and, via the WWW and a browser, could present multimedia material and information just as he or she would in a traditional classroom with all the students present.

The instructor could also release control of the students' machines to enable them to work on exercises, look for information, or communicate with other, remotely located students involved in a group project. The instructor could regain control at a future time to "discuss" an item with the entire class. In addition to presenting previously prepared information to the student machines, the instructor could give new information to all students by preparing it in advance for delivery, by typing it in, or by using voice and, eventually, real-time digital video. In this type of classroom, anything on the Web would become material for shared, real-time presentation and discussion.

Adding a simple capability to draw on the browser window would provide the users with "white board" interaction. Any changes that the instructor or a student made in this window could be seen by all the participants in the virtual classroom, and it would become easy to point out across the Net the important features of an article, a map, an image, or a 3-D drawing.

By generalizing the capability that allows one user to control or drive the software running on another user's machine when both are connected to the Internet, it becomes possible to bring any collaboration-capable software tool into the interaction.

In this way, specialized educational software could be integrated into the virtual classroom; an instructor could demonstrate to a remotely located student how to execute an application. The ability to run simulations on remote or local machines is another application that is very important in teaching computational science and indeed could be useful in teaching chemistry, physics, and other high school science subjects.

In the past, this application has been accomplished not with a browser, but with a series of File Transfer Protocols (FTPs), telnets, or other operations that allowed connectivity to another machine. Providing interaction with remote machines through a straightforward interface like a Web browser would make this capability available to a much larger audience. Building these types of applications for the Web requires much more power in the Web browser than we currently have.

In fact, the idea of a browser needs to give way to the more encompassing idea of a Web environment that is flexible and dynamic and can be customized to the needs of the moment. Java, a new programming language from Sun Microsystems, opens up these possibilities by allowing programs to be sent over the Web in a secure fashion. Programs that are executed locally when they arrive at the user's desktop are an example of "mobile code." The possibilities engendered by secure mobile code on the Internet are staggering.

Sun's Java is an example of a C++like language that was developed specifically to address network security considerations. The capability to send executing programs that can link dynamically with existing desktop browsers and other software means that whole applications, protocols, and interfaces can be sent over the Net with HTML documents. NCSA is evaluating the Java framework and working with Sun to make this technology available to educational users.

NCSA is also collaborating with the Open Software Foundation to evaluate Java's security features, with the University of Illinois Digital Library Initiative project to develop advanced search interfaces in Java, and with the Online Computer Library Center, Inc. to study the use of Hot Java for complex scientific documents. The use of mobile code (and Java is only one example of mobile code systems) very likely will revolutionize how students and teachers use the WWW, equivalent in impact to the introduction of Mosaic and the WWW a few years ago or to the advent of NCSA Telnet and FTP before that.

The collaborative engine developed in Java will allow users to share anything that can be sent over the Web, in addition to live sound and video. The basic Habanero engine will include a software interface that will allow any application to become collaborative by conforming to the interface. As in the above hypothetical scenario, a white board setup would allow users to share a drawing appearing on any page in the browser by sending drawing messages to the collaboration engine.

Any piece of data analysis or visualization software could become part of a collaborative session by exposing part of its interface to the Habanero engine, thereby allowing users to incorporate advanced or discipline-specific applications into their collaborative sessions. In addition, any collaborative session could be recorded, reviewed later, synopsized, annotated, and distributed to those who missed the virtual meeting or classroom session, with all the media and interactions of the original session intact.

Collaborative uses of Virtual Reality Modeling Language (VRML) would also be enhanced by the increased speed and would pave the way for the next generation of research and development of fully 3-D collaborative environments. NCSA's strategy builds on exploratory research done in the CAVE, a fully 3-D virtual environment with virtual presence of the collaborators in the form of "avatars," or rendered representations of the participants.

This technology is moving toward fully digital conferencing techniques that go beyond video and encompass a completely rendered, customizable, bandwidth-sensitive, 3-D representation of each participant, in a fully 3-D environment for the conference and any accompanying data or simulation results. Bandwidth and workstation capabilities available to users can define a spectrum of these kinds of environments, from full immersion in something like the CAVE, to VRML-based 3-D environments on widely available desktop systems.

The popularity of the Web as a means of information discovery and retrieval (the global electronic library metaphor), and as a foundation for electronic commerce (the electronic market metaphor), has tended to push into the background considerations about its use as a global research lab (the virtual institute or virtual classroom metaphor).

NCSA is focusing on developing a Web infrastructure that would change this and provide capabilities directly targeted on globally distributed research and learning communities. An example is the development of HyperNews (a Web-based bulletin board system) and of global annotation capabilities, which can be used as a foundation for virtual research colleges (in the classic sense) or research institutes on the Web. These kinds of Web-based virtual institutes could include most or all of the functions of a brick-and-mortar research institute.

In addition to participating in asynchronous collaborations via bulletin boards, e-mail, and the like, a visitor to the virtual institute could establish synchronous collaboration based on a chat session, a Collage session, a digital video teleconferencing center, a shared VRML scene, or any combination of these. With the VRML application, users visiting a VRML scene can "appear" in the scene via an icon and, with the aid of an integrated chat box, can communicate with other users that they can see. Future work aims toward a collaborative VRML environment, where users can run shared VRML simulations or take "group tours" through a VRML world. To provide some of this functionality, server-side capabilities must be enhanced and made available in forms as easily adoptable as current HyperText Transfer Protocol servers are. Support for manual searching, or browsing, already exists in the WWW; here the user selects links to follow from one document to the next across the Web of related documents. Automatic searching over the Web that uses the same links between documents requires standards across servers for query language, knowledge representation, and metadata semantics.

Automatic analysis of collections of interlinked documents can also help produce cross-collection indexes to optimize searching in fairly focused areas. Collaboration technologies and Repository framework can also allow users to contribute to the incremental self-organization of the Web. NCSA is currently developing a framework for educational information in Illinois called the Illinois Learning Mosaic (ILM) project. The ILM is being designed within the Repository framework of future Internet server software, so that any other information databases on the Internet built within this same Repository framework will automatically share data. Some of the current tools include a Web-based group calendar, chatting capability, capability for threaded discussion and group meetings, writing tools, document storage and publication tools, a project management tool, a forms tool, workspace management tools, and more.

Web-based Learning Systems

Understanding the student's knowledge base, as well as the structure of the instructional knowledge base is crucial to student modeling. As Web-based learning systems are becoming common place, how the knowledge domain is structured, in the design of Web-based instructions has been extensively researched. Student modeling, as the model of a learner, represents the computer system's belief about the learner's knowledge. In US, the Alberta Research Council's Student Modeling study, reported that in order to allow instruction to be individually designed, it is first necessary to capture the student's understanding of the subject. With this information, the difficulty of material, and any necessary remediation can be controlled within the instructional system. Building a student model involves defining; the "who", or the degree of specialization in defining who is modelled, and what the learner history is; the "what", or the goals, plans, attitudes, capabilites, knowledge, and beliefs of the learner; the "how" the model is to be acquired and maintained; and the "why" , including to whether to elicit information from the learner, to give assistance to the learner, to provide feedback to the learner, or to interpret learner behavior.

In maintaining the student model, the factors that need to be considered include the fact that students do not perform consistantly, forget information randomly, and then display large leaps in understanding. For an intelligent instructional system to be tailored to the student, the student model is the essential component in individualized learning. It is the student model that builds and maintains the system's understanding of the student. The knowledge base of the student model takes both domain and pedagogical knowledge into account.

The method to elicit a student model is closely tied to the approach. In the overlay approach, first the expert domain is modelled as a set of correct production rules. The learner is modelled as a subset of these correct rules, plus a set of incorrect production rules. Each new learner requires an individualized student model. In developing the student model, the type of knowledge (ie, declarative, procedural) to be defined must be determined. It has to be decided whether or not to include student goals, and how to include these. The methods used include the users outlining their own goals, providing self-documentation, and submitting answers to a pre-test.

The Internet links people world-wide, and contains a highly diverse, easy- to-update source of information. Web-based instruction is shown to be more useful for intellectual knowledge than affective knowledge, and is not appropriate if users do not have Internet connection, if the material requires large amounts of audio or video, or if the subject requires the teaching of physical skills.

The creation of instructions involves the organization of information to promote specific learning goals. It is critical to keep this a priority in the design of Web-based instructions. There are two schools of thought in the creation of learning instructions; objectivists and constructivists. Objectivists find a series of steps to lead the learner to the final goal. This final goal is defined in terms of behavior, ie "The learner will be able to demonstrate behavior".

This method does not take into account the individual learner's differences regarding prior knowledge or present motivation. It does expect a minimum prior skill relevant to the knowledge domain. This approach may work well for procedural knowledge, which can be exhibited, but is not as effective with declarative knowledge, and higher levels of learning. The constructivist approach differs from the objectivist in that the student takes control of the learning.

One example of this approach is the Cognitive Flexibility Theory. This theory deals with the special requirements for attaining advanced learning goals. It views the learning methods as having a multi-dimensional perspective with a criss-crossing of the subject matter in a non-linear fashion. The Internet is an ideal tool for this approach. The Hypermedia Design Model (HDM), in utilizing the above theory, defines the design methods as what knowledge the designer hopes will be attained by the learner, and how the learning environment is organized.

The learner methods are what the learner hopes to learn, and how the knowledge is accessed by the learner. In the HDM, the learner objectives are of the utmost importance. The HTM consists of the following steps;

Define the learning domain;

— The boundaries ,are set. The larger these are, the less detailed the knowledge will be.

— Identify the cases in the domain, which are the knowledge bits, plus the instructional elements, such as text, graphics, sound, and video.

The guided path creates specific trails through the knowledge domain. The design goals are identified and highlighted, using maps and maps in a criss-crossed landscape. The learner is led through this, returning to the same elements from many directions. The learner controlled path allows the learner to specify how to navigate without the aid of the design spcified trails.

Learners create their own objectives, regarding the domain, which supplies them with the necessary tools to explore it on their own, (ie, search engine, concept maps). Hypertext-based systems are described as static, and are often critisized for their lack of expert guidance in the instructional sequence. However, intelligent systems are often critisized for their structured tutoring and embedded expert's design as the basis for learning. One of the most common problems in hypertext systems, especially with novices, is disorientation, or becoming lost in the links.

A number of advanced navigational tools are used to prevent this. Punctual aids, such as transport buttons, and help buttons, assist the learner to move forward. Structural aids, such as maps, filters, and indexes, help the student to view the overall structure. Historical aids show the users where they have been. Although these navigational tools assist the learner to move in a non-linear manner, studies have shown that many students will still use the material in the same manner they would read a written text. This is dependent on the student's locus of control, prior knowledge of the domain, and familiarity with hypermedia.

Learners with an internal locus of control, strong domain knowledge, and high level of comfort with hypermedia, are more likely to use greater initiative with the navigational tools. In defining the cognitive models for structuring hypermedia, both the domain and pedagogical knowledge are considered. Domain knowledge includes declarative, structural, and procedural knowledge.

Pedagogical knowledge contains a knowledge of the domain structures, the state of the student understanding, knowledge of tutorial strategies, and a means to use these strategies to facilitate learning according to the domain structure and the student understanding.

Hypermedia Systems (HMS), which are based on hypertext, are non-sequential, non-linear methods of displaying text, graphics, sound, and video. They use interface design and advanced navigational tools, and assume that the student's interpretation is more meaningful that the expert's. Hypermedia Systems use a constructivist approach to learning, where learning is regarded as the formation of "constructs" of understanding by the learner. The learner builds the knowlegde based on previous understanding by interacting dynamically with the domain structure. HMS provide a suitable means for this approach because they allow the learner to take control. This system allows the learner to make an informed decision regarding where to proceed in the material. The hypertext is a node-link structure, which allows the user to move through the information using advanced navigational tools. The structure and the sequence is expert-defined, but the learner defines his own path to follow. This provides the students with the greatest opportunity to learn on their own.

Adaptive hypermedia involves the research of understanding student traits using computer interface. It attempts to trace student knowledge and provide individual advice, by creating an adaptive system with an interface management approach. A student model is used to adapt the display characteristics of the interface to the needs of the learner. One study involving adaptive hypermedia, at the Swedish Institute of Computer Science, uses stereotypical knowledge of the learner. This is derived from observing several users. It uses an adaptive search and filtering mechanism that involves the use of clustering and direct user input, and avoids the need for advanced organization of hypermedia knowledge. Another example is the Adaptive User Modeling System. This system addresses the two main problems users face with hypertext; navigation and comprehension. It allows objects to alter according to the user's knowledge state. There is an assumption here that the user will bypass familiar knowledge, but choose the knowledge areas they wish to learn.

Hypertext structures reflect a model of learning based on schemas. This knowledge exists in semantic memory, which is a network of interrelated concepts. In Semantic Net Architecture, such as Hypercard or Authorware, domain knowledge is organized as concept nodes.

These nodes are connected via links and menus, which describe the relationship between the nodes. The OCTR model of learning styles, describes "Orientation" as relating to the learner's prior knowledge, "Coaching" as apprenticeship learning, "Tuning" as finetuning the knowledge, and "Routining" as increasing student autonomy. This approach emphasizes the constructivist approach, and the creation of links between new knowledge and old.

In the node-link cognitive models, learning is the accumulation and organization of knowledge structures, which can be represented as nodes and links. The nodes are the declarative elements, and the links are the procedural and structural elements.

Following are the possibilities to learning on the Web;

- To use an expert's construction of the domain to form the basis for the creation of links and nodes.
- To incorporate advanced navigational devices such as concept maps.
- To provide online help, which may be intelligent help if the student is modelled.
- To use adaptive interface based on stereotypical user classes to modify the environment to suit the needs of the individual learner.

— To provide adaptive advise, and model the student's aquisition of knowledge through their use of the environment, (including navigational use, answers to questions, help requested), to intelligently suggest a preferred path through the knowledge base.

The above possibilities show how the use of student modeling can be related to learning on the Web. Online help may be specific to domain or generalized to more global assistance, (depending on whether the the problem occurs with the knowledge domain or with the tools). Adaptive interface applications and adaptive advice would both require use of intelligent systems, with student modeling being a requirement for development.

Students and Teachers Publishing in WWW

Today, publishers gain access to the part of the Internet known as the World Wide Web. Traditional publishers and their audiences are reevaluating the creation anddistribution of educational materials and all sorts of content, given changing curriculum standards, shifting distribution models, and opportunities for new types of electronic learning. Although the potential of the WWW as a multimedia printing press is obvious to all, many questions remain about the willingness of consumers and educators to pay for electronic information and about the kinds of content and exchanges that best suit this medium.

The long-term implications for educational and mainstream publishers as the WWW makes possible new types of content and new means of publishing, distribution, and learning. The ability for authors to create their own content and publish themselves on the

Web, and the ability for publishers to update their content, as well as to package and distribute information in new ways, makes this an exciting time to be in the publishing industry.

At the present time, there are four kinds of publishers dominate the Web: large commercial companies, small individual publishers, schools, and nonprofit organizations. In most cases, these publishers share two common goals: to reach a national or local audience with an interest in the issues of their particular niche, and to make publishing interactive.

In the past year alone, the number of publishers, schools, and educational organizations launching WWW sites has increased from perhaps 30 to over 1,800. K-12 schools publish portfolios of student research on the Web, educators use it to conduct research, and publishers launch corporate Web sites and catalogs that give them a greater sense of what their customers might want to do, buy, and link to online. Given these changes and the growing use and acceptance of the Web by educators and consumers.

In 1995, traditional education publishers began moving onto the WWW. Electronic Learning, the controlled-circulation educational technology magazine published by Scholastic for the past 10 years, recently cut back its print publication to a quarterly schedule but added a WWW site that is updated monthly. In the consumer field, the New York Times, Random House, Hearst, and Conde Nast have recently launched Web sites with areas meant to appeal to the home/school market.

The Discovery Channel, PBS, CNN, and other media companies that have veered into print with an eye to reaching the home/school market have gone onto the Web as well, promoting their television shows and supplementary print materials to great effect. And newspapers, late to the market, are coming in big and will play a significant role in driving educators and consumers onto the Web for current information and services.

The prevalent business models in use today are as follows:

— The Web site as an add-on or marketing tool for products sold through retail channels, such as books and videos, and for movie and television promotion.

— The Web site as a direct-mail vehicle and sales channel, with editorial content added to attract audiences to the catalog.

— The Web site as a means to promote and deliver subscription-based products published on the WWW, with a charge for access.

— The Web as a platform for publishing, with advertising as the revenue generator.

— The Web as a platform for subscription-based publishing.

The Web enables students and educators to publish their projects, writing, and curriculum materials in a way that is both similar to, and different from, traditional methods. While self- and small-press publishing is nothing new, the World Wide Web gives students and educators the opportunity to present their work to a potentially limitless audience throughout the world.

Only one-fifth of one percent of the approximately 100,000 K-12 schools in the United States currently have enough network access to develop their own Web sites. Yet, when one visits many of these 1,200-plus school sites and sees what they have published online, it is clear that the WWW indeed makes possible new kinds of publishing. The Web is enabling students to publish work not only in science an early and well-funded popular topic but also in many other areas.

Literary magazines and student "'zines" flourish around the country. Teachers are also using the Web to publish materials they once might have sought to publish first through more traditional channels. In Los Alamos, New Mexico, as part of a testbed known as the Sunrise Project, high school students and their teachers developed online math and science tutorials for their peers.

With the guidance of scientists at Los Alamos National Laboratory, the students produced units on the history of computing, basic hydrodynamics, and chaos theory. Classes logging into the site can turn to these materials in place of what Prentice-Hall or Simon and Schuster might offer.

In US, some of the most promising publishing efforts today come from and will continue to come from WWW entrepreneurs who recognize the participatory nature of the Web and are building sites to appeal to children and their teachers and parents. Nonprofits and education organizations seeking to build national education resources and virtual libraries face similar opportunities. These entrepreneurial creators recognize the need for focused content and tools to serve niche audiences.

Local and regional Web services, many supported by local newspapers, launch daily. These services have the potential to be strong partners for local educators and assets in building school/home connections. Often marketed through and with the local papers, these services can drive parents and students to a local school district or education consortium's WWW resources and information. New Jersey Online's Strong Words editorial current events project and its Election 96 package for kids which will be distributed without charge to online services around the country are examples of compelling Web projects directed at local audiences.

Today, Pathfinder or Playboy commands 5 million visitors per month for a module published on the Web. Through syndicating materials so that users access them through a local port, other publishers can gain the opportunity to reach an audience of the same size. If regional online services such as Boston.Com, New Jersey Online, Cleveland Online, and Portland Online, and educational sites such as the Mendocino, California, school district can all post the same project on their Web sites, inviting people to work with it through their access point, then that project can gain the same number of local viewers 5 million as would come to a national site.

As a national site, the project might never have had the marketing ability to draw in 5 million viewers. In some ways, the value of the WWW as a publishing and information distribution platform suggests that the Web is likely to evolve into a sort of high-bandwidth, "smart" TV, but with a degree of interactivity that TV has never had. On New Jersey Online, a site targeted at average users rather than technology wizards, 40 percent of the visitors download audio files, 15 percent download quicktime video files, and 10 percent post items in forums. On the Internet, the traffic in GIFS and images almost exceeds that of Usenet ASCII postings.

As AT&T and other telcos move audiences onto the Internet, they quickly will be joined by cable providers able to offer higher bandwidth access to the Web from home and school. Higher bandwidth will make it possible for a larger audience to experience and play a role in shaping the high-end tools, such as Shockwave, Java, television and video to the desktop, and Quicktime VR, that most of us only read about today.

Transaction and Authentication Tools Will Drive Business Growth As more and more educators and publishers move onto the Web, one area where the heavy hitters will shake out from the crowd is in the area of server tools, particularly the ability to offer direct sales transaction on the WWW and the ability to authenticate visitors to a site. Transaction capability, as it is generally referred to, enables visitors to purchase items online.

Whether it is used to sell books online or purchase the right to view an article, this is a critical capability. Authentication the ability for a server to create a unique I.D. for a user, retain that information over a series of Web visitors or sessions, and grant access privileges accordingly is the other key technical capability that will make some publishers more competitive than others. Authentication tools must be in place in order for Web users to employ personalization and customization tools, which allow a user to shape a WWW service to fit her needs.

Digital Archives for Teaching and Learning

Today new emerging technologies can be powerful allies in efforts to improve teaching and learning. For technologies to play a truly comprehensive role in reshaping the nature of schooling, however, they must support a broader vision of educational change. The phenomenal growth of the World Wide Web and the rapid development of multimedia technologies are making a wide range of information resources available to the public in ways that were heretofore impossible. Yahoo, the company that provides indexing and search tools for Internet resources, claims that there are 50,000 new Web servers coming online each week.

In US, the Center for Children and Technology has long been committed to a vision of schools and classrooms in which reasoning and problem solving are emphasized, students and teachers help each other learn, students and teachers are motivated and genuinely engaged, the learning environment is responsive to students, teachers use authentic assessment practices, and students learn and effectively apply complex thinking skills and discipline-based knowledge. Technologies that are well designed and well integrated into instruction can help bring about and sustain these kinds of changes in United States' classrooms.

Communications technologies provide teachers and students with opportunities to share, discuss, and exchange ideas with larger communities of learners. Simulations, microworlds, and other discovery-oriented programs create environments in which students can apply thinking skills to solve real-world problems, students can work readily together in groups, and teachers--freed from certain classroom management tasks--can become guides and coaches to students.

Software composition tools, such as word processors, scanners, desktop publishing programs, and video cameras, enable students to express what they know in the form of tangible products, and these products in turn can stimulate further conversation and learning and offer new forms of assessment. Digital storage media, with their great capacity and flexibility, allow teachers and students to pursue a wide range of inquiries into complex subject matter that are tailored to individual interests and needs, and this can motivate students to learn more.

The digital archives being developed by museums, libraries, and other archival institutions are among the most exciting resources driving educational interest in information-based, multimedia technologies. The World Wide Web gives teachers and students opportunities to work with an extraordinary array of authentic materials and up-to-date information. It is precisely the depth, scope, and multiple media nature of such collections that makes them particularly challenging to structure and present in ways that are truly useful to educators and their students. Too often, the developers of various online educational resources have neglected the particular interests of and significant constraints faced by educators.

The creation of digital libraries and archives provides an opportunity to address the design concerns of teachers and students in a challenging but highly rewarding context. The growth of information archives has the potential to achieve the following goals:

— Provide information at any time and in any place;

— Provide access to collections of multimedia information that integrate text, image, graphics, audio, video, and other continuous media;

— Make it possible for users to personalize or customize how they access and represent information for example, by "harvesting" only relevant information and avoiding information overload; and

— Radically enhance collaborative intellectual activities, including research, learning, and design, by reducing barriers of geography, organizational distance, and time.

US' Center for Children and Technology is currently involved in two major initiatives to study and improve the design and use of large archives of scholarly, cultural, and scientific materials for Kindergarter education. In the first project, the Center is collaborating with the Digital Archives group at the Library of Congress to explore how large collections of primary source documents related to American history can be made useful to Kindergarter educators and their students. In a second project, American Natural History Museum's resources are predominantly visual, consisting of objects and images, a main goal of its educational projects is to help people learn how find, look at, think about, and understand visual resources.

The museum also has a rich store of human resources: more than 200 scientists who are world-renowned experts in natural history. As part of its educational efforts, the museum is considering how to incorporate this expertise into designs for digital resources in ways that are judicious yet responsive.

Classroom teachers face a number of obstacles in using and interpreting information-rich resources, and making them relevant to their students. Teachers have different purposes and initially bring different training to the job. There is abundant evidence demonstrating that access and training are key factors that consistently complicate efforts to integrate technology into the classroom. Gaining access to technology resources—particularly the high-speed network connections required to connect to the World Wide Web--is often the first hurdle that schools must overcome.

Limited finances and lack of community awareness can make this a significant hurdle for school districts. It is also well documented that the ongoing training of teachers in how to integrate technology resources in the curriculum is just as important as basic access. Professional development opportunities are often the first items cut from district budgets, leaving teachers in the position of having to seek training and support on their own.

While these issues continue to be chronic challenges for technology integration efforts, two related problems are particularly relevant to thinking about the design of online resources for educators: teacher time and limited contexts or incentives for intellectual exploration. Teachers lack the kind of time that many scientists and scholarly researchers take for granted. Anyone who has spent time researching a paper in the library knows that the process of serendipitous inquiry is often at the heart of discovery—previously unrecognized connections are made and ideas grow through the contemplative process of browsing.

But teachers are often hobbled bureaucratically in their opportunities for the kind of intellectual exploration that is a hallmark of the jobs of scholars and scientists. The nature of schooling is such that most teachers are required to teach a curriculum that they played little or no role in designing and have only limited opportunities to adapt. Teachers are commonly viewed as implementers of state- and district-mandated curricula rather than shapers and interpreters of powerful ideas and methodologies. Often teacher education is built on these assumptions as well. These constraints are brought to the fore when teachers begin to work with the kinds of resources that academic scholars and scientists use. It is the job of scholars and scientists to make new knowledge based on their engagement with these resources.

If digital archives are to be of genuine value to elementary and secondary educators and their students, we must think differently and creatively about how best to support them in making substantive and relevant use of these resources. There are three key design considerations are central to this task. To make large digital archives accessible and engaging for the community, the following issues need to be addressed: teacher ownership, student engagement, and education-relevant search engines.

Developers of print and multimedia educational materials often assume that for their products to be used productively in classrooms, they must be made "teacher proof"--designed in a way that leaves little or no room for experimentation or invention by teachers and students. For example, teachers' guides, rather than creating opportunities for interpretation and ownership, often contain lockstep approaches to teaching and learning. This approach is being challenged widely by educators and researchers who advocate classrooms based on active, constructive teaching and learning processes: solving problems, communicating, reasoning, exploring, inventing, and proving. Increasingly, professional teaching associations and groups involved in education reform are seeking to articulate standards for students that emphasize thinking over memorization.

Although these efforts have gone a long way toward reshaping of the classroom teacher's roles and responsibilities, the publishing industry is still heavily dominated by a mindset that discourages inventiveness in teachers and students. The decentralized architecture of the Internet offers opportunities to build resources for teachers that are not governed by the preconceptions of educational publishers.

The World Wide Web has the potential to serve as an alternative forum, in which developers and designers can experiment with formats that enable educators to bring archival resources into their curricula in ways that make sense to them. The ownership—the process of generating ideas and strategies that make sense within the particular circumstances of one's own classroom and curriculum—is a key to successful use of digital archives.

One possible design approach is to provide teachers with an analytical tool kit that can support different kinds of analyses of resource materials. Analytic tools—such as story boards, spreadsheets, image analysis tools, databases, timelines, templates that describe the content and structure of documents, and resource tools that enable teachers to construct relevant content links—could help teachers evaluate and assemble their own information resources.

For example, if teachers and students are studying the history of the civil rights movement and have access to a digital archive containing photographs of key historical events associated with this period, they can use a timeline tool to construct their own understandings of the narrative events that define the era. If students are studying the growth and decline of the bluefin tuna population, they could use a spreadsheet template to chart, visualize, and help interpret the collected information. Rather than building lesson plans that tell teachers how and when to use archival materials, designers of digital educational resources could develop activity templates that illustrate potential uses of their tools, and could make them available through the World Wide Web.

In some cases, as with story boards or image analysis tools, the templates would be the tools themselves. In other cases, the templates would illustrate ways to use archival materials with off-the-shelf spreadsheets, databases, and timelines. Online conversation spaces would be a key component this tool-based approach. Here teachers could generate and share ideas online about how to use analytic tools with different types of information archives.

US' Center for Children and Technology has worked closely with teachers at the elementary, middle, and high school levels in developing multiple media materials for teaching and learning. The most engaging materials are developmentally relevant--they recognize the understandings and concerns of students at different age levels. In the elementary grades, a student's sense of self is very important, and students develop better understanding in all disciplines when they can connect the subject of study to their own lives.

In elementary social studies, for example, teachers might use photographs, diaries, and other historical artifacts to encourage students to compare what life was like at a particular time in the past with life nowadays. Students might also use timelines, maps, and other visual aids to put past events in chronological order, draw connections among them, and make sense of a sea of information. Designers of resources for the elementary level can make concepts that often seem abstract and remote more familiar and accessible by building in creative ways for children to look and investigate.

Students at the middle schoold age enjoy inquiries and arguments, and archival materials can become evidence for solving a larger intellectual quest or puzzle. Middle school students relish problems of interpretation; by piecing together information from a number of different documents or artifacts, they can begin to develop a better understanding of the meaning of each source and can draw conclusions based on the evidence.

In the humanities, for example, historical narratives, documents, photographs, oral histories, and art can be used to build hypotheses about the historical context in which the sources were created. One compelling way to use archival materials with this age group is to construct a mystery that students answer by hunting for and piecing together clues contained in or across digital archives; this kind of information hunt can be part of a larger inquiry. At the high school level, students are capable of sophisticated inquiry; they also need to feel passionate about and connected to the issues they are studying.

Building connections between the subject area being studied and the issues of real concern to high school students is of paramount importance. Issues of fairness, leadership, and responsibility are examples of themes that can stimulate students to engage with archival materials. For example, students can use scientific databases as core resources for local environmental projects. Or they can use archives that contain historical advertisements to compare past representations of women with their contemporary portrayals. The best informants for developers are likely to be the students and teachers themselves.

One of the most complex tasks associated with using archival materials effectively is the ability to search and browse through large quantities of information in a way that makes conceptual and logistical sense. Indexing schemes that work well for a classroom teacher are likely to be very different from those that function effectively for a scientist or scholar. Many of the indexing schemes currently used by digital libraries and other archival institutions are based on a standard bibliographic categorization system.

Institutions that digitize material find this to be the most efficient way of referencing materials while preserving traditional categorizing system familiar to researchers, scholars, and archivists. But this system was developed during an era when people had to come to libraries, and materials had to be physically organized on shelves. The digital world redefines the concept of categorization and offers new possibilities. To make the best use of the more extensive and flexible digital resources, teachers and students need to be able to build their own approaches to cataloguing archival materials.

As teachers work with an archive and become familiar with its contents, they need to be able to generate their own categories of key terms or thematic topics and use them to organize materials. This not only saves time, but enables teachers to build interpretations of the material that are relevant to the curriculum and to their students' strategies for learning. For example, a middle school teacher could build an index organized around themes that are central to the study of the Civil

War, such as bravery and heroes, or could organize a database on polar wildlife around such themes as habitats, hunting practices, and survival strategies. Because these alternative search schemes require teachers and students to think through their systems of categorization, they also have instructional value. A number of issues must be addressed if new cataloguing tools are to have pragmatic value.

Sharing teacher-built pathways over the World Wide Web is one way to make a wide range of different approaches to and uses of materials broadly available to the education community. Since this process will undoubtedly lead to differences in interpretation—where one person sees poverty, another may see instances of self-determination—teachers will need opportunities to discuss and debate their approaches.

3

Higher Education in 21st Century: Vision and Action

Higher education is now regarded as an institution not only for developing knowledge and training young minds, but for disseminating and applying such knowledge as well. The 20th century will be remembered for its intellectual discoveries of relativity and quantum mechanics, and for the interpretation of the structure of DNA-discoveries that have enabled researchers to unravel some of nature's secrets and the fundamental behaviour of some of its life forms. The university's utilitarian perception of its mission, now regarded with greater emphasis and urgency, has come about largely as a result of these breakthroughs of knowledge in the natural sciences.

Among the consequences of these discoveries could be listed the fantastic development of information technology and high-tech industries, the increase in life-expectancy (chiefly because of advances in medical research and nutritional science), and increased food security (derived from genetic engineering research). In all these, the university has provided much of the leadership; with the partnership of government and its agents, industry and international agencies either as research collaborators or as funding bodies. It is such achievements, such triumphs of science, that have led to a revision of Newman's dictum that higher educational institutions should pursue knowledge only for its own sake. Of course there will continue to be programmes of liberal education devoted entirely to scholarly study of the major works of other scholars to help clarify and possibly modify one's previously held convictions. Pure scholarship will remain with us because of the persistence of the cherished value of freedom of thought and enquiry, that intellectual value upon which the life of the university as a place of research and teaching depends. But in recent times, the immense contributions that university research has made to the national economy ironically places in jeopardy the future funding of such work. The university itself appears to be moving away from its ancient tradition of pursuing pure inquiry for its own sake precisely because of the pressures felt from underfunding.

The current triumphs of research are due in large measure to the provision of adequate financial support from government, from the private sector (through its industries) and from international agencies. The successes of the newly emerging economies in South East Asia-the present economic crises notwithstanding-provide sufficient evidence that in a science and technology-driven economy, it is the university that must be the powerhouse of the 'knowledge economy.' Now governments everywhere are expecting the university to fulfil its role as a major agent of economic growth. However, there is a price to pay for this. The injection of public funds into the university for research requires accountability that may be directed by an outside body and not by reliance upon the university's own evaluative procedures. This may impact negatively on a tenet the university holds so dear: respect for academic freedom and autonomy of choice in conducting one's own research.

In the same way, industry in the private sector is accountable to its shareholders who are typically more interested in their profits than in the pursuit of knowledge for its own sake. Shareholders are likely to favour programmes and projects that yield immediately applicable results. The effect is that basic research will be the loser. Will the university have the moral tenacity and related resources to balance its cherished values of free inquiry and intellectual honesty? Going after government and industry-supported research could lead to long-term consequences that are not easy to predict. The challenge now is to work out ways of catering for the interests of both parties in the research partnership. There is also the problem of research conducted outside the university.

The total government expenditure for research is often shared between the university and other specialised national research institutes or centres, while multinational industries have their own laboratories for research. The conduct of advanced research is no longer solely the preserve of the university. Research results obtained in national research institutes as well as in industry may be classified and so may remain unknown to the research public, sometimes until two or more decades have passed. No longer is all knowledge readily disseminated to all those capable of benefiting from it. This situation clearly undermines the important normative principle of the universality of knowledge, a principle that is treasured by the university and by

International Council for Science (ICSU). The freedom to pursue research and to publish one's results, the freedom to communicate among researchers and to disseminate such research information-these cherished rights-are thereby compromised with predictably morbid consequences for the educational training of the next generation of researchers. How to contend with this constraint is surely a challenge that must be addressed.

These considerations indicate that inadequate funding, leading to the need to generate additional income from other sources, is one reason for the university and its researchers to move toward applied research at the expense of basic research. The need for funding has yielded the marginalization of research motivated by a sense of curiosity generating from the intuition and the sheer intellectual power of individual minds. Yet, fostering such work remains one of the basic missions of any higher educational institution, perhaps all the more so during times of socio-economic crisis.

Prior to the demise of one of the superpowers, national agencies used to support basic research principally for its potential applications in the military and in commerce. But now they have less reason to invest in it. Yet everyone recognizes the economic and social benefits of basic research: it produces background knowledge, it develops research skills, new techniques, instruments and methods that in turn yield economic benefits over a much broader range of production sectors. Also there is a symbiotic relation between basic research and technology, with each moving ahead increasingly faster because of the impact that one has upon the other. Thus inadequate funding for basic research has an immediate deteriorating effect not only on higher educational institutions themselves but on national economies. We need to continue to create the necessary infrastructure for basic research 'to fulfill its mandate as a creative manifestation of the human spirit.'

Information technology has proven to be a powerful aid to the researcher; but its potential has yet to be fully exploited. Its recent forays into the higher education industry, through the establishment of the 'Virtual University', has led some to forecast the demise of the traditional university structure as it is presently constituted. This is because of the several advantages the 'virtual university' has over the traditional one: it encourages collaboration between universities and staff in distant locations; it affords the ready availability of first class libraries to students in varied institutions; and it is an excellent tool for cutting down costs. All that the internet is encouraging is the possibility of providing at lower cost the capacity to unite spatially disparate people. In this way, it enlarges the research community to include those outside one's physical neighbourhood, so that people with shared interests can interact while working in different places on the globe. These are exciting possibilities of which even Cardinal Newman would have approved.

The applications of some research in science and technology have proven extremely hazardous to humanity. This utilitarian criterion—the mandate to apply knowledge, to pursue dominion over the earth—is plagued with danger and measures should be put in place to protect mankind and our environs. Currently, questions are being raised concerning the desirability and even the purpose of some of the research carried out in higher educational institutions. For although these institutions provide the technical tools of civilisation, they do not at present provide any guidance for their use.

They are neither interested in ultimate ends nor can they predict ultimate consequences.

Typically, researchers are now faced with questions concerning the consequences of their work: what will be the consequences of biochemical weapons research for future generations, or of nuclear waste disposal, or of human cloning and other genetic experiments? How can our planet be saved from the current as well as for the future generations? Here we are dealing not just with technological and ecological questions but with moral dilemmas as well. The university cannot remain wholly indifferent to all values other than its cherished prizes of the search for truth and for funds, important though these quests may be. The good members of society, duly trained by the university, should go into life conscious of the deeper issues at stake and of the values involved in them. Truth and its applications must be pursued with responsibility, and it is for this reason that ICSU has created a Committee on Responsibility and Ethics in Science, charged with the duty of helping to find solutions to problems concerning ethics and responsibility in the conduct of science. ICSU aims to ensure that the contributions science makes to humanity will be for our common well-being and for humane social progress.

For, without such ethical vigilance, the distrust that some of the public currently has about science will most likely intensify at great cost to the progress of science. It is the challenge of the researcher to ensure that the two values of freedom and responsibility in the conduct of research are kept in their proper perspective, if the researcher is not to encourage the rejection of progress or modernity as an item of reactionary dogma.

The International Dimension of Higher Education and Research In his Metaphysics, Aristotle claimed that all men by nature desire to know, and in most cases they also desire to apply their knowledge. It is because of man's insatiable desire to know and to apply his knowledge that institutions of higher education exist at all. The economic progress that industrialised nations have enjoyed was hastened because of the existence of the relevant indigenous capability in a social environment that nurtured scholarship.

The gap between the developed and the developing worlds, which is widening at an increasing pace, will be narrowed only if the necessary infrastructure and local supports for high education and research exist within the developing world. While most governments of the developing countries are facing serious economic crises, in the long run it will be to their advantage if a reasonable percentage of their GNP provides the resource necessary for the promotion of quality higher education and capacity-building in research. The advanced countries can also contribute in the effort to create an indigenous base for research by helping to equip researchers of the developing world for full participation in knowledge-based socio-economic development. Working as a researcher in a less than sound environment, with few exceptions, means working in complete isolation. Having himself experienced such loneliness while working in his own country.

There scientists of the Third World get the chance to interact with their colleagues from the industrialised world while at the same time they continue to contribute to the capacity-building of scientists in their own countries. This world will be a better place for all if such institutional experiments could be replicated in other research areas. The challenge, then, is for the world's community of higher educational institutions and researchers to make hope a reality, by finding ways to build bridges between the worlds of North and South, First and Third, men and women. The challenge is to ensure that all scientists, irrespective of where they might find themselves, will be suitably positioned to contribute their best toward solving the world's complex problems, thereby giving substance to the international nature and universality of knowledge.

The curricula of some of the most well-known universities encourage too early a specialisation for the student. A science student specialises in the study of nature but not of man; student of the humanities concentrates upon man, to the complete neglect of nature. Some policy makers are students of the humanities with little or no interest in how the technological gadgets that they regularly use came about. Similarly, some scientists are hardly conversant with the appreciation of poetry or art or music. The public will better appreciate the work of the researcher if he has been prepared with an understanding of that public in all its dimensions. Indeed, our educational system should be guided by the scientific worldview that has emerged in this century, that is the Copenhagen interpretation of quantum mechanics that states that there exist several mutually exclusive but complementary approaches to reality, since nature and society are too subtle to be described from any single viewpoint.

The education of the scientist should include training in the social sciences, and that of the social scientist should include training in the natural sciences, so that it is possible for them both to apply their fullest potentials to national life and development. One of our challenges as we enter the next millennium is to establish meaningful and extensive dialogue across and between disciplines to deal more effectively with some of the outstanding questions in the arts and the sciences.

Still in the 21st century, we are unable to reconcile two of the major discoveries of the 20th century, quantum theory and the theory of gravitation. We are reminded of the dilemma faced by the 19th century researchers between Newtonian mechanics and electromagnetism. Its resolution in the early part of this century set the stage for some of the advances in knowledge already referred to. Are we to witness in the next century a synthesis of quantum mechanics and Einstein's gravitation theory? And what impact will such a feat have on mankind should research succeed in the endeavour? Without doubt, the major problem 20th century research has created is how to sustain development so as to meet the needs of the present generation without compromising the needs of the future generation. As is well-known development is closely linked to environmental change.

Two major causative factors have been identified as responsible for the degradation of the environment, with serious implications for the future of planet Earth. These are the increased consumption patterns and life-styles of the affluent industrialised countries, and high population growth rates in the developing countries. Sustaining these life-styles and catering for the minimum needs of the global community have led to a considerable pressure on our natural resources. For example, energy sources are among the vital ingredients for economic activities as well as for people's daily lives. Fossil fuels which are the principal source of energy are responsible for heavy damage to the environment, contributing to the increase in carbon dioxide, the chief greenhouse gas. They are also a non-renewable source of energy. And yet energy consumption in the world is expected to increase.

And so, in order not to compromise the needs of future generations, the challenge to the researcher whether at a higher educational institution or in industry, is to either identify alternative sources of energy which are renewable and are environmentally-friendly, or if we are to live with non-renewable sources, to find ways of decreasing the carbon dioxide emitted by fossil fuels. How to achieve population stabilization has to be considered not only from a purely economic point of view but from human and cultural aspects as well. Happiness in some cultures means having many children while in others it is having one or none at all. All researchers, social and natural, basic and applied, have a role to play in our attempt to encourage a globally applicable plan for sustainable development.

Research on the management of the environment, is global and interdisciplinary. Fortunately, meaningful cooperation and collaboration is now possible because of information technology. We need to take advantage of this very useful technology. No doubt, the 21st century will raise even more problems but in the midst of difficulties lie challenges and opportunities. We need to ask ourselves what sort of human society we want to build in the next century; it must surely be one dominated by science and technology, but which engages the participation of all researchers. In all our endeavours we should let the following admonishing words of Einstein be our guiding principle for the next millennium.Concern for man himself and his fate must always form the chief interest of all technical endeavours; concern for the great unsolved problems of the organisation of labour and the distribution of goods in order that the creations of our minds shall be a blessing and not a curse to mankind.

Governments should continue to fund basic research to levels which will enable the University fulfil better its role as a major agent of economic growth,

a) Governments of developing countries must create the necessary social environment that nurtures scholarship; they should also provide a reasonable percentage of their GNP to promote quality higher education and capacity-building in research.

b) International organisations and researchers in the developed countries must help break the isolation often experienced by researchers working in developing countries, through such methods as creation of centres of excellence twinning and sandwich post-graduate programmes.

Governments especially from the developing countries are invited to study the opportunities afforded by the new information technology towards establishing 'virtual universities', 'Higher educational institutions and research institutes outside the higher educational set-up need to collaborate to promote the principle of universality of knowledge, Higher educational institutions should ensure that the education of the researcher includes training in both the natural and social sciences, nature and society being too subtle to be described from one single viewpoint only, International organisations including International Council for Science (ICSU) and the International Social Science Council (ISSC), must prepare guidelines for their members concerning the ethics and responsibility in the conduct of their research, ICSU, ISSC, and other international organisations including those n the engineering sciences and industry should collaborate more fully to address the effects of overpopulation and of man-made environmental changes on our planet.

Third World Academy of Sciences (TWAS)

Experience has shown that no country can achieve sustainable economic and social development without the support of a minimum core of indigenous, highly skilled and innovative scientists, technologists and other professionals, who can undertake basic and applied research essential to national development. This view is currently shared by a number of leading economists in the world.

In the majority of developing countries, especially the Least Developed Countries (LDCs), there is an acute shortage of world-class professionals. This is largely due to the failure of the institutions of higher education to attract, properly train and retain these professionals. The reasons are well-known. They are mainly attributed to the deteriorating infrastructure in universities and the acute shortage of leadership due to declining budgets and the brain drain. In addition, there has been a substantial increase in the student body, resulting in the over-production of poorly qualified graduates. Basic sciences are the worst hit by this crisis.

The challenge, therefore, is how to reverse this situation and create opportunities to attract and train young talents and sustain them to conduct problem-solving research. In many developing countries there is a strong political will to change and invest more in education and research but they are crippled by debt and globalisation problems.

International Cooperation Strategies

Centres of excellence in education and research in developing countries can jointly play a significant role in uplifting the status of higher education in developing countries, especially in the LDCs.

— We need to identify these centres (TWNSO/TWAS/ South Centre project).

— We need to form thematic networks of these centres working in similar fields and provide them with modern communication technologies to facilitate their interaction.

— We need to establish comprehensive graduate and postgraduate training programmes at these centres and offer attractive fellowships to talented students to pursue their studies at these centres. The demand for such programmes is very high.

— We need to link these networks of centres of excellence in the South with their counterparts in the North and facilitate joint research programmes and exchanges of professionals.

Joint international action co-sponsored by governments and major development aid organizations, including the World Bank, the regional Banks and UNDP, to establish regional foundations to provide funds to improve the quality of higher education in the developing world. A foundation for the African region is most needed. It should have a capital fund of about one billion US dollars, the income of which could be utilized to improve the infrastructure for research and training in institutions of higher education provide competitive fellowships to talented students to pursue postgraduate research and training at centres of excellence in the South; counteract the brain drain by providing attractive conditions and incentives to leading indigenous scientists and other professionals; facilitate the flow of world-class scientists and other professionals from the North to the South to assist in building local capacities in higher education.

Integration of Research Development

As we move into the future to relate to the multicultural diversity, we must make fullest use of distance education, continuing education, interdisciplinary education, using the powerful new tools being provided by science and technology, and not necessarily keeping to the institutional frameworks we have created and nurtured so far. An important aspect would be to increase public understanding of science, particularly to make it intelligible, exciting and show its relevance.

Science and technology are a manifestation of human creativity at the highest level, with profound implications for society. But, as a search for truth, for an understanding of nature and in creating the enormous edifice of knowledge that we have today, it is undoubtedly an intrinsic part of Culture, perhaps a different face of culture on account of its philosophy and method, from that of the art science in its internal functioning is universal but it must derive from the multicultural culture of our global society; it is the latter, which makes human society so productive and so interesting.

Universal Networking

In exploring this theme of universal networking, we would like to touch on first, the context in which we all now find ourselves, with some comments on where we are now, and examine the opportunities we are afforded, and the challenges that we in higher education and in government will have to meet.

The Nature of Information and Communication Technologies: There are two particular aspects of the context that would like to mention, within which higher education functions. One view of our society is that a new wave of economic and social activity, associated with profound technological change, is replacing the industrial age. In this paradigm, information and communication technologies (ICTs) are 'the key to bringing in new flexible working practices, ridding, bureaucracy of its numerous dysfunctions, and allowing economies of scope, rather than economies of scale to be achieved'. A number of researchers have analysed the impact that the new technologies have had on society. They find on the one hand, the potential for moving towards a more egalitarian society, in which there are hugely expanded opportunities for accessing and exchanging information. But they also find, on the other hand, evidence for the emergence of new social divisions between those who hold much information and those who hold little, the information rich and the 'information poor'. They also find some evidence for the use of these technologies as a means of introducing subtle forms of social control.

Yet however one views the effects of the changes in technology there is no doubt that they have impinged on the nature of information and communication in our institutions of government and of higher education. The coming of the personal computer to our institutions has enabled far-reaching changes in working practices to be developed. The combination of computers and telecommunications has brought about new and differing ways of organizing work. The electronic interchange of data allows faster, more accurate and more efficient flows of data between our institutions, and, within higher education, between academics and students, researchers and funding bodies, university administrators and academic staff. Two particular characteristics of information and communication technologies are worth mentioning.

— The ability to produce information which enables the organisation into which it has been introduced to reflect on that information and, as a result, introduce changes.A good example is a university library where the computerised circulation and control systems supply the professional librarians with detailed information on their customers' preferences, use patterns of the books, and requirements. Thus the data generated by the processes of issuing, returning and reserving books can be used to reshape the way libraries handle the books so that they become more efficient in the use of their stock.

— Communicating and networking information. The networking of information can be used for a range of activities, some of which lead inevitably to control by others. Governing the Information Age give four main capabilities of these networks, each of value to the researcher.

— Electronic networks can permit the integration of data which are held in different computer files, in different information systems, in different places and, even, in different organizations or jurisdictions.

— Electronic networks allow for the cross-matching of data, enabling new kinds of information to emerge, information which can significantly extend the 'intelligence' possessed by those who have access to such processes.

— Networking can bestow much more flexibility and precision in the targeting, tailoring and differentiation of information flowing to and from specific groups of businesses, customers cr citizens. and,

— The flexibility and connectivity associated with electronic networks can permit organizations and individuals, alike, to acquire much more autonomy and selectivity in the ways in which they retrieve, disseminate and communicate information.

Each characteristic offers positive benefits to higher education, either in its administrative practice, or its research. Many of our universities see themselves as global institutions. And the demand to learn is expanding exponentially throughout the world. Equality of opportunity in seeking access to higher education is still far from achieved. Whereas participation at tertiary levels in OECD countries is between 30 and 50 per cent, in non-OECD countries, East Asia and the Pacific Islands it is below 15% and in South Asia around 5%. Sub-Saharan Africa has even lower participation rates. The World Bank has indicated that by 2025 as many as 150 million individuals will be seeking higher education.

Most of the new demand, however, will come from the countries with low incomes where the infrastructure needed to meet that demand will be the least developed. New ways of making education available to these communities need to be found. Already a number of developments have been established which make use of a learner centred, flexible, technology-driven system of education available throughout the globe. These can be single institutions or partnerships, mergers and consortia. One example of an established body which offers distance learning is Open Learning Australia which acts as a broker to make courses from Australian Universities available to far-flung students in remote locations.

A new development is the growth of degree providers who are in the private, for-profit sector. Most are based in the US and include the University of Phoenix which has 48000 degree-credit students at 57 learning centres in 12 states: it offers an on-line campus and specialises in particular areas at the BA completion and master's decree levels, especially in business, IT and teacher education.

The explosion of distance learning programmes is very marked within industry, some of which hreaten university provision. Kaiser Permanente, in the US health field, offers on 300 distance learning sites, bachelor's and master's degrees for nurses and continuing education for doctors. Vice president of the American Association for Higher Education is that the inherently global nature of distance education will lead to the establishment of major international combines. He asks 'What would the postsecondary marketplace look like if (say) Microsoft Deutsche Telekom, International Thomson and the University of California combined to offer UC courses and degrees world wide. In time, its only competitor could be a combine of like standing and deep pockets: an IBM-Elsevier-NEC-Oxford combine, for example."

International networks for mutual cooperation and benefit in relation to university projects have been lone, established. There are four types of inter-university networks:

— *The associations and learned societies*—These include formal consortia of universities such as the Council of European Rectors, and the many international learned societies such as own. The Society for Research into Higher Education. Information is disseminated through professional groups who are able to reflect on and evaluate new developments which affect the universities. Research based networks can also provide a forum for initiating further collaborative projects.

— *Inter university Ccooperation projects, joint european projects*—Small international research networks frequently develop, often stimulated by European Union financing. These carry out research on a particular topic over a certain period of time. They often continue to function after the research grant is finished, and are run by the researchers themselves. Major European Union programmes such as Erasmus and Tempus also fit into this grouping. Usually they are organised as discipline-orientated networks and are most likely to continue after the project has ended if their members can continue to meet under the aegis of a discipline based learned society.

— *Partnership with others Bodies*—An example of such partnerships was the European Union Comett Programme which involved universities and business enterprises through a regional framework. Although that programme has ended, similar examples of international industry/university networks can be found.

— *Institutional Networks*—These have developed notably over the last decade with universities in one country seeking links with others, sometimes with a view to establishing student mobility arrangements, joint research initiatives, and academic staff exchange. The networks frequently deal with mobility, information, exchange, lobbying and putting in tenders.

Establishing links with other universities offers several advantages: not least the ability to focus a university's attention on the areas in which it excels and to find companion universities to provide strength in other fields. The organisation of networks can vary considerably. Networks, after all, are essentially complex systems which function within their own political and social environment. Some can be informed groups, with loosely attached participants, open to all who wish to join. Others can be formal, closed organisations with legal status such as joint ventures and strategic alliances.

4

Restructuring Teacher's Work

The comprehensive changes in teachers' roles would contribute to higher student achievement. This change promoted changes in teachers' roles in school governance, collegial relations, and the classroom. The relationship of these changes to one another, and weighed the likelihood that they had the capacity to affect core educational practices. Theoretically, this is situated in the available literature on teachers' collegial relations; participation in shared decision making; and classroom roles, relationships and practice. Three elementary schools served as the sites for intensive qualitative data collection completed over a two-year period. The schools differed in geographic location (two urban, one rural), but all enrolled a racially, ethnically and linguistically diverse population of students, and more than half of the students in each school qualified for free or reduced price lunch.

The multiple types and sources of data on teachers' professional roles, including: observations in classrooms, collegial interactions, and governance situations; interviews with teachers (including teacher leaders), parents, administrators, and students; and documents pertaining to the restructuring plans and process. Some schools introduced changes in classroom practice and roles, ranging from the adoption of multi-age classrooms to more modest innovations in curriculum or instruction. In only one case were changes in professional roles outside the classroom organized to support and sustain classroom changes. Two of the three schools introduced changes in staff organization (teacher teams) and leadership (governance committees), but underestimated the professional development and other supports that would in turn support changes in classroom practice. Altogether, it appears unlikely that the observed changes in professional roles were sufficiently well established and connected to affect core educational practice in the long run.

From 1880 to the present, little has changed in the organizational structures, instructional practices, and authority structures of teachers' work. Some authors theorized that this stability is due to the fact that school governance has been situated in the hands of individuals external to the classroom. Lortie has argued that it is due to the fact that much of teachers' work inside the classroom has been largely independent and individually-controlled. Still others have argued that teacher-centered instruction is the culprit. Whatever the reason, teachers' work today remains fairly similar to that of 100 years ago; it is characterized as individual work, with the governance power situated in the hands of individuals external to the classroom, and instruction that is largely teacher-centered.

The core of education practice as the teachers and students' role in learning and school practices, and how these ideas about knowledge and learning are manifested in teaching and the classroom. The structural arrangements of the school or classrooms such as physical layout, student grouping, as well as communication among parents, teachers and staff. In short, reforms have not affected what teachers and students do when they are together.

For example, the recommendations contained in California's elementary school reform blueprint, It's Elementary, touch on the learning environment of the classroom, diversity, and technology as well as organizational issues such as scheduling class work in larger blocks. But it consider the teacher's role in governance and only touched on some aspects of the teachers' role in classroom or collegial relationships. Thus, the prospects for changing the core of education were reduced. In 1990, California's School Restructuring Demonstration Program envisioned comprehensive changes in teachers' professional roles that would result in more "powerful learning" for students.

One of the purposes of California Senate Bill 1274 was to test the feasibility of large-scale systemic school reform, the hope being that the bill would affect school sites beyond the schools participating in the bill. In the final form, the bill included the following, "The demonstration of restructuring is intended to be a five-year effort aimed at improving student learning. The demonstration centers on the goal of engaging all students in powerful learning experiences, and a rich-thinking curriculum which empowers them to become life-long learners.

All students, regardless of race, ethnic, linguistic or socioeconomic background need to learn to think critically, solve problems individually or as part of a team, analyse and interpret new information, develop convincing arguments, and apply their knowledge to new situations. The demonstration invites educators to consider radical changes in the way schools and districts operate in order to create a better environment for engaging all students in powerful learning experiences and in a rich, meaning-centered curriculum".

Schools were asked to create new structures and practices that included increased professional collaboration and capacity-building, a greater number of diverse stake holders in decision-making processes, improved curriculum assessment and diverse instructional strategies, increased inquiry by examining students work, and better shaped specific strategies that impact the whole school.

The bill, although generally vague in meaning, would require changes in teachers' work to be successful. This approach of changing teachers' work to change the classroom is uncharacteristic of past reform bills that have virtually ignore teachers' work.

Moreover, the bill seems to touch on the issues outlined by Elmore's core theory. The call for professional collaboration and capacity building could affect the teachers and adult communication and relationships on the school level (collegial relations). The call for the inclusion of greater number of stakeholders in decision-making processes could require a change in teacher, parent and staff roles in school governance.

Finally, changes in curricular instructional strategies and the examination of student work could impact teacher and student roles in the classroom (classroom roles and relationships). In short, the bill would require changes in teachers' work in the areas of collegial relations, governance and classroom roles and relationships. Instead of once again studying why teachers' work has remained stable or why the core has not changed, SB 1274 allowed me to look at a bill that would require changing teachers' work in order to change the core.

Some of the focal schools, showing how they were positioned to undertake comprehensive restructuring, and recording the choices they made in the three areas of collegial relations, governance, and classroom roles, relationships and practice. Schools made restructuring choices based in part on SB 1274's theory that altering professional roles and relationships would improve academic achievement.

Web is a science and technology magnet school in a small urban district. Web Magnet school was created in 1990. As a magnet school, the school is designed to serve the district's high achieving students.

The school is located across the highway from the poorer neighborhood from which it draws most of its students, but the school itself is located in a middle to upper income area. Web does not screen its entering classes of kindergartners, but students transferring to Web from other schools are tested for high achievement levels in math and language arts.

Web's students routinely perform better on standardized tests than the rest of the district schools. The wait list for Web enrollment is very long; one parent reported waiting almost two years before her daughter could enter the school. Web serves 280 Pre K through 8th grade students. While the district is approximately 65% Latino and 35% African American, Web's student body is 62% African American, 30% Latino, 3% White, and 3% Asian, Pacific Islander, and Filipino. Twenty-three percent of the students are classified as LEP, which has grown from 7% in three years. Fifty one percent of the students qualify for free or reduced meals.

Web's staff consists of 10 classroom teachers, a science teacher, a principal, a computer teacher and a librarian. The staff is 71% white and 29% African American. This school has had two principals since the restructuring process began and both are African-American women. The science teacher is the only male staff member. Web's staff has experienced high turnover, and consequently, there are no staff members remaining who were at the school when the original 1274 grant was written. Teachers' responsibilities, in addition to teaching, include yard duty, bus duty, computer room duty and fellowship committee. Yard, bus, and computer duty consists of the supervision of children in the assigned areas before and after school. The fellowship committee is in charge of "school parties that keep the morale of everybody up".

Web teachers keep their classes for two years in a row (cycling), moving back and forth each year between two grades. For example, a 5th grade teacher will move with her class to 6th grade. Once the 6th graders move to the 7th grade, the teacher goes back to 5th grade and process begins again. In addition to cycling, Web focused its classroom restructuring efforts on the use of Integrated Thematic Instruction (ITI) as well as Brain Compatible Instruction in all of the classrooms. One thing that sets Web school apart from the two other schools is the union involvement. Several members of the staff were union leaders, and many teachers were very involved in union activities.

Olive Grove Elementary School serves 576 kindergarten through 6th graders in a largely rural area in Northern California. Between 1990 and 1992, the school's Hmong and Mien student population rose from almost nothing to 29 % of the student body. The school is still shaping its Limited English Proficiency (LEP) program in the wake of this population change.

Fifty-five percent of the students are white; 7% are Latino; and 7% are African American. Fifty-one percent come from families with income low enough to qualify for Aid to Families with Dependent Children (AFDC). The school is in the process of applying for Chapter One status based on the high number of students who qualify for free and reduced lunch.

Olive Grove's teaching staff consists of 23 classroom teachers, 14 aides, and a resource teacher. Three of the 23 classroom teachers are male. There are Hmong bilingual aides. The majority of the staff is white, and the principal is a white male. As part of their restructuring initiative, the school changed its classrooms to form multiage/ multiyear groupings.

Classrooms are either self-contained kindergarten, 1/2 combinations, or 3-6 clusters, which consist of approximately 7 third graders, 7 fourth graders, 7 fifth graders, and 7 sixth graders. Children stay with the same teacher and classmates in each of the groupings, culminating in four years with their 3-6 grade teacher. In addition, teachers are grouped in three K-6 grade teams, with approximately seven classrooms making up each team. The school has also adopted class meetings as an instructional change. Teachers are required to hold class meetings everyday. Class meetings begin with students and teacher sitting in a circle. They give complements, they discuss problems, and they discuss class business. The school has experienced little staff turnover since the grant began; 15 of the 23 teachers working when the grant was awarded in 1991 are still on site, as is the principal. The average years of teaching experience for the staff is 10 years.

At Olive Grove, we also found changes in professional roles and practice, but, unlike at Trent, the changes occurred first and most clearly in the classrooms. As the first step in Olive Grove's restructuring process, they moved to a multiage/multiyear configuration. In moving to this structure, teachers' roles and practices changed inside the classroom.

However, these changes were not anticipated. Teachers no longer used textbooks, and teachers stopped using directed lessons because techniques such as individualized packets made the varying ages of the students easier to teach and control. In addition, to cope with the multiage configuration, teachers needed students to help each other which allowed the "student as teacher" role to arise.

Teachers could not always work with all levels at once, so teachers had to move from being the one who asked the majority of questions and gave the majority of answers to one of many teachers in the room. Finally, this change in structure led Olive Grove's teachers to change their focus. They moved from a focus on curriculum to a focus on classroom management, control of behavior and socialization. After these changes to professional roles and practices occurred inside the classroom, Olive Grove attempted to change teachers' roles outside of the classroom through the creation of action teams.

Although Olive Grove made bold changes in their classrooms, their efforts fell short of the ultimate goal of increasing student achievement. The staff lost focus of the goal and began to focus on control. Since they did not have a mechanism in place to evaluate their efforts, they were unaware of the difficulties, and thus, they were unable to refocus their work.

Web, did not demonstrate clear changes to professional roles inside or outside of the classroom. Web, more than the other two schools, continues to function as a "typical" school. Teachers continued to be isolated and administrators continued to lead.

However, it is important to note that Web had uniform practices across the school. The small school size enabled the administrator to spend her time checking each classroom weekly to make sure there was evidence of ITI and Brain Compatible Instruction in place. This technique is obviously one way to make change happen at a small school, but it led to low teacher morale, high turnover and superficial adoption of techniques. Web's reforms may not have resulted in many changes for a number of reasons. It could be the lack of professional development training for new teachers, the high turnover, or the fact that as a small school, the teachers at Web already wear many hats.

At a small school such as Web, teachers must take on many roles and responsibilities because they have fewer support staff than a larger school. Thus, maybe there was no shift in teachers' roles from what is typically expected because teachers' roles at Web were not truly typical to begin with. New teachers (new to the profession and the school) were less likely to adopt their school's reform efforts. For example, at Web, all of the experienced teachers used Brain Compatible techniques in their classrooms, but the new teachers resisted this change.

Teacher Education in 21st Century

As we entered into the twenty-first century, the outcomes, consequences, and results of teacher education have become critical topics in nearly all of the state and national policy debates about teacher preparation and licensure as well as in the development of many of the privately and publicly funded research agendas related to teacher and student learning. Teacher education reform over the last fifty years has been driven by a series of questions about policy and practice. The question that is currently driving reform and policy in teacher education is what we refer to as 'the outcomes question.' This question asks how we should conceptualise and define the outcomes of teacher education for teacher learning, professional practice, and student learning, as well as how, by whom, and for what purposes these outcomes should be documented, demonstrated, and/or measured. We suggest that the outcomes question in teacher education is being conceptualized and constructed in quite different ways depending on the policy, research, and practice contexts in which the question is posed as well as on the political and professional motives of the posers. This chapter begins with an overview of the policy context, including those reforms and initiatives that have most influenced how outcomes are currently being constructed, debated, and enacted in teacher education. There are three major 'take' on the outcomes question in teacher education—outcomes as the long-term or general impacts of teacher education, outcomes as teacher candidates' scores on high stakes teacher tests, and outcomes as the professional performances of teacher candidates, particularly their demonstrated ability to influence student learning. For each of these approaches to outcomes, we examine underlying assumptions about teaching and schooling, the evidence and criteria used for evaluation, units of analysis, and consequences for the profession.

We point out that how we construct outcomes in teacher education (including how we make the case that some outcomes matter more than others) legitimizes but also undermines particular points of view about the purposes of schooling, the nature of teaching and learning, and the role of teacher education in educational reform. In public opinion polls of what concerns Americans most, education has ranked higher than the economy, the environment, and even crime.

The recent history of teacher education—roughly the last half century—has been analyzed in terms of philosophical and epistemological positions, historical trends, and paradigms of inquiry. Another way to think about and trace teacher education reform, however, is in terms of the major questions that have driven the field and the varying and sometimes competing ways these questions are constructed, debated, and enacted in research, policy, and practice. Along these lines, a very loosely chronological (and necessarily simplified) list of the major questions that have driven teacher education reform over the last 50 years might go something like this: the attributes question, the effectiveness question, the knowledge question, and what proposing we now think of as "the outcomes question" in teacher education. Each of these questions both shaped and was shaped by the political climate, the degree and kind of public attention to K-12 schooling, the perceived supply and demand of teachers, federal and state policies and funding programs, perceptions of teacher education as a profession and an area of scholarship that ought to be located (or not) in colleges and universities, and emerging and competing paradigms and programs of research on teaching, teacher learning, and teaching/learning/curriculum in the subject areas.

The effectiveness question focused different issues: "What are the teaching strategies and processes used by effective teachers, and, what teacher education processes are most effective in ensuring that prospective teachers learn these strategies?" This question drove many of the developments and reforms in teacher education during the late 1960s through the mid 1980s. Influenced by new studies of the "scientific basis of teaching" and by empirical evidence about effective teaching strategies, many teacher education programs developed systems for evaluating prospective teachers according to scientific objectives and stated performance criteria. Checklists and other forms of assessment attempted to align classroom teachers' practices with the criteria used by fieldwork supervisors to evaluate the practice of teacher candidates and also with teacher education processes, programs, and language. Some of the other questions that shaped this period arose at least partly in response to perceived flaws in the effectiveness question. New questions rooted in anthropological and sociolinguistic theories about the meanings of classroom events for participants, for example, countered the effectiveness question and pointed to what was left out of discussions that focused on effective teacher behaviors.

Public concern about the quality of teaching and teacher education, the knowledge question drove the field from the early 1980s through the late 1990s. This question became mantra throughout the field, "What should teachers know and be able to do?" and/or, its companion, "What should the knowledge base of teacher education be?" At the heart of the knowledge question was the desire to professionalize teaching and teacher education by building a common knowledge base for the profession. Building on early research about teachers' thinking and on emerging knowledge in the various subject matter disciplines related to children's learning, the knowledge question moved the field away from an emphasis on what effective teachers do to a focus on what they know and need to know, the knowledge sources they use, how they organize and evaluate knowledge, and how they learn to construct new knowledge that is appropriate for differing local contexts, particularly for increasingly diverse learners.

Versions of the knowledge question identified and made distinctions among formal and practical knowledge, pedagogical content knowledge, case knowledge, craft knowledge; knowledge in action, reflection on knowledge, culturally relevant knowledge, and local knowledge generated through teacher research and/or action research. Prompted in part by new programs of research and in part by changing accreditation standards, the knowledge question drove major policies and program revisions in teacher education intended to ensure that the burgeoning codified knowledge base was at the center of the curriculum. Some versions of the knowledge question concentrated on the contexts within which prospective teachers could gain the knowledge and practices they need.

As we close the twentieth century and open the twenty-first, the major question that is driving the field is the outcomes question in teacher education. Before turning to the outcomes question, however, several other comments are important. First it is important to point out that the questions have sketched above are not simply research questions, although each of them has research aspects, and several have spawned major programs of empirical study. Each of them also has to do with policy and practice in teacher education and with the intersections as well as disconnects among the three. More important to note, however, is the fact that each of these animating questions is also in some fundamental way a question about the priorities and goals of the profession. Thoughtful article about the relationships between mathematics research and National Council of Teachers of Mathematics (NCTM) standards, the rightness or legitimacy of priorities and goals are questions of value and belief rather than questions of evidence that can suggest educational policies based on varying levels of confidence.

There has not been complete consensus in teacher education at any point over the last half century—nor is there now—about which questions are the right ones to ask. There have always been—and hopefully will continue to be—competing questions as well as questions that critique, play off of, and take on the major animating issues. Thus my short list knowingly leaves out a host of important issues and critical questions that have been explored energetically by practitioners, policy makers, and researchers in teacher education. Finally it is important to note that none of the questions have loosely associated with particular time periods was settled during that time period or disappeared from consideration after that time. Rather many of the questions that drive the field during particular eras are periodically recycled, reemphasized, and rethreaded into new and current intersections of research, practice, and policy in ways that may or may not appear to be different from their previous iterations.

For example, some of the questions about intellectual rigor in teacher education programs and the questionable scholarship of teacher education faculty that were prominent in the late 1950s and early 1960s reemerged in the 1980s. Even though the 'new' critiques apparently had little to offer that was different from the old, they were nonetheless different in that they emerged in the context of a different social and political climate. Similarly, some of the underlying assumptions of 1970s and 80s questions about the relationships of teaching and learning processes and products are being recycled into some current versions of the outcomes question in teacher education, and of course some outcomes questions were also explored in the early and mid 1980s. Old questions, however, are never just "same ole" old questions. They are instead "new" old questions because they have a different import and a different set of implications when they are woven into the tapestry of a changed and changing political, social, and economic time.

As we enter the twenty-first century, the outcomes, consequences, and results of teacher education have become critical topics in nearly all of the state and national policy debates about teacher preparation and licensure as well as in the development of many of the privately and publicly funded research agendas related to teacher and student learning. If the major question that drove the field during the last fifteen years was, "What should teachers and teacher candidates know and be able to do?" then the driving question for the last three or four has been, "How will we know when teachers and teacher candidates know and can do what they ought to know and be able to do?"

The context of reform in teacher education has been analyzed and described at great length from policy, curricular, organizational, and political perspectives. The outcomes debate is deeply embedded in the movement to professionalize teaching and to secure for teaching and teacher education a legitimate place among other health and human services professions. As is now well-documented, there has been a major effort over the last 15 years to codify and disseminate the formal knowledge base for teaching and teacher education in order to insure that teacher education is no longer a normative, natural, or intuitive process. Prompted in large part by nationwide criticisms of teaching and teacher education in the early and mid 1980s and by early work about teachers' thinking and knowledge, the professionalization movement was intended to make teacher education a state-of-the-art field by establishing an official and formal body of knowledge that distinguished professional educators from lay persons.

The development of standards for the profession has been a central part of the professionalization movement. Since the mid 1980s, the National Council for the Accreditation of Teacher Education (NCATE) has evaluated teacher preparation programs according to the professional knowledge bases and later the conceptual frameworks that shaped and connected the various coursework and fieldwork pieces of the curriculum. The National Board for Professional Teaching Standards (NBPTS) was established in 1987 as the first professional organization in the teaching profession to establish standards for the advanced certification of highly experienced and successful teachers. These were parallel to the model performance-based licensing standards developed by the Interstate New Teacher Assessment and

Support Consortium (INTASC), which was initiated in 1987 by the Council of Chief State School Officers to support the work of states in rethinking and reinventing teacher preparation and teacher licensing.

NCATE 2000 standards also offer performance standards in keeping with those of NBPTS and INTASC. This means that there are major efforts now well underway to develop a common national system of accreditation of "professionally grounded and performance-based standards for education, licensing, and certification" that is remarkably broad-based in its support and connects the accreditation of teacher preparation institutions with initial state licensing systems as well as systems for the advanced certification of experienced teachers. All of these center on authentic assessment of teacher performance. Notwithstanding the critique that professional standards for teaching and teacher education are largely provisional and unvalidated—based on a consensus of professional educators and an emerging knowledge base rather than on tested outcomes and solid evidence, standards are now part of state licensing requirements in most states are play a major role in the outcomes context.

Part of the professionalization of teaching and teacher education was mounting recognition that training models were inadequate to the major tasks of teaching and school reform, and new models of professional development for prospective and experienced teachers were required. In fact, as we enter the new century, it is now being suggested that there is a "new paradigm" for professional development and a "new professional consensus" about what teacher education and teacher learning need to look like in order to handle the new tasks of teaching and learning in restructured schools. The general orientation of the "new" approach to professional development is more constructivist than transmission- oriented; it is based on the recognition that both prospective and experienced teachers (like all learners) bring prior knowledge and experience to all new learning situations, which are social and specific.

In addition, it is now generally understood that teacher learning takes place over time rather than in isolated moments in time, and that active learning requires opportunities to link previous knowledge with new understandings. It also has been widely acknowledged that professional development needs to be linked to educational reform and needs to focus on 'culture-building' not skills training. It is generally agreed that professional development that is linked to student learning and curricular reform should be embedded in the daily life of schools and should feature opportunities for teachers to inquire systematically about how teaching practice constructs different kinds of learning opportunities for students. These new understandings about teacher learning are consistent and intertwined with the emerging standards for the profession.

At the same time that researchers and practitioners in teaching and teacher education were working to build and codify a knowledge base, new frameworks for teaching, learning, and curriculum in almost every K-12 subject area were also being developed by the discipline-based professional organizations such as the National Council of Teachers of Mathematics (NCTM) and the National Council of Teachers of English (NCTE). These were based on new understandings about learning, cognition, and the socio-psycho-cultural construction of subject matter understandings. These were intended to promote teaching for meaning and understanding and explicitly to avoid narrow emphases on skills development and rote learning. New curriculum frameworks were eventually implemented in almost every state, and in most of these, they were coupled with new standards for K-12 student achievement. In most states, new teaching and learning standards were eventually accompanied by high stakes paper and pencil assessments intended to be tightly aligned with the knowledge and skills outlined in the new curriculum frameworks, which in turn were to be tightly aligned with the new knowledge bases in each of the disciplinary areas as established by the professional organizations.

What is closest to day-to-day work of teacher educators are the new outcomes-based approaches to evaluating teacher preparation programs and institutions. An outcomes-based approach is now in effect at NCATE, the major teacher education accrediting agency. Emphasizing outcomes rather than inputs was also a major reason for the founding of newcomer accrediting organization, Teacher Education Accreditation Council (TEAC). Although fewer than half of the nation's teacher preparation institutions are currently accredited, NCATE-accredited institutions produce two thirds of the nation's teachers. In addition, NCATE has relationships with 40-some states, and some are moving to require all teacher preparation institutions to seek accreditation from either NCATE or TEAC. NCATE 2000's new focus on outcomes has been described as a "paradigm shift from inputs to outputs", a 'bold' and 'daring... plunge into the world of performance assessment and performance standards", and a "major shift from curriculum- oriented standards to performance-based standards that focus on what teacher candidates know and are able to do". NCATE's prior standards were described by critics as merely "counting courses" or focusing on curriculum content instead of paying attention to results. The new standards focus on what teacher candidates can actually do in schools and classrooms by emphasizing performance, particularly in relation to students' learning.

The new standards, which received final approval in 2000, are effective for all institutions seeking NCATE accreditation during or after Fall 2001. NCATE's new system will require schools of education to provide performance evidence of candidate competence, including state licensing examination results as well as summarized and sampled performance evidence of candidates' knowledge and skill. The stated rationale for the first major section of the new standards, "Candidate Performance," makes this emphasis clear:

> The public expects that teachers of their children have sufficient knowledge of content to help all students meet standards for P-12 education. The teaching profession itself believes that student learning is the goal of teaching. NCATE's Standard 1 reinforces the importance of this goal by requiring that teacher candidates know their content or subject matter, can teach, and can help all students learn . .
>
> Candidates for all professional education roles are expected to demonstrate positive effects on student learning. Teachers and teacher candidates should have student learning as the focus of their work...Primary documentation for this standard will be candidates' performance data prepared for national and/or state review ...[including] performance assessment data collected internally by the unit and external data such as results on state licensing tests and other assessments.

The new NCATE standards are in keeping with movement to professionalize teaching and also consistent with recent developments in specialized accreditation organizations more generally, where the emphasis has shifted from inputs to outcomes measures.

The aspects of the policy context for the outcomes mentioned so far are in sync with one another in certain important ways —the development of standards for subject matter teaching, new understandings of teacher learning, new standards for the accreditation of teacher education institutions, and the efforts of NCTAF, NBPTS, INTASC, and NCATE to unify teacher preparation, licensing, and certification. All of these are consistent with the first item on the list—the movement to establish teaching as a legitimate profession with a well-established knowledge base, jurisdictional responsibility for defining and acting on professional problems, and clear principles or standards for professional practice.

Each of these initiatives works from but also builds on the dual premises that caring, competent, and qualified teachers are essential to insuring rigorous learning opportunities for all children in America's schools and that upgrading teacher education and credentialing for the profession are necessary for ensuring that all children have such teachers. As is now well known, however, the professionalization movement is not the only national agenda related to teaching and teacher education. There is also a well publicized and well-funded movement to deregulate teacher education by dismantling teacher education institutions and breaking up the monopoly that the profession (i.e., schools of education, professional accrediting agencies, and many state licensing departments) has, according to its critics, too long enjoyed.

The deregulation movement, well-funded by conservative political groups like the Heritage Foundation, the Pioneer Institute, and the Fordham Foundation, begins with a premise that is radically different from the premises of professionalization. Those who support deregulation assert that teacher education programs and most of the requirements of state licensing agencies are unnecessary hurdles that keep bright young people out of teaching and focus on social goals (even "social engineering") rather than academic achievement. Denigrating professionalization efforts as the "romance of regulation", the Fordham Foundation's 250 page volume on how to get "better schools" and "better teachers", for example, intentionally frames its agenda in opposition to efforts to professionalize teaching and teacher education. The Fordham Foundation "manifesto" asserts:

> Today in response to widening concern about teacher quality, most states are tightening the regulatory vise, making it harder to enter teaching by piling on new requirements for certification. On the advice of some highly visible education groups, such as the National Commission on Teaching and America's Future, these states are also attempting to 'professionalize' teacher preparation by raising admissions criteria for training programs and ensuring that these programs are all accredited by the National Council for the Accreditation of Teacher Education (NCATE). That organization is currently toughening its own standards to make accredited programs longer, more demanding, and more focused on avant-garde education ideas and social and political concerns...

The regulatory strategy that states have followed for at least the past generation has failed. The unfortunate results are obvious: able liberal arts graduates avoid teaching, those who endure the process of acquiring pedagogical degrees refer to them as 'Mickey Mouse' programs, and over time the problems of supply and quality have been exacerbated. When a strategy fails, it does not make much sense to do the same thing with redoubled effort. Yet that is what many states are now doing.

Lest anyone think they eschew all regulations related to teacher education, editors of the Fordham volume concede that some regulation is necessary:

> Every child should be able to count on having a teacher who has a solid general education, who possesses deep subject area knowledge, and who has no record of misbehavior. The state has an obligation to ensure that all prospective teachers meet this minimal standard.

High stakes testing as the primary way to ensure teachers' subject matter knowledge, and a heavy emphasis in schools on academic achievement, order, and discipline. Part of a larger conservative political agenda for the privatization of American education, the deregulation movement is an influential part of the policy context in teacher education, it is playing a major role in the ways we construct outcomes in teacher education.

The different ways outcomes are being constructed in teacher education rest on differing assumptions about what teachers and teacher candidates should know and be able to do, what K-12 students should know and be able to do, what counts as evidence of "knowing" and "doing," and what the ultimate purposes of schooling should be. Different premises about the purposes of schooling mean different ways of demonstrating that teacher education programs and procedures are 'accountable,' 'effective,' or 'value-added.' Despite these differences, however, most discussions about teacher education outcomes have to do with the connection between teacher education and student learning. In a certain sense, every debate related to outcomes assumes that the ultimate goal of teacher education is student learning and that there are certain measures that can be used to indicate the degree to which this outcome is or is not being achieved by teacher candidates, K-12 students, teacher educators, higher education institutions, local or state policies, and the education profession itself.

It is important to note that unanimity about the outcomes questions we should be asking begins and ends here, at this rather surface level of understanding. If we move one level deeper in terms of specificity or elaboration, we uncover disagreement. If we attempt to describe the relationship between teacher learning and professional practice, attempt to explain what we mean by teacher learning and student learning, attempt to elaborate the theoretical bases and consequences of the kinds of student learning we are trying to account for, or even attempt to define what we mean by 'students', we uncover differences, some of which represent deep philosophical and political divides. Notwithstanding the growing—and many say unprecedented—consensus about standards for teaching and teacher education, it is important to acknowledge that there is considerable variation both within and outside the profession in terms of how outcomes are being constructed and upon what grounds they are being debated.

There are three major ways of constructing outcomes in teacher education are currently receiving major attention and visibility nationally, at the state level, and within teacher education institutions: the long-term or general impacts of teacher education as a profession; the aggregated scores on teacher tests of teacher candidates, teacher preparation programs, and/or higher education institutions; and the professional performances expected of teachers and teacher candidates. In some policy and practice contexts, one or more of these is used in combination with others to guide decisions about distribution of resources, licensing and accreditation privileges, and relative rankings of programs, institutions, and individuals.

Outcome as 'teacher test results' What impact should preservice teacher education be expected to have on teacher test results? What results on teacher tests should be expected of teacher candidates, teacher education programs. Outcome as 'professional performance' What professional performances should teacher candidates be expected to demonstrate? How should teacher candidates and teacher education programs/institutions be expected to document, analyze, and evaluate these professional performances?

The first major take on the outcomes question concerns the long-term or general impact of teacher education on teacher knowledge, teacher preparedness, teacher attrition, teacher ratings, and student achievement. Explorations of these questions in teacher education are located within much larger debates about teacher quality and teacher qualifications, teacher licensing and certification, professional standards for teaching and curriculum, and the use of student achievement as a valid evaluation measure for teachers and schools. Various studies have analyzed whether teacher candidates who have completed approved teacher education programs stay in teaching longer than those without such preparation, whether their attitudes and knowledge about teaching and learning are different, whether they feel more committed to teaching than others or more prepared to teach, and whether their principals rate them higher or lower than others. Studies have also compared the teaching ratings of liberal arts graduates with those prepared in pedagogy and/or have compared the teaching effectiveness, including the classroom management skills, of those with minimal versus extensive subject matter knowledge and/or minimal versus full preparation in teaching. Other studies have considered whether education and subject matter preparation predict teaching performance of teacher candidates and/or have an impact on students' achievement. There is a great deal of attention currently to sorting out the results of these studies and drawing policy conclusions from them.

The issue that is most visible and most highly contested has to do with the impact of teacher education on K-12 students' learning. Debated in the research literature and in the media, is being explored primarily through meta-analyses and/or syntheses of previous and current work in order to make recommendations about teacher education as state policy that is either value-added or not, either a good investment or not. In these high stakes debates, teacher education at the preservice level is not considered by itself but as one of several factors related to the quality and qualifications of teachers. The unit of analysis is not teacher candidates—individually or collectively—or even teacher preparation programs and institutions. Rather the unit of analysis is the profession itself—teacher preparation as one aspect of a broad category referred to as teacher qualifications, which includes scores on licensure examinations, graduate level degrees, years of experience, preparation in the subject matter area of certification as well as in pedagogy, type and extent of certification in the teaching area, and amount of money spent by school districts on professional development.

Student learning is generally defined as student gains on achievement tests, often reading and mathematics in grades one through twelve. The relationship between the two is taken to be the percentage of variance in student gains accounted for by teacher qualifications when other variables are held constant or adjusted. The pertinent units of analysis are aggregated student achievement scores and general indices of teacher qualifications that include multiple features. The impact of teacher education are at the heart of many policy debates related to the initial preparation of teachers as well as teachers' continuing professional development. These have enormous implications for how states (and now the federal government) support and invest in the improvement of schooling, how higher education institutions support and invest in teacher education programs and schools of education, and how school districts establish and maintain hiring and reward systems as well as local programs of ongoing professional development.

Constructing the outcomes of teacher education as long-term impact on students' achievement is part of NCTAF's larger campaign to provide qualified and competent teachers for all students by emphasizing and aligning professional standards across initial teacher preparation, teacher licensure, and teacher certification at the state and regional levels. This take on the outcomes question provides little information about the impact of teacher education disaggregated from teacher qualifications more generally, nor does it address the relative merit of various approaches to teacher education, although there is related research that does so. But this was never the point of constructing outcomes as long-term impact of teacher qualifications on students' achievement. The point was to demonstrate that teacher education, as part of teacher professionalization more broadly, was and is a good investment—for state policy makers, for higher education institutions, and for the future of a democratic society.

Another conclusion about long-term impact as an outcome of teacher education. Some economists offer analyses of teacher preparation, licensing and certification that support the deregulation of teacher education and seek to limit the power of the educational community to control the profession.

The fact that some of the same evidence is used to make two exceedingly different cases about teacher education is confusing to say the least. The evidence concerning the relationship of teacher education and student learning outcomes continue, and they are growing increasingly heated.

Problem of Teacher Education

Part of the difference in conclusions about the long- term outcomes of teacher education may lie in the details of the ways terms are defined and data are selected for these analyses. For example, there are major differences across reports in what is included under 'alternate programs,' what it means to be 'fully qualified,' or 'to have a major' in one's area of certification. The accumulation of many small differences in definitions of terms and data analysis procedures may account for some of the major statistical differences and the contradictory conclusions of these two major syntheses. But the differences may also be partly explained by differences in the way the problem of teacher education is framed in the first place and how these different constructions shape the ways terms are defined, procedures are established for data selection, results are manipulated, and interpretive frameworks are developed.

The teacher tests now required for initial licensing in most US states suggest another highly visible way that outcomes are being constructed in teacher education. The construction of test scores as outcomes is in a certain sense a subset of the preceding construction in that the test scores of prospective teachers are often taken to be one facet of the long-term impact of teacher education. However, because teacher tests have been given so much recent attention and weight, it is worth considering them separately.

The teacher tests are connected to larger discussions about quality, licensing, standards, and assessment. Teacher tests are also related to the long history of criticisms of teachers as mediocre students, semi-skilled workers, less than literate individuals, and members of a minor or not quite profession. With initial licensing tests, what is measured (and taken to be an indication of what prospective teachers have learned) is usually some combination of general knowledge, including communication and literacy skills, with knowledge of specific subject matter and pedagogy, both of which are demonstrated on a paper and pencil exam.

Although teacher test scores have probably received more publicity and more public outcry than any other recent measure of outcomes, they are linked to teacher performance and K-12 student learning primarily through presumption rather than empirical evidence and/or are considered in combination with other measures of teacher expertise or teacher qualifications that are difficult to untangle as I noted a moment ago. There is little evidence that large-scale implementation of statewide teacher testing programs is affecting the actual classroom performance of teachers, although there is some evidence that testing has an impact on the 'quality' of those entering and remaining in teaching where quality is defined as other test scores, grade point averages, and similar measures.

Of particular importance in the Higher Education Act are the mandatory accountability requirements, which stipulate that all states and colleges/universities receiving federal dollars must provide annual information on the performance of all teacher candidates recommended by an institution on each measure required for licensure. As has been widely broadcast, these data are to be compiled into institutional and state "report cards" intended to serve as indicators of the fitness of the teacher education enterprise and will provide public (and no doubt highly politicized) rankings of teacher education institutions in the U.S. By switching the unit of analysis from individuals to institutions, recent testing arrangements locate the responsibility for teacher education outcomes squarely at the feet of colleges and universities, some of which will be seriously threatened with closure when the new regulations go into effect.

In some states, it has even been suggested that a major result of teacher tests has been to discredit schools of education and provide ammunition for those who would like to close them. In a strange sort of contradiction, teacher tests in some places are now being framed in the media as both outcomes of teacher education (i.e., teacher education programs and institutions get public blame for low test scores), and, at the same time, prerequisites for teacher education programs (i.e., candidates in some institutions are now being required to take certain portions of tests in order to be admitted to programs in the first place). Constructing outcomes in teacher education as scores on teacher tests creates a number of problems and has important consequences for the pool of candidates entering the profession. Some statewide teacher tests, for example, are anathematic to the concepts and knowledge taught in teacher education programs, particularly in terms of conceptions of literacy, views of student learning, and notions of growth and progress. Unfortunately, at exactly the same time that we are supposedly interested in recruiting a more diverse pool of teacher candidates, teacher tests are working as gate keepers to keep some potential teachers out.

Fear of poor performance on teachers tests is leading some schools of education to change admissions standards with the consequence that fewer students are applying, and there is increasing evidence that the implementation of teacher tests—like other tests historically that are biased against minorities—may be playing a role in the decline of minority participation in the teaching profession. Further, although some studies have also considered whether teacher candidates prepared in fully-accredited teacher education programs score higher on teacher tests than those prepared in other teacher education programs and/or those with no teacher preparation, there is little evidence that teacher test scores are related to actual teaching performance in classrooms or to students' learning.

The third take on the outcomes question—and the one that is closest to the everyday work of many teacher educators—has to do with the professional performances that teacher candidates should be expected to demonstrate, including the ways candidates and teacher educators document, analyze, and evaluate these performances. This version of outcomes is located within larger debates about authentic assessments of teaching that result in student learning, the shift from "inputs" to "outputs" as the basis of professional accreditation reviews of teacher education institutions, the development of quality assurance mechanisms based on professional standards that are consistent across the professional lifespan, and a growing body of literature that examines the relationships of inquiry, knowledge, professional practice, and teacher education pedagogy.

Constructing teacher education outcomes in terms of the professional performances of teacher candidates begins with the premise that there is a professional knowledge base in teaching and teacher education based on general consensus about what it is that teachers and teacher candidates should know and be able to do. The obvious next step, then, is to ask how teacher educators will know when and if individual teacher candidates know and can do what they ought to know and be able to do. A related and larger issue is how evaluators will know when and if teacher education programs and institutions are preparing teachers who know and can do what they ought to know and be able to do. In a recent historical sketch of performance assessment, today's emphasis on performance assessment in K-12 education is part of a larger sea change in educational measurement that highlights the "3 P's—performance, portfolios, and products" and that has captured "the linguistic high ground, just as the term 'minimum competency testing' did in the 1970s".

The performance assessment is based on the same technology as all assessments—obtaining a small piece or sample of a candidate's behavior drawn from the larger domain of knowledge and skill it is assumed to be part of and then using the candidate's performance on that sample to make inferences about his or her likely performance on the entire domain. Defining performance assessment broadly, there are three ways to sample behavior from a larger domain—requiring an examinee to construct or supply oral or written answers to some set of questions, requiring him or her to perform an act that will be evaluated according to certain criteria, or requiring him or her to produce a product of some kind.

In teacher education, performance assessment is intended to evaluate teacher candidates' ability to produce "products" and complete "authentic tasks" that closely resemble the real work of teaching and do so in ways that are aligned with consistent internal and external standards and criteria. The notion of professional performance as outcome is a central to new partnerships among accrediting, licensing, and certification agencies across states and the nation. Performance as outcome is also implicated in the debate between NCATE and TEAC as accrediting agencies, including disagreements about whether the latter is a threat to professionalization or a useful and appropriate accrediting alternative for many institutions. Performance as outcome is behind the move in some states to require all teacher education institutions to seek either NCATE or TEAC accreditation as well as other new state requirements that teacher education programs provide evidence that teacher candidates have state-of-the-art knowledge and a demonstrable impact on K-12 students' learning.

5

Transformations in Higher Education: Challenges and Opportunities

Education has a far greater intrinsic value than the monetary worth of a degree in the marketplace. Phat private businesses enter this arena with little experience and fewer qualifications as providers of higher education. But we must acknowledge that they also enter with fewer of the entrenched traditions that have made colleges and universities so inflexible and slow to respond to the changing needs of students.

In their 1958 book, *Higher Education In Transition: An American History, 1636 - 1956*, Brubacher and Rudy recount the fascinating history of the evolution of the present layered structure of the American educational system. Beginning with village schools and academies, they founded colleges patterned after English four-year colleges and then added what were known as preparatory schools. Next they added to the colleges graduate and professional schools on the German model. Then inserted transitional institutions, the junior high school or middle school, and the junior college, now commonly called community college. At every stage of this creation process, educators vigorously debated the purposes and the proper "thickness" of each layer, and the circumstances and conditions that should attend a student's transition from one layer to the next. Although traces of these debates persist today, this gradually accreted sedimentary structure has largely hardened into something with the apparent hardness of stone. It seems that it is time to revive the vigorous debate of a century ago and reconsider the whole structure of the American education system.

Business and government leaders are less interested in what kind of a general degree a student has than in knowing more precisely what he or she knows and can do. Rather than continue to rely on diplomas or degrees, we ought to consider developing a more detailed suite of certification that would give a truer picture both are students knowledge and of their skills. Perhaps the most powerful driver of change in the universities is information technology. One of the most frequently expressed concerns in discussions of the impact of information technology on education is that it may isolate students from their teachers and one another, dehumanise the process of education, and destroy the academic communities.

Information technology might disrupt traditional modes of academic research and undergraduate education, sometimes ideally pictured as a professor and a graduate student working together at a laboratory bench in an intimate mentor-apprentice relationship. The fearful overlook the fact that, in many fields, that idyllic model has long since been abandoned. Perhaps the most salient example is that of experimental elementary particle physics.

Decades ago, the size and cost of the basic tool of the field, the particle accelerator, outgrew the financial capacity of any single scientist, any single university, and most single nations. The result today is a very few international laboratories where single experiments occupy teams of hundreds of physicists for a decade, and cost hundreds of millions of dollars. The life of a faculty member engaged in academic research of this sort bears little resemblance to the conventional ideal. A colleague who for several years managed a normal campus teaching load in Cambridge (Massachusetts) while running a major experiment at DESY in Hamburg, at the cost of a weekly transatlantic round trip, once described himself as holding an endowed chair on Lufthansa. The graduate students of another colleague calculated his annual average speed by dividing his annual air mileage by the number of hours in a year and came up with a value of about 35 mph. Information technology did not cause this to happen, but it did make it all possible.

It is worth remembering that the World Wide Web was originally invented by a British programmer to serve the communication needs of a mere couple of thousand elementary particle physicists spread around world. For the immediate future, while all these changes take place, we must continue to adapt to the duality that accompanies any great cultural shift. We must continue to juggle information that we receive and store electronically and on paper; to teach and take classes on campus and online; to interface physically and virtually; to search the stacks and comb the shelves and surf the Web until we have all the information we need.

The use to which any new technology is put depends on who controls it. To a skilled cabinet-maker, a laser-guided router is a tool which assists in the creation of better cabinets. To a profit-seeking firm, it is a machine which reduces the costs of production by requiring less labor per cabinet or by allowing the replacement of skilled labor with lesser-skilled labor - cheaper, of course - for some of the procedures of cabinet-making. Much of the history of capitalism can be written as a sequence of invasions in which the control of production in industry after industry shifts from crafts persons to capitalist enterprises. In most of these industries we can identify a critical point - usually based on a newly available technology - at which the successful invasion of craft-based production began.

As one of the last centers of craft-based production, higher education has enjoyed an anomalous position within the capitalist economy. Capitalism needs us as a producer of an educated labor force. So legislatures fund us - within obvious limitations - and some individual capitalists earn the esteem of their peers by funding various aspects of higher education or even founding entire universities However, we have only retained this independence because higher education has not yet become completely susceptible to the methods of command and control typical of capitalist enterprise. The faculty still have a governance role at most colleges and universities. Aside from the large lecture hall with section meetings conducted by teaching assistants, there have not yet been many ways to exploit economies of scale in higher education.

There have been few technological developments other than printing and the copy machine that have had much effect on how university faculties and students produce education. As in the first universities of medieval Europe, higher education is still a labor-intensive product in which the labor force itself must be highly educated. Capitalists have needed the universities and colleges to provide them with engineers, managers and other professionals. Capitalists have earned profits supplying goods and services - from construction to textbooks to computers - to these educational institutions. But there has been no profit in producing higher education itself. It has become part of the necessary infrastructure of capitalism, rather like a road system, and its operation has best been left to the state.

The accelerating power and falling prices of computers; the Internet; computerized data banks; the proliferation of basic computer skills within the college-age population: all are factors making higher education ripe for invasion by capitalist enterprise. It is now possible to earn a profit providing higher education, or at least something that will pass for higher education in the eyes of its "consumers." Online education, in particular, may become capital's major beachhead in its incursion into this new territory. Marx traced the process by which simple tools - under the control and often even the ownership of crafts persons - evolved into machines and systems of machines which were under the control of capitalists. But the modern computer is both tool and machine.

Higher education is still in the sphere of craft production and the crafts persons continue to have a voice in how this production takes place. Professors look to the new technologies for opportunities to improve the quality of the work and to provide better access to educational materials for the students. And computer-mediated education offers us quite a bit:

— Physical location will no longer be a primary criteria for students selecting courses. A student looking for a

Survey of Economics course, for example, will be able to surf the Web and examine syllabi in order to pick the course that best meets his or her needs. This also benefits the professor as more of the students will be committed to the course from the beginning.

— Students can be linked in new ways. When their papers are posted electronically, they can read each others papers - the professor can direct a student who has trouble with concluding paragraphs to look over some papers with good concluding paragraphs. This would be a cumbersome process if we tried to accomplish it through copying and physically circulating student papers.

— Updating of materials becomes simpler and faster as more sources become available online.

— The tedious part of managing a course can be automated and improved. The student can get a response on exams which provides links to the appropriate materials. Grades can be calculated automatically. This leaves more time for commenting on student papers, reading essay answers more carefully, or for any of the more important aspects of teaching.

— Students can fit more of their coursework into convenient times. The worker with rotating shifts and the salesperson who has to travel can take online courses.

— Educational opportunities for the hearing-impaired or mobility-impaired student and/or professor are expanded.

The profit-seeking firm sees these technological breakthroughs in a completely different light:

— There is a global market for a product which has virtually no transportation costs.

— No classrooms are necessary. Instructors will work out of their homes, so they don't even have to be provided with offices. Except for some specialized software, the equipment required is strictly off-the-shelf. All of these factors reduce the start-up costs and the risks.

— The production of education can be broken down into sub-assemblies. High-cost labor can be used only where necessary - for course design, course updating, and development of specialized software. Standardization of the product allows for a more extensive division of labor. The actual instructors will only have to meet the minimal requirements for accreditation and can be paid very little. Since the instructors will be, for the most part, following a script, this work can be carried out by high-turnover labor, much like McDonald's or Taco Bell.

— Every activity in the virtual college leaves an electronic trail. All work can be monitored and quantified: the time an instructor takes to answer a student e-mail; the percentage of each instructor's students that continue to enroll in the college; or any deviations from the approved script in the instructor's answers to student questions. It will even be feasible to pay instructors on a piecework basis instead of by the credit hour.

Today's institutions of higher education - whether state-supported or private non-profit - are facing a new threat. For the first time in the histories, we face potential competition from the for-profit private sector. Driven only by the quest for profits, these firms do not share the ethics, the values, or the concept of what constitutes good higher education. Since the instructor can be anywhere, these education firms will not be restricted by local labor markets: they will be able to hire instructors at very low pay rates. Accreditation may pose some temporary problems, but online colleges will be able to shop around to find the region with the loosest accreditation policies.

The relentless drive of capital to spread its tentacles into every area of human life is a powerful force. But the traditions of higher education have deep roots, some going back 700 years or more. While we often decry institutional inertia when we want to introduce new courses or programs, this resistance to change becomes the ally when we find ourselves threatened by forces from outside of the institutions of higher education. Among the many possibilities of how this will unfold, two potential scenarios stand out: one leads to the dismantling of higher education as we know it today; in the other we use the new technologies to improve higher education and keep the for-profit schools at bay - at least until the development of artificial intelligence software that can display most college professors.

The first scenario could lead to the takeover of lower- and middle-level higher education by private firms, leaving only the top research institutions functioning as traditional universities:

— Private colleges start by 'cherry picking.' They go for the older students, many of whom are employed by firms that pay their tuition. They concentrate on the programs with the largest number of majors, such as education and business. Phoenix University, which accepts only students who are 23 or older and are employed, is already pursuing this strategy.

— In some of the programs that are most susceptible to standardization, these firms will be able to undercut the fees charged by state-supported institutions, even though these fees only cover a small part of the total cost. Community college students in Washington state currently pay $250 to take a five-credit course. The student fees cover about 20 percent of the cost of the state's community college system. A for-profit college that is totally online might charge $200 while paying the instructor $1,500 [8]. With an average class size of 20 students, there will be $2,500 per course to cover the other costs and provide profits.

— The state-supported colleges begin to look like high-cost operations when compared with the private virtual colleges.

— The large corporations that have tuition-reimbursement programs start complaining to the legislatures that they are paying twice - once through the taxes that support the public colleges and again when they pay tuition for their employees at the for-profit schools. Soon there is a movement afoot to finance most of the state's higher education through a voucher program - and the vouchers can be used to pay the for-profit colleges as well as for the traditional colleges.

The second scenario is far more palatable. But bucking the current tide of capitalist expansion will require much foresight and some favorable luck:

— The public colleges establish ourselves as providers of online education before the for-profits get very far with their plans.

— Online programs become hallmarks of quality in online education.

— We use veteran faculty, but only faculty who wish to teach via the new technologies.

— The for-profit virtual colleges make serious mistakes. Too many of their green instructors cannot adequately answer student questions. The scripts developed by their course designers are too rigid and not updated often enough.

— Tradition and inertia provide us with some breathing space. In the minds of much of the public, the existing core of state-supported and private non-profit universities, colleges and community colleges are the providers of education.

If we try to ignore the new technologies, we will be swept away by those who harness this electronic force. We must recognize that the information technologies are powerful tools that, in the hands of skilled crafts persons, can improve the quality of the service that we produce. If we fail in this endeavor, we will meet the new technologies as labor-displacing machinery which will assist capital in its conquest of one of the few remaining fields of craft-based production.

However, the trend towards automation of higher education as implemented in North American universities today is a battle between students and professors on one side, and university administrations and companies with "educational products" to sell on the other. It is not a progressive trend towards a new era at all, but a regressive trend, towards the rather old era of mass-production, standardization and purely commercial interests. Recent events at two large North American universities signal dramatically that we have entered a new era in higher education, one which is rapidly drawing the halls of academe into the age of automation.

In mid- summer the UCLA administration launched its historic "Instructional Enhancement Initiative" requiring computer Web sites for all of its arts and sciences courses by the start of the Fall term, the first time that a major university has made mandatory the use of computer telecommunications technology in the delivery of higher education. In partnership with several private corporations, moreover, UCLA has spawned its own for-profit company, headed by a former UCLA vice chancellor, to peddle online education. This past spring in Toronto, meanwhile, the full-time faculty of York University, Canada's third largest, ended an historic two-month strike having secured for the first time anywhere formal contractual protection against precisely the kind of administrative action being taken by UCLA. The unprecedented faculty job action, the longest university strike in English Canadian history, was taken partly in response to unilateral administrative initiatives in the implementation of instructional technology, the most egregious example of which was an official solicitation to private corporations inviting them to permanently place their logo on a university online course in return for a $10,000 contribution to courseware development.

As at UCLA, the York University administration has spawned its own subsidiary, directed by the vice president for research and several deans and dedicated, in collaboration with a consortium of private sector firms, to the commercial development and exploitation of online education. Significantly, at both UCLA and York, the presumably cyber-happy students have given clear indication that they are not exactly enthusiastic about the prospect of a high-tech academic future, recommending against the Initiative at UCLA and at York lending their support to striking faculty and launching their own independent investigation of the commercial, pedagogical, and ethical implications of online educational technology. This Fall the student handbook distributed annually to all students by the York Federation of Students contained a warning about the dangers of online education.

At the very outset of this new age of higher education, the lines have already been drawn in the struggle which will ultimately determine its shape. On the one side university administrators and their myriad commercial partners, on the other those who constitute the core relation of education: students and teachers. It is no accident, then, that the high-tech transformation of higher education is being initiated and implemented from the top down, either without any student and faculty involvement in the decision-making or despite it.

At UCLA the administration launched their Initiative during the summer when many faculty are away and there was little possibility of faculty oversight or governance; faculty were thus left out of the loop and kept in the dark about the new web requirement until the last moment. And UCLA administrators also went ahead with its Initiative, which is funded by a new compulsory student fee, despite the formal student recommendation against it. Similarly the initiatives of the York administration in the deployment of computer technology in education were taken without faculty oversight and deliberation much less student involvement. What is driving this headlong rush to implement new technology with so little regard for deliberation of the pedagogical and economic costs and at the risk of student and faculty alienation and opposition? A short answer might be the fear of getting left behind, the incessant pressures of "progress". But there is more to it. For the universities are not simply undergoing a technological transformation. Beneath that change, and camouflaged by it, lies another: the commercialization of higher education.

The major change to befall the universities over the last two decades has been the identification of the campus as a significant site of capital accumulation, a change in social perception which has resulted in the systematic conversion of intellectual activity into intellectual capital and, hence, intellectual property. There have been two general phases of this transformation. The first, which began twenty years ago and is still underway, entailed the commoditization of the research function of the university, transforming scientific and engineering knowledge into commercially viable proprietary products that could be owned and bought and sold in the market. The second, which we are now witnessing, entails the commoditization of the educational function of the university, transforming courses into courseware, the activity of instruction itself into commercially viable proprietary products that can be owned and bought and sold in the market. In the first phase the universities became the site of production and sale of patents and exclusive licenses. In the second, they are becoming the site of production of - as well as the chief market for - copyrighted videos, courseware, CD-ROMs, and Web sites.

The first phase began in the mid-1970's when, in the wake of the oil crisis and intensifying international competition, corporate and political leaders of the major industrialized countries of the world recognized that they were losing their monopoly over the world's heavy industries and that, in the future, their supremacy would depend upon their monopoly over the knowledge which had become the lifeblood of the new so-called "knowledge-based" industries (space, electronics, computers, materials, telecommunications, and bioengineering). This focus upon "intellectual capital" turned their attention to the universities as its chief source, implicating the universities as never before in the economic machinery. In the view of capital, the universities had become too important to be left to the universities.

Within a decade there was a proliferation of industrial partnerships and new proprietary arrangements, as industrialists and their campus counterparts invented ways to socialize the risks and costs of creating this knowledge while privatizing the benefits. This unprecedented collaboration gave rise to an elaborate web of interlocking directorates between corporate and academic boardrooms and the foundation of joint lobbying efforts epitomized by the work of the Business-Higher Education Forum. The chief accomplishment of the combined effort, in addition to a relaxation of anti-trust regulations and greater tax incentives for corporate funding of university research, was the 1980 reform of the patent law which for the first time gave the universities automatic ownership of patents resulting from federal government grants. Laboratory knowledge now became patents, that is Intellectual capital and intellectual property.

As patent holding companies, the universities set about at once to codify their intellectual property policies, develop the infrastructure for the conduct of commercially-viable research, cultivate their corporate ties, and create the mechanisms for marketing their new commodity, exclusive licenses to their patents. The result of this first phase of university commoditization was a wholesale reallocation of university resources toward its research function at the expense of its educational function. Class sizes swelled, teaching staffs and instructional resources were reduced, salaries were frozen, and curricular offerings were cut to the bone. At the same time, tuition soared to subsidize the creation and maintenance of the commercial infrastructure (and correspondingly bloated administration) that has never really paid off. In the end students were paying more for their education and getting less, and the campuses were in crisis.

The second phase of the commercialization of academia, the commoditization of instruction, is touted as the solution to the crisis engendered by the first. Ignoring the true sources of the financial debacle - an expensive and low-yielding commercial infrastructure and greatly expanded administrative costs - the champions of computer-based instruction focus their attention rather upon increasing the efficiencies of already overextended teachers. And they ignore as well the fact that their high-tech remedies are bound only to compound the problem, increasing further, rather then reducing, the costs of higher education. (Experience to date demonstrates clearly that computer-based teaching, with its limitless demands upon instructor time and vastly expanded overhead requirements - equipment, upgrades, maintenance, and technical and administrative support staff - costs more not less than traditional education, whatever the reductions in direct labor, hence the need for outside funding and student technology fees). Little wonder, then, that teachers and students are reluctant to embrace this new panacea. Their hesitation reflects not fear but wisdom.

But this second transformation of higher education is not the work of teachers or students, the presumed beneficiaries of improved education, because it is not really about education at all. That's just the name of the market. The foremost promoters of this transformation are rather the vendors of the network hardware, software, and "content" - Apple, IBM, Bell, the cable companies, Microsoft, and the edutainment and publishing companies Disney, Simon and Schuster, Prentice-Hall, et al. - who view education as a market for their wares, a market estimated by the Lehman Brothers investment firm potentially to be worth several hundred billion dollars. "Investment opportunity in the education industry has never been better," one of their reports proclaimed, indicating that this will be "the focus industry" for lucrative investment in the future, replacing the health care industry.

It is important to emphasize that, for all the democratic rhetoric about extending educational access to those unable to get to the campus, the campus remains the real market for these products, where students outnumber their distance learning counterparts six-to-one. In addition to the vendors, corporate training advocates view online education as yet another way of bringing their problem- solving, information- processing, "just-in-time" educated employees up to profit- making speed. Beyond their ambitious in-house training programs, which have incorporated computer-based instructional methods pioneered by the military, they envision the transformation of the delivery of higher education as a means of supplying their properly-prepared personnel at public expense.

The third major promoters of this transformation are the university administrators, who see it as a way of giving their institutions a fashionably forward-looking image. More importantly, they view computer-based instruction as a means of reducing their direct labor and plant maintenance costs - fewer teachers and classrooms - while at the same time undermining the autonomy and independence of faculty. At the same time, they are hoping to get a piece of the commercial action for their institutions or themselves, as vendors in their own right of software and content. University administrators are supported in this enterprise by a number of private foundations, trade associations, and academic-corporate consortia which are promoting the use of the new technologies with increasing intensity.

Behind this effort are the ubiquitous technozealots who simply view computers as the panacea for everything, because they like to play with them. With the avid encouragement of their private sector and university patrons, they forge ahead, without support for their pedagogical claims about the alleged enhancement of education, without any real evidence of productivity improvement, and without any effective demand from either students or teachers.

In addition to York and UCLA, universities throughout North America are rapidly being overtaken by this second phase of commercialization. There are the stand-alone virtual institutions like University of Phoenix, the wired private institutions like the New School for Social Research, the campuses of state universities like the University of Maryland and the new Gulf-Coast campus of the University of Florida. On the state level, the states of Arizona and California have initiated their own state-wide virtual university projects, while a consortia of western "Smart States" have launched their own ambitious effort to wire all of their campuses into an online educational network. In Canada, a national effort has been undertaken, spearheaded by the Telelearning Research Network centered at Simon Fraser University in Vancouver, to bring most of the nation's higher education institutions into a "Virtual U" network.

The overriding commercial intent and market orientation behind these initiatives is explicit, as is illustrated by the most ambitious U. S. effort to date, the Western Governors' Virtual University Project, whose stated goals are to "expand the marketplace for instructional materials, courseware, and programs utilizing advanced technology," "expand the marketplace for demonstrated competence," and "identify and remove barriers to the free functioning of these markets, particularly barriers posed by statutes, policies, and administrative rules and regulations."

Start up funds for the project come from the private sector, specifically from Educational Management Group, the educational arm of the world's largest educational publisher Simon and Schuster and the proprietary impulse behind their largesse is made clear by Simon and Schuster CEO Jonathan Newcomb: "The use of interactive technology is causing a fundamental shift away from the physical classroom toward anytime, anywhere learning - the model for post secondary education in the twenty-first century." This transformation is being made possible by "advances in digital technology, coupled with the protection of copyright in cyberspace." Similarly, the national effort to develop the "Virtual U" customized educational software platform in Canada is directed by an industrial consortium which includes Kodak, IBM, Microsoft, McGraw- Hill, Prentice-Hall, Rogers Cablesystems, Unitel, Novasys, Nortel, Bell Canada, and

MPR Teltech, a research subsidiary of GTE. The commercial thrust behind the project is explicit here too. Predicting a potential fifty billion dollar Canadian market, the project proposal emphasizes the adoption of "an intellectual property policy that will encourage researchers and industry to commercialize their innovations" and anticipates the development of "a number of commercially marketable hardware and software products and services," including "courseware and other learning products." The two directors of the project, Simon Fraser University professors, have formed their own company to peddle these products in collaboration with the university. At the same time, the nearby University of British Columbia has recently spun off the private WEB-CT company to peddle its own educational Web site software, WEB-CT, the software designed by one of its computer science professors and now being used by UCLA. In recent months, WEB-CT has entered into production and distribution relationships with Silicon Graphics and Prentice-Hall and is fast becoming a major player in the American as well as Canadian higher education market.

The implications of the commoditization of university instruction are two-fold in nature, those relating to the university as a site of the production of the commodities and those relating to the university as a market for them. The first raises for the faculty traditional labor issues about the introduction of new technologies of production. The second raises for students major questions about costs, coercion, privacy, equity, and the quality of education. With the commoditization of instruction, teachers as labor are drawn into a production process designed for the efficient creation of instructional commodities, and hence become subject to all the pressures that have befallen production workers in other industries undergoing rapid technological transformation from above. In this context faculty have much more in common with the historic plight of other skilled workers than they care to acknowledge. Like these others, their activity is being restructured, via the technology, in order to reduce their autonomy, independence, and control over their work and to place workplace knowledge and control as much as possible into the hands of the administration.

As in other industries, the technology is being deployed by management primarily to discipline, de-skill, and displace labor. Once faculty and courses go online, administrators gain much greater direct control over faculty performance and course content than ever before and the potential for administrative scrutiny, supervision, regimentation, discipline and even censorship increase dramatically. At the same time, the use of the technology entails an inevitable extension of working time and an intensification of work as faculty struggle at all hours of the day and night to stay on top of the technology and respond, via chat rooms, virtual office hours, and e-mail, to both students and administrators to whom they have now become instantly and continuously accessible. The technology also allows for much more careful administrative monitoring of faculty availability, activities, and responsiveness. Once faculty put their course material online, moreover, the knowledge and course design skill embodied in that material is taken out of their possession, transferred to the machinery and placed in the hands of the administration.

The administration is now in a position to hire less skilled, and hence cheaper, workers to deliver the technologically prepackaged course. It also allows the administration, which claims ownership of this commodity, to peddle the course elsewhere without the original designer's involvement or even knowledge, much less financial interest. The buyers of this packaged commodity, meanwhile, other academic institutions, are able thereby to contract out, and hence outsource, the work of their own employees and thus reduce their reliance upon their in-house teaching staff.

Most important, once the faculty converts its courses to courseware, their services are in the long run no longer required. They become redundant, and when they leave, their work remains behind. In Kurt Vonnegut's classic novel Player Piano the ace machinist Rudy Hertz is flattered by the automation engineers who tell him his genius will be immortalized. They buy him a beer. They capture his skills on tape. Then they fire him. Today faculty are falling for the same tired line, that their brilliance will be broadcast online to millions. Perhaps, but without their further participation. Some skeptical faculty insist that what they do cannot possibly be automated, and they are right. But it will be automated anyway, whatever the loss in educational quality. Because education, again, is not what all this is about; it's about making money.

The new technology of education, like the automation of other industries, robs faculty of their knowledge and skills, their control over their working lives, the product of their labor, and, ultimately, their means of livelihood. None of this is speculation. This Fall the UCLA faculty, at administration request, have dutifully or grudgingly placed their course work - ranging from just syllabi and assignments to the entire body of course lectures and notes - at the disposal of their administration, to be used online, without asking who will own it much less how it will eventually be used and with what consequences.

At York University, untenured faculty have been required to put their courses on video, CD- ROM or the Internet or lose their job. They have then been hired to teach their own now automated course at a fraction of their former compensation. The New School in New York now routinely hires outside contractors from around the country, mostly unemployed PhDs, to design online courses. The designers are not hired as employees but are simply paid a modest flat fee and are required to surrender to the university all rights to their course. The New School then offers the course without having to employ anyone. And this is just the beginning. Educom, the academic-corporate consortium, has recently established their Learning Infrastructure Initiative which includes the detailed study of what professors do, breaking the faculty job down in classic Tayloristic fashion into discrete tasks, and determining what parts can be automated or outsourced.

Toward this end, university administrators are coercing or enticing faculty into compliance, placing the greatest pressures on the most vulnerable. They are using the academic incentive and promotion structure to reward cooperation and discourage dissent. At the same time they are mounting an intensifying propaganda campaign to portray faculty as incompetent, hide-bound, recalcitrant, inefficient, ineffective, and expensive - in short, in need of improvement or replacement through instructional technologies. Faculty are portrayed above all as obstructionist, as standing in the way of progress and forestalling the panacea of virtual education allegedly demanded by students, their parents, and the public.

The York University faculty had heard it all. Yet still they fought vigorously and ultimately successfully to preserve quality education and protect themselves from administrative assault. During their long strike they countered such administration propaganda with the truth about what was happening to higher education and eventually won the support of students, the media, and the public. Most important, they secured a new contract containing unique and unprecedented provisions which, if effectively enforced, give faculty members direct and unambiguous control over all decisions relating to the automation of instruction, including veto power. According to the contract, all decisions regarding the use of technology as a supplement to classroom instruction or as a means of alternative delivery (including the use of video, CD-ROM's, Internet Web sites, computer-mediated conferencing, etc.) "shall be consistent with the pedagogic and academic judgments and principles of the faculty member employee as to the appropriateness of the use of technology in the circumstances." The contract also guarantees that "a faculty member will not be required to convert a course without his or her agreement." Thus, the York faculty will be able to ensure that the new technology, if and when used, will contribute to a genuine enhancement rather than a degradation of the quality of education, while at the same time preserving their positions, their autonomy, and their academic freedom. The battle is far from won, but it is a start.

The second set of implications stemming from the commoditization of instruction involve the transformation of the university into a market for the commodities being produced. Administrative propaganda routinely alludes to an alleged student demand for the new instructional products. At UCLA officials are betting that their high-tech agenda will be "student driven", as students insist that faculty make fuller use of the Web site technology in their courses. To date, however, there has been no such demand on the part of students, no serious study of it, and no evidence for it. Indeed, the few times students have been given a voice, they have rejected the initiatives hands down, especially when they were required to pay for it. At UCLA, students recommended against the Instructional Enhancement Initiative. At the University of British Columbia, home of the WEB-CT software being used at UCLA, students voted in a referendum four-to-one against a similar initiative, despite a lengthy administration campaign promising them a more secure place in the high tech future. Administrators at both institutions have tended to dismiss, ignore, or explain away these negative student decisions, but there is a message here: students want the genuine face-to-face education they paid for not a cyber-counterfeit.

Nevertheless, administrators at both UCLA and UBC decided to proceed with the their agenda anyway, desperate to create a market and secure some return on their investment in the information technology infrastructure. Thus, they are creating a market by fiat, compelling students to become users and hence consumers of the hardware, software, and content products as a condition of getting an education, whatever their interest or ability to pay. Can all students equally afford this capital-intensive education?

Another key ethical issue relates to the use of student online activities. Few students realize that their computer-based courses are often thinly-veiled field trials for product and market development, that while they are studying their courses, their courses are studying them.

In Canada, for example, universities have been given royalty-free licenses to Virtual U software in return for providing data on its use to the vendors. Thus, all online activity including communications between students and professors and among students are monitored, automatically logged and archived by the system for use by the vendor. Students enrolled in courses using Virtual U software are in fact formally designated "experimental subjects." Because federal monies were used to develop the software and underwrite the field trials, vendors were compelled to comply with ethical guidelines on the experimental use of human subjects.

Higher Educational Training

Marketing higher educational training as a commodity in the global economy presents an opportunity to reform the costly practices that hamper the international competitiveness of American universities. Designating those who matriculate as "clients" and "customers" rather than "students" encapsulates a proper businesslike attitude, but universities have barely begun to cheapen higher education sufficiently to assure consumer satisfaction. It is time to examine how to implement money-saving educational reforms and the likely consequences those reforms will have for higher education. Maintenance of faculties constitutes American universities' most costly problem as they get ready for the new millennium.

Higher educational training has been a labor intensive process. Personnel costs, of which salaries and benefits for tenured faculty take up the lion's share, typically account for about 90 percent of operating budgets. While progress has been made in cutting these costs - larger class enrollments, buyouts and early retirements of senior faculty, increased use of teaching assistants and part timers, and holding salary and benefits increases below inflation - most universities have barely begun to realize the savings offered by new instructional technologies. The largest savings can be achieved through elimination of classroom lectures. These lectures, which originated in the Greek academy, have been anachronistic since the invention of the printing press. But where a book might not match the aural-visual experience of a fine lecture, online access to the virtual classroom certainly can. The Internet provides the power for customers to call up an instructor's lectures at their convenience and to access supplementary materials in multi-media formats that relate to those lectures.

As the Internet reaches a global market, local universities no longer need to limit their course instruction to their own - and let's face it - sometimes mediocre faculty. Instead, they can offer choice among the world's greatest instructors online. Once arrangements for outsourcing the desired courses have been made with the managers and instructors at the appropriate institutions, local universities can effectively become franchises of greater institutions. They can offer their customers the finest courses of instruction from Harvard, Oxford or Heidelberg, or if their customers so desire, from Hillsdale, Liberty Baptist or Motorola. And because they won't need to maintain many faculty to teach on their own campuses, they can offer these courses at a fraction of their present cost. The market will determine the best courses to offer, and the economies of scale will afford even greater savings. To the extent that interaction among customers and instructors is demanded, information can be exchanged via electronic mail. If demand for online chat groups for some courses is strong, they can be established, moderated by local teaching assistants. We already have inexpensive cameras that can project each user's image, and "whiteboards" that permit simultaneous sharing and editing of a document. And better yet, as the technology improves, customers will be able not only to view their classmates and documents on screen, but, with the click of mouse, to immerse themselves in the chatroom in which the group's interaction takes place.

Higher educational training, is too important to leave it mainly in the control of the faculties of traditional institutions. Private corporations, which already offer universities a multitude of educational materials and services, will find it profitable to franchise courses themselves. The marketing of Speaker Gingrich's course on renewing America has already provided a model. Moreover, the competition from non-traditional educational suppliers, such as the University of Phoenix, Glenn R. Jones's International University, Michael Milken's Knowledge Universe, or "in-house" corporate universities, will surely force the managers of established universities to improve the cost efficiency with which they deliver their products.

Using the Internet is not as yet suitable for presenting some courses. Laboratory experiments that cannot be readily simulated, aspects of physical education, ROTC, dance, engineering, architectural design, and the use of musical instruments, for instance, still require facilities where students and instructors meet one another in person. A well-managed university, however, should be able to keep courses that require these facilities to a minimum. With proper planning, the savings generated from eliminating lecture halls, classrooms, and most undergraduate laboratories should be second only to those realized from downsizing faculty and outsourcing courses. Research represents the third area where savings can be achieved. Traditionally, American universities have underwritten scholarly projects for which funding from external sources has not been available, particularly in the humanities and social sciences. They have maintained elephantine research libraries and expensive computer centers, which members of the university community could access without charge, and they have set aside internal funds, which faculty and affiliated researchers on campus might tap. Undergraduates, who comprise the universities' principal clients and customers, however, usually have little or no use for these facilities. In this era of global competition American universities can no longer afford to offer researchers such freebies. As researchers in the physical, engineering, and medical sciences have long understood, the only research worth doing is that which others are willing to pay for.

The Internet provides a solution that virtually eliminates costly libraries and computer centers. Digitized libraries, accessible through the Internet, offer the customer more volumes, periodicals and documents than any single university library could physically contain. Such ready access obviates the need for all but a small reference division on campus, staffed by a few information specialists. The money saved from not having to purchase, catalogue, store and lend materials, not to mention the savings from downsized library staffing and capital budgets, can be used to buy licenses for customers to access commonly used documents. Such access can be marketed as a tuition benefit or for a nominal charge. And universities can also maintain good will by permitting researchers to download more specialized material at cost or for a very good price.

Except for occasionally needing to access regional supercomputers, customers and even most researchers already get sufficient computing power from appropriately linked servers and work stations. Moreover, universally applicable software languages like Java may soon enable customers to deploy a new generation of inexpensive personal computers that can download almost any decent application "as needed." Better yet, these computers will reduce the number of laboratories that universities must maintain for distributed computing on campus. The savings obtained from downsizing of campus computer laboratories can be used to offer customers one of the new computers as a tuition benefit.

Reform of personnel practices represents the final major area of savings. For too long American universities have paid professors to study and to think as opposed to teach or to produce valuable research. Professors enjoy more protection from the vicissitudes of the job market than any other occupational category in the free economy, save perhaps CEO and the classified civil service. Such practices are no longer economically viable. American universities will need to increase their faculties' economic productivity if they expect to survive in the global market. They can no longer afford workers whose primary duties involve thought and study. Managers will have to evaluate professorial performance for the net income generated from teaching, research, and community service. If a department's income falls short in one category or another, professors must be assigned to additional duties within or without their departments to protect the university's bottom line.

Some faculty may become specialists in teaching popular courses, in person or over the Internet. Others may specialize in lucrative research enterprises in lieu of teaching. Still others may earn their keep acting as community organizers or consultants. Once faculties are sufficiently motivated, the possibilities are endless. Managers can encourage flexibility and decentralized initiatives by offering bonuses to individuals, departments, or interdisciplinary programs or projects that show the most profit. They can also track alumni contributions and offer bonuses for long term customer satisfaction. But ultimately, the key to survival is ending tenure as we know it. As competing universities must spend more and more to recruit and retain their most profitable undergraduate customers, they cannot be expected to carry their workers through lean times as well as fat. Academic freedom needs to be protected by tenure, but tenure must be balanced against economic exigency. When a department or program cannot produce sufficient income to cover its costs, downsizing is in order.

Here flexibility and decentralization can be employed to protect academic freedom. Managers can follow Northwestern University's lead in distinguishing between "appointment" and "employment." In times of economic stress, departments can be instructed to designate the appointments of a certain number of professors as tenured but without employment, that is, tenured but without salary. Alternatively, the conduct of Warsaw's Jewish Police under the Third Reich can serve as a model: the departments or programs can decide for themselves which professors to eliminate in order to meet their designated downsized quotas. When implementing these reforms, however, local universities still must use creative marketing to retain nearby customers who might otherwise shop for their courses over the Internet. Local universities have the comparative advantage of offering personal consultation at a lesser price than their competitors. They also have a comparative advantage in offering laboratory facilities and meeting rooms locally for courses that need them or for occasions when customers demand them.

Beyond that, local universities can offer their customers attractive resort facilities, such as low price memberships in campus entertainment centers, gymnasiums, swimming pools and health clubs. Some universities may even be able to piece together groups of faculty whose research, teaching or community expertise gains sufficient notoriety locally or through the Internet to induce customers to matriculate. But the biggest local advantage can be found in the universities' athletic enterprises. Harvard may be known for its academic prowess, but how much mass media coverage does it get in prime time or on weekends? And how many pay to see its varsity football or basketball teams? By professionalizing their varsity athletics, many universities have been remarkably successful in fostering the loyalty of local supporters, not to mention increasing their proprietary sales of university clothing and paraphernalia. A smart marketing campaign can turn a significant number of these fans into clients and customers.

The commodification of higher educational training provides the impetus for reform of costly practices of American universities. To survive in the global market universities need to implement four types of reform:

— downsizing faculty by replacing classroom lectures with both asynchronous and simultaneous interactive sessions on the Internet;

— minimizing the need for instructional laboratories, lecture halls, and other physical spaces for teaching on campus;

— cutting research costs through use of digital libraries and networked computers, eliminating valueless scholarship, and charging a fair price for support services that universities formerly gave for free;

— ending tenure as we know it and using appropriate economic criteria to evaluate each professor's teaching, research, and community service.

— universities can supplement these reforms with expanded investment in recreational facilities and in varsity athletic enterprises.

In order to succeed with implementing all of these reforms, university managers will have to overcome the troglodytes who resist marketing higher education as a commodity. These reactionaries argue that education in the arts and sciences is also an experience that provides worthwhile non-material benefits that enrich a person's life over time, and they often cite philosophies of education that run back at least to Thomas Jefferson.

In the global economy, however, customers see higher education as training and credentialing to secure jobs that provide better remuneration. The American public understands that every major endeavor - with the possible exception of religion - needs to be evaluated on a commercial basis. What makes American universities the envy of most of the world? Why do large numbers of foreign students flock to them? Institutions of higher education in United States are considered superior because they 'have delivered a lucrative educational product for a competitive price, not because they have been subsidized with public tax dollars and charitable donations.

Learning Assistance

The primary mission of early colleges such as Harvard and Yale was to train clergy and to preserve and maintain the cultural norms that were brought from Europe. The goal was to provide an educated elite who could lead the new society. This was supported by statements such as the following made at a 17th century Harvard commencement address. While the goal of preserving traditional norms was widely accepted as the primary mission of the early colleges, it was not without its challenges. In the 17th century at Harvard, for example, ten percent of its student body came from families listed as artisans, seamen and servants and it continued to reserve places for poorer students whose tuition was paid either through work or assessments on the wealthier students.

In 1654 an "Indian College" was founded at Harvard to fulfill part of its charter to reach out to the local native American population. One entire room was to be devoted to this endeavor; however, it failed because the president complained that the facility was being under used and also because of the "unspoken assumption that the Indians should aspire to the same social and cultural ends as the whites." It is apparent that the colleges, while attempting to reach out to more diverse populations, were not willing to modify their curricula to meet individual needs. An attempt was made by Thomas Jefferson in 1779 at the college of William and Mary to reform this uncompromising attitude toward minority populations. He recommended that instead of trying to christianize the Indians through schooling the college should try to understand the Indian culture by studying its laws, language, religions, etc.. and then constructing grammars and vocabularies which would become areas for further study. This recommendation was rejected, but it demonstrates again the tension between the traditional purposes of education and the reformist ideas that were continuously being proposed.

Somewhat later, Francis Wayland, president of Brown University, proposed one of the most democratic missions for a college of the time. He described the college as the "center of intelligence for all classes" and developed a university extension division that included classes taught by the faculty of Brown. His program lasted until 1854 when "unmistakable evidence began to accumulate that the quality of the student body was deteriorating." There was also a widespread perception that he had lowered the standards of the bachelor's degree with his innovative "partial" coursework that did not lead to a degree. Other schools tried to provide an alternative opportunity for those students who had not received sufficient college preparatory training by offering different degrees. Instead of the traditional liberal arts degree, the bachelor of philosophy and the bachelor of science degrees were designed, but again the feeling was widespread that they led to a lowering of standards.

Even though these attempts at reform were put on hold at this time, they reflected the constant struggle to " Americanize" higher education, and they seemed to mirror the changing needs of those attending college. In the 17th century, seventy percent of the college graduates went into the ministry while in the 18th century that percentage dropped to twenty percent and by 1840 it was less than ten percent.

The "qualified" students during this time were narrowly defined as males with the proper family background. Preparation for higher education consisted mainly of private tutoring with each individual tutor deciding when the student was ready for the more formal study offered at the colleges. In 1700 the requirement for college entrance was a demonstrated knowledge of Greek and Latin along with evidence of a good moral character. Yale added an arithmetic exam to its entrance requirements in 1745. " Qualified" students were not numerous during this early period. Harvard only had 465 graduates in the entire 17th century and in 1710 there were only 36 students at Yale and 123 at Harvard. This small pool of appropriate students coupled with the lack of secondary schools and standardized preparation forced the colleges to admit and then accommodate students with minimal training. It was during this time that the President of Vassar College declared that "the range of student achievement extends to a point lower than any scale could measure. "

In order to extend educational opportunity to a broader population, colleges like Amherst and Williams were founded to accommodate those who could not afford the education offered by Harvard and Yale. These schools helped to open the doors to education, but they also had the effect of segregating those students who, due to their lesser means, were most likely less prepared. The students at Williams were described as "...rough, brown featured, schoolmaster-looking, half-bumpkin, half-scholar, in black, ill-cut broadcloth..." Although standardized preparation for college was unknown during this period, it was assumed that all students, once accepted, would proceed at the same pace and with the same instructional delivery techniques. Students were assigned a tutor who was charged with reading their lessons to them and then listening to their recitations to verify that they had memorized the given text.

While the learning needs of students were not considered individually, colleges did recognize that to cover expenses, they needed to accept students who were not ready for college study. To this end, preparatory departments were formed . Designed to provide the academic preparation that students had not received earlier, these departments proliferated on college campuses; indeed, " at many institutions preparatory enrollments matched or exceeded the 'regular' college enrollments." This can be explained in part by the lack of secondary schools at the time; students came to college lacking the basic skills of spelling, writing, geography and mathematics. Viewed as secondary schools within colleges, these programs delivered training that often led to a six year program for underprepared students. One of the most enduring preparatory departments was developed at the University of Wisconsin. It was designed in 1849 to "bridge the gap" and lasted until 1880 although it was continuously under fire from the faculty.

Those colleges without preparatory departments often offered pre-college courses and/or tutoring to those students who needed assistance. Students who were admitted on a "conditional" basis were required to fulfill certain criteria such as attending extra classes, receiving individual tutoring or taking special classes. In addition to the resources offered by the colleges themselves were proprietary tutoring schools. These private enterprises delivered tutoring in college and college preparatory coursework as well as provided instruction to prepare students for college entrance examinations.

College in the first half of the 19th century was not directly tied to professional aspirations; rather, it was simply designed to provide the elements necessary for the life of a gentleman. The curriculum provided for this training was borrowed from the classical tradition and mainly offered coursework in Greek, Latin and mathematics. The education was expected to discipline the mind by providing it with difficult material and forcing recitation to prove its effectiveness. The Yale Report of 1828 reinforced this notion with its implication that the difficulty of the ancient languages led to a strengthening of character and a mental power that would serve students well in whatever they chose to pursue after college.

Even though the notion of a classical curriculum and training for an elitist group of gentlemen was the majority opinion, there was ongoing tension. Educators and statesmen led the debate over both the relevancy of the curriculum and the students it was serving. The debate and tension was fueled by a speech delivered in 1837 at Harvard by Ralph Waldo Emerson who promoted the idea of "adapting education to the individual" and "developing a distinctively American intellectual culture." Prior to this in 1756, the College of Philadelphia had adopted a more comprehensive curriculum by including coursework for those interested in mechanic arts as well as the learned professions. Harvard later led the movement to incorporate an elective system into the curriculum and thus better meet the needs of individual students. It was regularly a source of conflict as the classicists thought it was lowering the educational standards of the institution.

Another attempt to revise the curriculum came from Henry Tappan at the University of Michigan. He proposed extending the traditional studies to include such areas as fine arts, industrial arts, civil engineering and science. He also set up a scientific curriculum as an integral part of the college. His rationale, however, was fairly elitist as he declared that the student who chose this "barely useful" course of study may become hooked on education and eventually proceed to the study of what was "ideal and beautiful". To this seemingly liberal attitude toward broadening the curriculum, however, Tappan added that American colleges had for too long taught courses that belonged in lower schools and that admission standards were too low. He asked, " And of what avail could the learned professors and preparations of a University be to juvenile students?" He felt that admitting such raw, undisciplined students was a "palpable absurdity."

Tappan's striving for a comprehensive university with coursework designed to meet a variety of student needs coupled with his concern over a lowering of standards both summarizes this period of higher education and provides a framework for the decades to come.

During 1862 - 1960, the federal government became directly involved in the educational system at all levels. Its influence was felt in higher education as a result of several initiatives including the Morrill Acts, equal opportunity legislation, and the G.I. Bill. This period also witnessed the development and rapid growth of the junior college. Together, these landmarks created the climate for change, a change which expanded the earlier purpose of higher education. While it is true that the purpose of higher education became broader during this period, it did not occur without tension. This time the tension was often reflected internally as colleges developed distinctive units within their own walls and also between colleges as institutions with very different missions vied for funding.

In 1862 the first Morrill Act was signed by President Lincoln guaranteeing to each state 30,000 acres of land per congressman to be sold for the purpose of funding colleges dedicated to teaching agriculture and the mechanic arts. This was followed in 1890 by the second Morrill Act which reinforced the support for this broader educational mission and also prohibited the distribution of federal funding to states where discrimination persisted in higher education.

The developments following these Acts significantly changed the focus of higher education and led to its increased democratization. States followed the directives by establishing A & M universities, creating new colleges or in many cases increasing financial support to state universities in order to provide more technical training mainly in the area of agriculture. This new funding was controversial, especially in the Northeast where the private, classical institutions were well established and viewed federal intervention in higher education as threatening and inequitable. It also led to a new debate regarding purpose: should this new training be designed with a pure or an applied science focus?

Additional federal legislation in 1887 provided support for an applied focus with passage of the Hatch

Act. This legislation brought higher education even more directly to the general public by establishing extension courses for farmers and setting up experimental agricultural stations at the colleges. Thus, the agricultural schools resulting from the Morrill Acts became the first real attempt to popularize higher education and to consequently broaden its mission. It was not only from the areas of agriculture and mechanic arts that colleges and universities faced a challenge to the traditional purpose of higher education. Business leaders were calling for a curriculum that more directly prepared students for the professions.

There was increased articulation between colleges and the secondary school system at this time which also impacted the role of higher education. The Committee of Ten was appointed in 1892 by the National Educational Association to examine the curriculum of the high schools and the requirements for admission to college. The committee, composed of many prominent college presidents, recommended that many of the subjects recently added to the previously classical postsecondary curriculum, e.g., history and science, be taught at an earlier age so that students would have a more solid background and would be prepared to study in greater depth when enrolled in college.

At the same time, the Cornell University decided it needed to be more systematic in its admission of students by certificate, a method whereby students from certain secondary schools were exempt from taking entrance examinations and admitted on the basis of their secondary certificates. By the mid-1880's, the problem of admission by certificate had grown into a University controversy. President Charles Kendall Adams, who had succeeded President White, told the board the chief fault with this method of admission was the absence of any provision 'for an examination of the quality of work done at the schools whose pupils sought admission without examination' . As a result, systematic 'inquiries in regard to the schools from which application is made' was proposed by Adams. The purpose was to determine if 'students making such applicaton are properly prepared to go on with the work of the freshman class'...In addition to improving the process and quality of the preparation of the students admitted, this approach kept Cornell 'constantly en rapport with the preparatory schools'. Before retiring as president of the University, Andrew Dickson White had called for greater interaction between the university and the secondary schools. In his final message to the board, White called for the University to push its 'roots'...'down into and throughout the public school system.' He said this would give strength back to the university as well as bring new strength to the lower school.

Partly as a result of the Committee of Ten report, secondary schools become stronger and more standardized in the early 20th century. Consequently, college leaders began to discuss the implications this held for the role of their institutions. Since students now were studying more subjects before entering college, there were suggestions to shorten the length of time a student needed to spend in college. This led to the idea of a junior college within a four year institution. The University of Chicago established such a two year liberal studies division with the intent of creating a natural break for those not able to complete further study. A similar plan was created at the University of Minnesota with its two year general college where twenty percent of the students enrolled had failed elsewhere.

This notion of a junior college quickly became popular and by 1917, 76 such institutions had been founded. The President's Commission on Higher Education provided support for the movement by affirming that "...virtually 50 percent of the population has the ability to complete fourteen years of schooling, that is, through junior college and that nearly one third has the ability to complete a college course in liberal arts or professional training. For the first time, a minimum goal for college enrollment was established that would double the number of college students in the next 13 years. Even though this was met with opposition by some college educators who argued there were already too many students enrolled who could not do college work, it marked a new trend in American higher education. No longer was the purpose of college an exclusionary, elitist one.

As the junior college movement continued to develop in the first half of the twentieth century, it led to the proliferation of community colleges nationwide. Higher education became more of an expectation for the high school graduate: Whereas in 1900, 1.6 percent of the college-age population enrolled in college, by 1960 that percentage had increased to 22.2 percent. The question being asked in colleges by 1960 was no longer, " What knowledge is of most worth?" ; rather, " What knowledge yields the greatest tangible benefit to individuals or to society?" Indeed, the mission and purpose was changing again to meet the emerging needs of a democracy.

Not only were the numbers of students enrolling in higher education during this period higher than in any previous time, but their faces were quite different. No longer was college the elitist training ground for wealthy males with no particular professional goal other than perhaps the ministry. Farmers and those wanting to be trained for business or engineering began to look for institutions that could meet their needs. Women began to further their education, often at colleges designed as female-only, and following the Civil War, colleges were founded in the South expressly to provide an opportunity for the increasing numbers of black students seeking an advanced degree. Even though preparation in the secondary schools was becoming more standardized, it was not assumed that the students should be grouped for a common plan of study as it was in the 18th and early 19th centuries. Instead it seems that colleges did more to separate students based on differences in tested ability, goals, sex and ethnicity.

The admission requirements began to include the new College Entrance Examination; this enabled colleges to quantify differences between students more easily and to define their populations more precisely. Separate schools within colleges and universities were established to provide the curriculum for the new science, agriculture, and engineering students. These schools were considered by many to be "lesser" than their liberal arts counterparts and were chastised for admitting less qualified students. Even schools like Harvard created new degrees and certificates in order to accommodate less capable students. The junior colleges established within the universities were often used as termination points for those students who were not achieving.

At the end of two years, they were counseled out. The community college systems that mushroomed were yet another sorting point: With their open door admissions policies, they served as an accessible avenue for those denied admission elsewhere. They also provided an opportunity for further education to those with nontraditional goals such as continuing education for self improvement; training for a specific vocation; gaining credits for transfer to a 4 year institution and earning college credit while maintaining a home, family and job. Even though equal opportunity legislation had passed, and states were denied federal assistance if discrimination existed in their college admissions process, the policy of separate but equal was still followed especially in the South. This led to the founding of colleges such as Tuskegee and Howard that were developed to provide an opportunity for black students that had previously not existed.

Due to the lack of well established primary and secondary systems in the south, these black institutions provided instruction that would ordinarily have been considered below college level. In fact they were more successful in their funding efforts when they held to a trade school curriculum rather than attempt to offer the traditional liberal arts. The state legislatures were so adamant about this that at one black school the only way to offer Latin was to call it " Agricultural Latin." Women who desired a college education at this time experienced a similar situation. They frequently attended colleges designed for women only and due to an often inadequate secondary preparation the standards for these early colleges were low. While many educational leaders were opposed to college training for women and felt that admitting them would lower the standards of unversities in general, the female students were insistent that they receive a classical education similar to that offered to their male counterparts. Women and black students alike felt that the validity of their college training and the opportunity for advancement hinged on a traditional curriculum.

Even more discouraging was the deep-seated skepticism of the public with respect to the value of higher education for women. It was feared that such training would raise women above the duties of her 'station'. A man would not love a learned wife. Better far to teach young ladies to be "correct in their manners, respectable in their families, and agreeable in society."...They were such delicate creatures, so different in mental as well as physical make-up from men, that they would never be able to survive the prolonged intellectual effort. ...And likewise... The missionaries were warned by pessimists and opponents of education for blacks that they would soon reach a point beyond which the black's innate mental capacity would be unable to go. Some of the northern idealists, rejecting this counsel of despair, went to the other extreme of seeking to teach the freedmen, without adequate preparation, a full duplicate of the liberal-arts curriculum given in contemporary northern colleges. These attempts, of course, were ludicrous failures. The majority of the educational missionaries were far more realistic, however. Many of them realized that the illiterate farmer former slave would have to be introduced gradually to higher learning. They began by establishing primary departments where the three R's could be taught. As soon as a few students were sufficiently advanced, "normal" and theological departments were instituted.

One of the most significant new groups to attend college during this period was that of the veterans returning from World War II. The G.I. Bill of Rights, written with the assumption that few would take advantage of it, inspired more than one million veterans to enroll in college by the fall of 1946. These students, many of whom were married, had children and were working, represented a whole new generation of postsecondary students: often they were the first in their family to even think about continuing their education beyond high school. With the funding that accompanied the veterans, colleges initiated guidance centers, reading and study skills programs and tutoring services primarily to serve the new students.

Responding to Charles Eliot's lament in 1871 that freshmen entering Harvard exhibited "...bad spelling, incorrectness as well as inelegance of expression in writing, (and) ignorance of the simplest rules of punctuation", the University developed an entrance exam that included a written composition. By 1879, fifty percent of the applicants to Harvard were failing this exam and were admitted " on condition". This situation led the college to provide extra assistance in order to prepare the students for college-level classes.

By the 1890's the educators at Harvard were describing a literacy crisis among freshmen and formed a committee to examine the composition and rhetoric offerings at the college. The Harvard Reports, as they came to be known, linked poor writing to a lack of clear thinking and placed the blame on the educational system at the lower levels. President Eliot criticized the lack of time given to the teaching of English in both the secondary schools and the colleges and acknowledged that "...So little attention is paid to English at the preparatory schools that half of the time, labor, and money which the University spends upon English must be devoted to the mere elements of the subject."

In 1907 over one half of the newly admitted students at Harvard, Yale, Princeton and Columbia still did not meet the entrance requirements.As a result, these prestigious schools all added developmental courses to their curricula. The most common courses at this time consisted of remedial reading and study skills. By 1909 over 350 colleges were offering "How to Study" courses for underprepared students and by 1920, one hundred study habit books had been published.

A survey was sent to all state universities in 1929 asking if they provided remedial work in reading. Almost twenty five percent of the respondents indicated that they tried to identify poor readers upon admission and slightly fewer responded that they then provided remediation. Some of the schools made the remediation compulsory such as Ohio State University where all "probation" students were required to take remedial reading. The instruction consisted mainly of drills involving eye movements and tachistoscopes provided much of the training.

At Indiana University, studies were begun to determine reading levels of students and whether How to Study courses made a difference. Book found that in the fall of 1926, only twenty seven percent of the entering freshmen could articulate the main point of an assigned passage. He concluded that, "...the reading ability of college freshmen should be accurately determined; that special remedial instruction should be given to all who are found to be deficient in this regard; and that this instruction should be given in a special orientation or "how to study" course and given by an instructor who is specially interested in the work and well equipped to give the type of help which these students need." Such courses were offered at Indiana University using Book's textbook, Learning how to study and work effectively. The issue regarding reading instruction did not disappear. In fact an even stronger cry went out in 1948 as William S. Gray called for college reading to be taught to all students. He recommended that instruction include both content and personal reading. An indication of how widespread the notion of college reading had become was the formation of its own professional organization, the Southwest Reading Conference. Precollege courses increased in popularity during this period. In 1926 the University of Buffalo required that all entering students who fell in the lower ranks of their high school class enroll in a three week study course which was held prior to the start of school. At the end of the course, a few students were "debarred" from admission to the university and others who were considered "doubtful" were given a reduced academic load.

Many of the black colleges throughout the South provided an excellent range of programs designed to facilitate opportunities for high school students who were still not receiving adequate academic preparation from the elementary and secondary schools. The authors of a survey describing these offerings stated, " ...such efforts deserve general support for student expenses and institutional costs from foundations, state and Federal governments, and all individuals wishing to equalize opportunities for higher education among the young people. More important, since these varied efforts are now still in a formative stage, the opportunity exists to coordinate them as they develop to assure the widespread adoption of demonstrably superior practices and to make certain that the needs of all deserving students everywhere are met." These innovative programs included preparatory opportunities which brought high school students to campus for coursework in basic skills as well as for seminars in science. Precollege programs lasting from one hour a day to 14 hours a day for 8 weeks at the Tuskegee Institute were designed to " obviate the need for remedial work after the student has entered college." One initiative, the Southern Teaching Program, Inc., brought graduate students from Yale Law School to 13 black colleges for the summer to provide instruction.

Of the black colleges surveyed, only four reported that they provided no remedial instruction during the academic year. The programs described were required, often carried credit and foreshadowed the variety that would appear nationwide starting in the 60's and 70's. Basically five approaches were implemented to "rectify the deficiencies of incoming students": special courses; intensified sections of regular courses; tutoring; clinical work and a reduced schedule of instruction. Interestingly, the clinical work, while the most expensive alternative, was the most popular among students due to its individualized nature and the fact that it was viewed, "...more as an effort to improve themselves than as evidence that they are academically inferior..."

It seems evident that colleges were beginning to acknowledge their role in providing assistance to those students who were not academically prepared. Some were willing to grant credit for the coursework, and even hired a fulltime staff and provided special training for those responsible for delivering the assistance. Colleges offered the coursework from a variety of departments including English, Education and Psychology. Schools such as Harvard discovered that the title of the course affected the willingness of students to enroll. Once

Harvard changed its "Remedial Reading" course to " The Reading Class", enrollment increased dramatically. From thirty reluctant freshmen per year, the classes began to attract hundreds of freshmen, upper classmen, graduate students, and even professors from the law school.

During 1960s, the concept of open admissions challenged many of the earlier assumptions that had gradually been losing status over the years, and the surge of grass-roots colleges ensured that educational diversity is a difference to be cherished. The voices of change were perhaps louder and clearer than in earlier periods, but the tension also became more obvious. The debate over opening doors while maintaining standards entered the public domain with a roar. Not only were educators involved in the debate, but everyone seemed to have a opinion. College administrators often assumed the role of reformists defending their institutions against those who charged that standards were declining.

The rapid growth of new types of colleges which were designed expressly to serve the needs of nontraditional students provides the clearest picture of higher education during this period. In 1970 there were more than 1,000 junior and community colleges serving 2 million students. The critical issue facing these schools was how " to make good on the implied promise of the open door". Providing access was one thing; facilitating success was quite another. Gleazer suggested that these schools learn as much as possible about the needs of the community; that they meet the students where they are, and that they provide assistance to students to clarify their goals and identify their talents. This was quite revolutionary compared to earlier decades where the curriculum was fixed, and the student was left to figure out just how to fit in and succeed.

A wide range of institutions challenged the former assumptions of higher education. College study was now considered more of a right than a privilege; it provided for social mobility and also offered a curriculum increasingly relevant to an individual's life goals, both professional and personal. Flexibility was built in as colleges began to recognize that the life circumstances of students had to be accommodated. Classes were scheduled for both daytime and evening hours, weekdays and weekends. Options for fulltime or part time study needed to be provided so that students could take one course at a time or several in order to fulfill the requirements for a certificate or a degree which could now be either a two year Associate's degree or the more traditional four year Bachelor of Arts or Science. The educational choices multiplied to meet the needs, and demands, of the public.

Cross described some of the colleges offering alternative delivery systems which demonstrate how the new, broader purposes of higher education were being met. These systems included work/study programs that connected the business world directly to higher education; TV colleges that extended coursework to both urban and rural populations; correspondence schools that allowed students to learn at their own pace in their own home; and schools that gave credit for life experiences. Schools were founded that reached out to specific populations who had previously been denied access to college. In Harlem, a no-cost night college opened that offered babysitting services as well as tutoring to students who were mostly unskilled workers. Schools for Native Americans, Chicanos, and Blacks came into existence with precollege programs that offered tutoring, basic skills and counseling. The Carnegie Commission, writing in 1973, described an "educational revolution" in the sixties where colleges and universities moved from providing "mass higher education" to providing "universal access". The final report states, " The current transition to universal access to college involves the guarantee of a place for every high school student who wishes to enter higher education, the introduction of more remedial work, the adaptation to the interests of new groups of students regardless of age...It is a transformation of fundamental historic proportions."

As colleges opened their doors wider and as the number of unskilled positions in the job market dropped to fifteen percent in 1979 , individuals who had never considered a postsecondary education filled the seats of classrooms everywhere. A major shift from earlier decades occured as 75.4 % of all adults had a high school degree in 1970 and by 1993, this increased to 87%. Cross has described these students, who often ranked in the lowest third of their high school class, as being passive toward learning and bringing with them a fear of failure.The failure syndrome had been deeply embedded in them from years of non-achievement in the earlier grades, and the students had often become passive in the process. These new students also were often the first generation of their families to attend college and represented a wider range of socioeconomic levels, and ethnic and cultural backgrounds than did earlier students. More women and adults entered the world of postsecondary education. Indeed, it is not unheard of today for a 65 year old grandmother to graduate from college. From 1972 to 1982, the number of adult learners, aged 25 to 34, attending college increased by seventy percent while those over the age of 35 increased by seventy five percent.

These difficulties have to do with the age at which young men can get prepared for college, and therefore with the ages at which boys pass the successive stages of their earlier education. The average age of admission to Harvard College has been rising for sixty years past, and has now reached the extravagant limit of eighteen years and ten months. Harvard College is not at all peculiar in this respect; indeed, many of the colleges find their young men older still at entrance. The average college graduate is undoubtedly nearly twenty-three years old at graduation. Since many of the new students entering college were either misprepared because they had not expected to pursue a postsecondary education or were returning to school after a lengthy hiatus, they often needed support systems to complete the transition to college. Hardin offered several assumptions regarding these students. First, they may have been underprepared, but they were not incapable or ineducable. Second, the reasons for an earlier lack of achievement are complex, and third they could be overcome with the proper support system. Fourth, given adequate time and opportunity, the new students could succeed and, finally, these students needed assistance with social and personal concerns as well as academic needs.

In addition to the students already described, other populations started coming through the doors of higher education. Beginning with the Rehabilitation Act of1973, students with disabilities were granted easier access to college and also given assurances of academic assistance. Continuing to 1990, with passage of the Americans with Disabilities Act , access for the disabled became a matter of course for all postsecondary institutions. Schools have been charged to provide "reasonable accommodation" , and the number of disabled students attending college has grown steadily from the 1970's in part due to increased support systems provided by the elementary and secondary schools. By 1994, 75% of disabled adults had completed high school, and 14,994 seniors took special editions of the SAT designed for the disabled.

Another significant population in terms of growth in higher education is that of international students and students for whom English is their second language. Academic assistance is frequently offered to them through formal coursework or more informal "conversation" groups in order to improve communication skills as well as to promote a better understanding of the cultural differences they experience in the classroom. Tutors who speak a second language are frequently hired to provide supplemental support. This new population also brings a unique opportunity for reciprocal learning as cultural diversity workshops abound and are often offered through the learning assistance unit.

Over one thousand Women's Studies courses were offered in 1973. These courses along with Ethnic Studies and others new to the traditional college curriculum continued to grow exponentially throughout the sixties and into the seventies. Students demanded relevant coursework, and universities accommodated them by expanding existing departments and often organizing new ones. Requirements were relaxed, and students were frequently allowed to construct their own academic programs. Along with this freedom of choice, however, came risk and the subsequent "opportunity to fail". The open door often turned into a "revolving door" with students dropping out and stopping out regularly. This led to a highly charged debate about the lowering of standards, often followed by the call to raise admission standards and close the doors of opportunity to the thousands of new students.

Not everyone, however, believed in locking out the new students. With the decade of the eighties came attempts to combine access with excellence. Robert McCabe, President of Miami-Dade Community College, summed up one school of thought when he said: "It is clear that standards have declined in American education at all levels....It is most important that we raise student expectations...The college should assume responsibility for assisting individuals to succeed, and an ordered curriculum should be instituted to deal with reading, writing, and computational deficiencies first, so that all students benefit from attendance."He further suggested that colleges hold to high standards, not by excluding students; rather, by requiring developmental coursework when test scores indicate the need. He advocated early advising where the student would be apprised of strengths and weaknesses and directed into appropriate classes. To this he added that schools should develop systems that would allow variable time frames for course completion and that students who need assistance be given a reduced load.

The philosophy expressed by McCabe was also supported by other educators such as Patricia Cross who declared that many students needed assistance while overcoming their fear of failure. John Roeuche advocated a more intensive, directed program of academic assistance. He was critical of the "bandaid" approach where a student in need of help was given a few remedial classes along with a full academic load. Instead, he suggested an integrated skills program which a student would complete before entering the regular curriculum. The efforts of Miami-Dade Community College in Florida reflected the attempts during the eighties to hold to standards while providing the academic assistance needed by so many students. In a switch from the two earlier decades, the faculty at Miami-Dade developed a prescribed general education, interdisciplinary core that all students would be required to take. In addition, the school began to administer a test to all first time students that assessed their skill levels in reading, writing and computation. Using the test scores plus pertinent personal information, the school placed students in appropriate developmental courses, limited their academic loads, and restricted their enrollment in certain courses. As a consequence of this program, students who took part were nine times more likely to graduate than those who did not participate.

Miami-Dade's new programming was undertaken with the help of a grant from the Fund for the Improvement of Postsecondary Education which demonstrated the growth of public support for helping students who needed assistance. In the fall of 1989, seventy four percent of colleges and universities offered at least one remedial course and twenty percent awarded degree credit for these courses. Two-thirds of the institutions gave institutional credit and only one-tenth awarded no credit at all. The question was no longer " Should we provide learning assistance to the underprepared student?" Rather educators were asking, " How should we provide learning assistance to provide the best opportunity for success to the underprepared student?"

Academic support units expanded to provide services for disabled students. Services include the taping of textbooks; testing accommodations, e.g., untimed, oral delivery and response, computer-assisted; the provision of notetakers and individualized supplemental instruction. Often these services provide a multi-faceted approach as they attempt to address social and emotional needs in addition to the academic ones. Counseling components have been added to many college programs for the learning disabled as well as pre-college, transitional offerings designed to create support networks and to increase self esteem. At Adelphi University, preliminary data indicated a 84% persistence for learning disabled students who participated in a holistic, pre-college program. This rate compared favorably to the overall persistence of 60% for the regular students at the University.

A gradual change in terminology used to describe learning assistance programs emerged which indicated changing perspectives toward the underprepared student. While the term "remedial" was still applied to programs through the early sixties, it was often used interchangeably in the late sixties and seventies with the term "compensatory". This became a popular term in education following equal rights legislation which funded programs designed to help students make up for earlier discrimination and poverty. According to Clowes, " Compensatory education in higher education would take the form of remediation activities such as preparatory and supplementary work...all with a program to provide an enriching experience beyond the academic environment to counter balance a non-supportive home environment.

Clowes included remediation within this definition of compensatory education for all too often its meaning has not been clear. The term remedial has implied a more limited approach toward the student, and has primarily described programs which focus on correcting specific skill areas. It was reflective of a "medical model" approach to learning assistance where "treatments" were prescribed for discrete problems with little consideration given to the whole "patient", and subsequently evaluated for effectiveness. If they didn't work, then quite likely, they were repeated with the assumption that additional time would make a difference. Both terms, remedial and compensatory, have contributed to the negative connotation associated with the programs and the students that they were meant to describe. They have tended to focus on weaknesses and highlight the differences between these students and those enrolled in the more advanced college curriculum.

As learning assistance has become more acceptable and more integral to the well-being of higher education, a new term has come into use which reflects this shift in perspective. The more current term, "developmental" originally came from the field of student personnel and was applied, beginning in the late seventies, to programs that took a more comprehensive view of the individual student and sought to promote growth in both academic and personal areas. It infers that a college or university should provide a comprehensive support system that meets students where they are and combines assistance in academic areas with personal counseling. Rather than focusing solely on weak skill areas, a developmental approach assumes that everyone has talents and is strong in some area. By acknowledging these strengths while building those areas that are underdeveloped, a more positive tone is established with the student.

One significant aspect of this shift in perspective is that all students are potentially developmental students:

the talented mathematician may need help to write an English essay; the fine musician may seek assistance with Geometry; the overzealous high achiever may need time management skills and personal counseling, and the student who needs help at Harvard may not need the same help at Triton Community College. With a continued emphasis on the developmental nature of learning assistance, it seems that it has earned a permanent spot in higher education. Although some states are currently trying to relegate developmental education programs to two year, community colleges a great deal of effective programming is firmly in place among four year institutions.

Recent research has shown the effectiveness of these programs both in terms of persistence toward graduation and success in more advanced coursework: forty eight percent of the students enrolled in developmental coursework at research universities graduate and over ninety percent of those who pass Developmental English go on to pass College English. Similar statistics exist for Developmental Math and Reading courses. These statistics along with the wide range of students who will continue to enter colleges and universities and the democratic philosophy of higher education that urges accessibility along with maintaining standards ensure that developmental education will be around well into the twenty first century.

6

Higher Education in India

We are in the midst of a revolution in the delivery of academic programmes of all kinds internationally. So far, commentators have focused largely on the positive aspects of the revolution. Increased access, lower costs, and the advent of a truly global market for higher education are all cited as favourable trends, especially when governments are cutting back on higher education spending at the same time that demands for access are increasing worldwide. Enrolments have expanded dramatically—from 40 to 80 million worldwide in the past two decades, and with likely increases of another 20 million in the coming decade, most of it in developing countries.

In India, the University Grants Commission (UGC), an apex body in the field of higher education is responsible for coordination, determination and maintenance of standards in higher education. It advises the Central and State Governments on the measures necessary for the improvement of university education besides framing regulations on various aspects of higher education. It also determines disbursement of funds for maintenance and development of Central/State

Universities, and some colleges which qualify for such assistance.

UGC: Programmes and Policies

The Commission's Policy for development of undergraduate and post-graduate education in the colleges during the Ninth Plan period will have the following main aims/objectives: (i) improvement of standards and quality of education; (ii) removal of social disparities and regional imbalances in higher educational facilities. Restructuring of courses including developing career thrust in the coursesl; (iii) grant of autonomous status to qualifying colleges. To achieve these objectives, the Commission will provide assistance to the colleges which fulfil the minimum eligibility conditions and have the necessary viability and potential and are striving for better standards.

During the Ninth Plan, the UGC has launched many new schemes under the broad headings of (a) Relevance and Quality, (b) Access and Equity, (c) Extra Moral/ Adult, Continuing Education and Outreach and (d) Management of Education and Resource Mobilisation. The Pay Review Committee submitted its report to the Commission on 28 May 1997.

The report was sent to the Universities, Teachers' Associations and State Education Secretaries for higher education. The Commission had wide ranging discussions on the recommendations of the Pay Review Committee. The UGC is finalising its notification on qualification and service conditions based on the Pay Committee Report in consultation with the MHRD. The Commission has been striving to develop human resources and towards this end it provides assistance for various programmes which enable teachers and researchers to upgrade professional competence and keep abreast of the latest developments in their disciplines. Assistance for various types of Scholarships and Fellowships is provided to achieve this objective. Junior Research Fellowship is awarded to those research scholars who have qualified in the national level tests conducted by the UGC, CSIR, GATE, etc. Teachers in universities and colleges are given an opportunity to pursue research for a brief period of time without having to undertake full teaching responsibilities. During the year under report, the Commission continued the scheme of Visiting Faculty in the universities so as to provide teaching/research assignments outside Kashmir to the teachers from Kashmir University and its affiliated colleges due to disturbed conditions there.

Research and studies in emerging and inter-disciplinary areas: Courses like Super -conductivity, Atmospheric 'Science, Environmental Education, Computer Application, etc. are included under this scheme. The total number of universities supported under the Super -conductivity programme up to November 1998, was 35. It is supporting seven universities under the Atmospheric science programme. Courses in the emerging areas like computer application, functional Hindi, biotechnology, environment education, energy education, electronics, futurology, business administration, communication and remote sensing were being reviewed during the year under report.

Innovative programmes: The scheme aims at providing a framework for assistance to a limited number of innovative projects, not covered by other UGC schemes, within the available resources of the UGC. Some of the innovative programmes include Cognitive Science, Mathematical Modelling and Designing through Computer graphics, Development of Microscale Experiments in Chemistry, setting up of Human Rights department in a university, development of Terracotta mural, etc. The two programmes, viz. Courses in Emerging Areas and Innovative Programmes were integrated during the year and named Innovative Programmes for implementation during the Ninth Plan period. The Superconductivity R and D programme and the Atmospheric Science Programme are also now part of the Innovative Programmes.

Area studies programme: The Commission is providing assistance to centres identified as Area Study Centres for undertaking studies relating to problems and culture of a given area and developing interdisciplinary research and teaching within a comparative framework. The focus is on such countries and regions with which India has had close and direct contact. There were 20 such centres being funded in 17 universities.

Vocationalisation of education at the first degree level: The UGC launched the scheme of Career Orientation of Education at the first degree level in the universities and colleges in 199495, in conformity with the National Policy on Education. Under the scheme, universities/ colleges would introduce one to three vocational courses in 35 subjects identified by the Core Committee.There are inbuilt training programmes for equipping teachers of the respective institutions for teaching the vocational subjects which are arranged for them through identified nodal institutions.The UGC has identified areas to cater to the needs of under-developed and rural sectors specially women, tribal and hilly regions.

Subject panels: The UGC has panels of experts to advise it on measures to enhance the quality of teaching and research in various subjects, to prepare status reports regarding research and teaching facilities available in the universities, to indicate thrust areas, and to advise the Commission on other relevant matters. The recommendations of these panels contribute to updating and modernising courses and introducing new dimensions in teaching and research. There are 28 subject panels in various disciplines of Science, Humanities and Social Sciences. A major task taken up by these panels during the year was to revise the syllabus for the NET examination.

Autonomous colleges: The concept of autonomous colleges is aimed at providing academic freedom for potential colleges by way of designing their curricula, evolving new methods of teaching, research and learning, framing own rules for admission, prescribing own courses of study and conduct of examinations. Under the scheme of autonomous colleges, a college declared autonomous by its affiliating university is fully accountable for the content and quality of education it imparts. Such a college is also responsible for setting up its own examination papers and for the conduct of examinations. The college evaluates the students for the award of degrees which will be accepted by the parent university. Up to November 1998, 123 colleges were functioning as autonomous colleges spread over eight States, viz. Tamil Nadu, Andhra Pradesh, Madhya Pradesh, Orissa, Uttar Pradesh, Gujarat, Maharashtra and Himachal Pradesh.

Teacher recruitment: During the year, the Commission conducted qualifying test for determining the eligibility for lecturership and for award of Junior Research

Fellowship in Humanities and Social Sciences. Similar test in science subjects was conducted jointly by the UGC and the CSIR.

Teacher training: Under the Academic Staff Orientation Scheme for orientation of newly recruited and in-service college and university lecturers, the 45 Academic Staff Colleges identified by the Commission organised orientation programmes for new teachers and refresher courses for in-service teachers.

Improvement in efficiency: The Commission provided grants for setting up computer centres in 125 universities up to November 1998. Also, assistance was provided for upgradation of computer facilities in the computer centres of various universities. In addition, the Commission provided assistance to 3,137 colleges up to November 1998 for installing computer facilities. Universities were also assisted by the UGC for introducing Computer Application paper at PG level in all subjects wherever there was relevant need for it. As many as 13 universities were assisted under the scheme up to November 1998.

Development of engineering/technology and management education: The UGC provides financial assistance to the universities /institutions for their Engineering and Technology Departments to enable them to carry out various programmes of higher education and research. Assistance was provided to 11 Technological Universities and 25 State/ Central/ Deemed to be Universities. A new scheme 'Technology for Women' in women universities was introduced during 1998-99 for providing financial assistance for introduction of under-graduate courses in Engineering and Technology. Under the scheme, assistance would be provided for recurring and non-recurring items for a period of five years from the date of implementation of the course. To begin with, five women universities have been identified under the scheme during the Ninth Plan.

COSIST scheme: One hundred sixty-five departments have been assisted under the scheme of strengthening Infrastructure in Science and Technology Education (COSIST) and research till November 1998. Assistance under this programme is a one-time input. Departments supported under COSIST have been given functional autonomy. The infrastructural facilities extended through COSIST support have attracted additional funds not only from funding agencies in India but also from abroad and have improved teaching instructions both at the post-graduate and research level by enhancing the quality of teaching, particularly the experimental part of the courses.

Common facilities and services: The UGC assists a large number of centres as national facilities. There are six Inter University Centres and 11 other Centres as national facilities/ Information Centres assisted by the UGC. The Inter-University Centres are namely Nuclear Science Centre, Delhi, Inter-University Centre for Astronomy and Astro-physics, Pune, Inter-University Consortium for DAE Facilities, Indore, National Assessment and Accreditation Council, Bangalore, Information and Library Network (INFLIBNET), Ahmedabad and Consortium of Educational Communication, New Delhi.

Education international: Education International (EI), a commercial organisation, has been set up by the MHRD and the UGC under the overall supervision of CEC. El has a mandate to promote and sell educational programmes available with CEC, IGNOU, NCERT and NOS in the international market. It also markets CEC programmes nationwide.

Educational outreach activities: The Commission deputes university/college teachers to work with Bharat Gyan Vigyan Samithi on wholetime basis for nationwide literacy movement. Fifteen Teacher Fellowships have also been provided for this purpose. Population Education programme, assisted by the UGC, is implemented by the universities as part of the United Nations Population Fund (UNPF)-UGC project through the Population Education Resource Centres (PERCs). The guidelines for the scheme of Adult and Continuing Education, Extension and Field Outreach activities were revised for the Ninth Plan period. The Ninth Plan guidelines involve the following programmes:

— Vocational/ career -oriented programmes

— Equivalency programme

— Quality of life improvement programme

— Leadership and human resource development programme

— Social and citizenship role awareness programme

— Individual interest programme.

Facilities for SCs/STs,and the weaker sections: In order to ensure effective implementation of reservation Policy for SCs and STs, the UGC provides assistance to universities/ deemed to be universities for the establishment of SC/ST Cells. The, Commission under this scheme provides some positions of staff for running these Cells. There is also a scheme of 'Remedial Coaching for Scheduled Castes and Scheduled Tribes' being implemented in universities and colleges which aims at improving the skills and linguistic proficiency of the students in various subjects and raising their level of comprehension in such subjects where quantitative techniques and laboratory work are involved. A significant policy decision taken during the year was to create a Central Pool Database in the UGC for SC/ST candidates to consider their candidature for teaching positions in universities and colleges.The Commission also continued to provide assistance to identified centres and cells (in universities and colleges, respectively) for conducting coaching classes for the educationally backward among minority communities for preparing them for competitive examinations other than the higher Civil Services as also classes for preparing students and providing training in shorthand/ typing, computer literacy, strengthening knowledge of English and regional languages, etc.

Under the scheme of Junior Research Fellowship, the Commission has reserved some positions for SC/ ST candidates out of the total number of such fellowships instituted for various universities. This is in addition to 50 fellowships which the Commission is directly awarding to SC/ST candidates. Also, the Commission has reserved 40 Research Associateships for SCs and STs. In order to provide opportunity to SC/ST teachers in affiliated colleges, 50 teacher fellowships have been earmarked for them to improve their qualifications by doing M.Phil/Ph.D. Relaxation has also been made in the criteria for financial assistance to colleges having SC/ ST enrolment and to those located in the backward regions. In order to oversee the implementation of the reservation policy in Central Universities, the Commission has appointed a

Monitoring Committee under the Chairmanship of the Secretary, UGC. A Standing Committee has also been constituted to consider various issues relating to the Reservation Policy for SC/ST candidates. The UGC has also been implementing the scheme of Integrated Education for Disabled Children with the initial financial support and sponsorship by the Department of Education, MHRD. The teachers and students trained under this programme are mainly placed in teaching general education to handicapped children in Integrated and Special Schools, Government Services, NGOs, research organisations, etc. as rehabilitation workers/ field workers to help the disabled community.

Revision of Pay Scales of University and College Teachers: The Pay Review Committee set up by the UGC under the chairmanship of Prof. R.P. Rastogi, former Vice- Chancellor, Banaras Hindu University submitted its report on 28 May 1997. After taking into consideration the recommendations made by the Committee, comments of the UGC, representations received from various quarters and the outcome of the wide-ranging discussions, the government announced revised pay scales and other conditions of service of university and college teachers on 27.7.98 and with further modifications on 6.11.98. Consequently the UGC finalised and notified the scheme of revised scales and service conditions on 24 December 1998. The changed pay structure and conditions of services of teachers ar2aimed at attracting talents to teaching in University and Colleges, awarding merits and promoting excellence in the profession. The State Governments have also been requested to adopt these scales for their university and college teachers. For this purpose the Centre has agreed to provide assistance to the extent of 80 per cent of the additional expenditure involved, for a period of five years.

Submission of Report by the Task Force on Amendments to the UGC Act: The Government of India constituted a Task Force under the Chairmanship of Prof. Amrik Singh, former Vice-Chancellor of Punjabi University, Patiala to examine the relevant provisions of the UGC Act with a view to suggest amendments in order to provide suitable safeguards against the incidence of fake universities and to empower the Commission to cope with the emerging challenges with confidence and to strengthen and restructure the Commission. The Task Force deliberated for over four months and submitted its report on 15 February 1999. The important recommendations of the Task Force are

(i) provision of five whole-time members in addition to the Chairperson;

(ii) increase in the number of members to 15 and of the nominated category, at least one-third should be women;

(iii) suitable punishment including a term of imprisonment fine ranging between one lakh and ten lakh rupees for contravening Sections 22 and 23 of the Act;

(iv) opportunity for establishment of private or self-financing universities in the country, subject to observance of rules made by the Government for the establishment of such universities; and

(v) the recognition of universities or institutions which may confer degrees including the operation of foreign universities /institutions in the country for running their courses and programme of studies.

Women's studies: Assistance is provided' by the UGC to universities and colleges for setting up Centres and Cells for Women's Studies. The Centres/ Cells are required to undertake research, develop curricula, and organise training and extension work in the areas of gender equity, economic self-reliance of women, girls' education, population issues, issues of human rights and social exploitation. These Centres/ Cells are not expected to be like other conventional departments of the universities, as they are not required to run courses that lead to under-graduate or a post-graduate degree.

Project on information and library network: This project was started by the UGC in the Seventh Plan with the aim of establishing a nationwide network of university libraries and information centres to organise library and information services based on sharing of library resources in the country and to promote academic interaction among academicians. The Centre is now an Inter -University Centre of the UGC. Main activities of the Centre include computerisation of libraries, upgrading the skill of existing library staff to work in the computerised library environment, establishment of networking facilities, creation of academic databases and organisation of information services. Various software packages required for library management services have been developed at this Centre. It has also developed an Integrated Library Management Software (ILMS) for management of libraries in collaboration with DESIDOC, for use in university libraries.

Promotion and preservation of Indian culture, heritage and values: The Commission continued to provide assistance on cent per cent basis under Plan funds for the promotion of Gandhian, Buddhist and Nehru studies. The assistance is provided for setting up centres for these studies, conducting programmes to acquaint teachers and students with their philosophy and ideas and for the purchase of books and journals relating to these studies. It was also decided during the year to introduce the scheme of promotion of Ambedkar Studies. Proposals in this regard have been invited from universities. The Commission has also been providing assistance for value-oriented education in order to foster among students and teachers alike such values which are necessary for retaining national identity and sustaining a peaceful and harmonious society. As part of value-oriented education, the Commission is also promoting the programmes of National Integration in collaboration with the Association of Indian Universities.

Human rights scheme: The Commission has initiated the Human Rights Scheme and guidelines for the same were framed for introduction of Human Rights courses at the P.G. /Certificate levels and for organising seminars, symposia and workshops. These guidelines form part of the UGC Ninth Plan Approach to Promotion of Human Rights Education in Universities and Colleges, 1998.

Promotion of physical education and sports: The Commission continued to provide assistance to universities and colleges for running the three-year degree course in physical education, health education and sports.

Resource mobilisation by universities: The Commission approved the revised Ninth Plan guidelines to support universities for their resource mobilisation efforts. The main objectives of the scheme are to encourage universities to mobilise resources by participation / contribution of society in their development and to encourage and enhance the flow of resources coming from the society for university development.

University-elementary education linkages: The UGC has been pursuing the universities to take up extension activities in social and economic areas in their areas. Realising that the Universalisation of Elementary Education remains a national goal and challenge and the universities are in a pivotal situation to join the movement, the UGC initiated dialogues, during the year, with academicians, educationists, NGO representatives and Vice-Chancellor to bring out a policy strategy paper on university-elementary education linkages. The UGC paper encourages university academic community to take up research, evaluation, training, development, etc. to support and strengthen the elementary school system in the areas of their operation. One such pilot initiative was arrived by the Mumbai University in a meeting taken by the Chairperson in Mumbai. The Department of Education has committed to support the universities' initiative by funds also under its various schemes meant for the NGO's programme for elementary education indicating for the training and research.

Financial Assistance

The central governmet have a scheme of financial assistance, which has been continuing from one plan period to the next plan period. Under the scheme, the MHRD has been providing financial assistance to some voluntary organisations /educational institutions. Assistance under the scheme is provided to institutions which are outside the university system and which are engaged in programme of innovative character. The institutions which have been receiving assistance from the Central Government are:

— Sri Aurobindo International Institute of Educational Research, Auroville, Tamil Nadu

— Sri Aurobindo International Centre of Education, Pondicherry

— Lok Bharati, Sanosra, Gujarat

— Mitraniketan, Vellanad, Kerala

Since assistance to the above institutions is being provided under the plan scheme, continuance of assistance from one plan period to the next plan period has to be decided at the end of every plan. In order to examine and to recommend the nature and quantum of assistance to be provided to these institutions during the Ninth Plan period, Visiting Committees were constituted by the MHRD to visit the institutions to make an on-the-spot assessment of their performance and to recommend nature and scope of future assistance during the Ninth Plan period.

The interest of foreigners in Higher Education is reflected in the large number of foreign scholars coming to India for doing research. Besides the research projects sponsored by the American Institute of Indian Studies, the United States Educational Foundation in India and the Shastri Indo-Canadian Institute, large number of scholars come for doing research either on self-funding basis or scholarships from their countries/other sources. During 1998-99, the number of research projects approved by the Ministry of Human Resource Development is 373. The Government has approved a number of bilateral agreements between Indian universities and their counterparts abroad. There has been significant increase in the number of bilateral international conferences/ symposia/ seminars/

workshops in collaboration with foreign universities. During the year 19 proposals for seminars/ symposia/ international conferences were approved on a variety of subjects under the aegis of universities, autonomous Organisations and Institutions of higher learning. The Government also approved 14 proposals of foreign scholars as visiting lecturers /professors in Indian universities in the country.

The United States Educational Foundation in India (USEFI) was established in February 1950 under a bilateral agreement as replaced by a new agreement in 1963 between the Government of India and the Government of United States of America to administer the Fullbright Educational Exchange Programme to promote mutual understanding between the people of the two countries by a wider exchange of knowledge and professional talents through educational contacts. During 1998-99, 21 visiting lecturers, 15 research scholars and 40 student professionals were given Fullbright grants ranging from 3 to 12 months. One grant was given to an Indian fellow under National Institute of Drug Abuse Programme of the Hubert H. Humphrey Fellowship. The USEFI also administers the East West Centre (EWC) grants by conducting workshops/senlinars on various themes involving Indian scholars at many of the EWC Institutes.

The Foundation also administers research scholar grants, short-term group programmes for school/college teachers, workshops/ seminars involving visiting American professors/ eminent Indian faculty for Indian college/university teachers in various fields besides the regular exchange programme. The American Institute of Indian Studies (AIIS), a consortium of about 50 major universities was established in 1960 with the approval of the Government of India to promote Indian studies, civilization and culture in the United States. The Institute awards Research and Language Fellowships. Five Group Projects were undertaken during the year under report. Five publications have also been brought out by the Institute. The Archives and Research Centre for Ethnomusiology continued its activities in computerising its library, field recordings and organising workshops. The AIIS Centre for Art and Archaeology published a comprehensive Bibliography on Imperial Gupta. The Institute has already published nine volumes of the Encyclopaedia of Indian Temple Architecture and work on more volumes is in progress. Considering the AIIS contribution to the academic world, the Board of Directors of Encyclopaedia, Britannica has established an Editorial Board to proceed further on the Encyclopaedia project. To celebrate the 50th year of India's Independence, the Institute brought out a volume entitled *Commemorating* the 50th Anniversary of India's Independence: India's World's and US Scholars. 1947-97.

A binational non-profit making organisation was established in 1968 by joint announcements of the Governments of India and Canada and signing a Memorandum of Understanding between the Government of India and the Shastri Indo-Canadian Institute for the operation of the Institute in India initially for a period of three years, which has been renewed from time to time. Action for renewal of agreement for a further period of five years, i.e. 1 April 1999 to 31 March 2004 is being initiated. The India Studies Programme of the Institute funded by the MHRD provides fellowship to Canadian scholars and supplies Indian imprints to Canadian Universities. The Government of India has approved visit of 22 scholars during 1998-99 under this programme.

The Canadian Studies Programme funded by the Foreign Affairs and International Trade, Canada offers fellowship to Indian scholars for research in Canada and also for visiting lecturerships for Canadian academics. It also supplies Canadian imprints to Indian universities. During 1998-99, 19 Indian scholars have been selected for the fellowship. The CIDI-SICI Project (CSP) funded by the Canadian International Development Agency runs the partnership programme, the journalism programme, the distinguished speaker programme and the summer programme in India. The partnership programme which proved to be a very popular component of the CSP has entered its second phase. The Institute is ready to start eleven partnership projects in the area of Development related to Environment, Gender, Social and Economic Reform and private sector development. The Institute in its role as a mediator and catalyst in academic and non-academic collaborative initiatives between India and Canada was honoured by the Governor General of Canada on 31 March 1998 during his official visit to India.

Higher Education Institutions

Some of the major higher education institutions of india are the following:

— *Visva-Bharati*: Visva-Bharati, an educational institution founded by Guru Rabindranath Tagore, was incorporated as a Central University by the Visva-Bharati Act, 195 1. The University imparts education from the Primary School level to Post-Graduate and Doctorate levels. It has 11 Institutes—eight at Santiniketan and three at

Sriniketan. As on 31 March 1998, there were 6,336 students on the rolls of the University including its School Sections. The total strength of teaching and non-teaching staff was 506 and 1586, respectively. A few new courses, namely, B.A. (Vocational), functional course in Hindi, two-year post graduate course in Biotechnology and two-year M.Sc. (Agriculture) course in Horticulture have been introduced. The library of the University has a total collection of 3,59,601 books and 2,592 journals. In addition, 2,89,128 books are housed at 12 Sectional Libraries of the University. Implementation of the Information and Library Network programme started in January 1998 is in progress. While the major focus of development was rightly pointed out towards modernisation of both academic institutions and administrative management, rural segment of Visva-Bharati, i.e. Sriniketan has been taken up with some priority with creation of CAREER (Centre for Advanced Rural Education, Extension and Research) and CSV (Centre for Science in Villages). The avenue for exploring the potential strength of the adjoining villages has been extended enormously. With the establishment of Nirman Bhavan (Building Centre), a project under the sponsorship of HUDCO for creating facilities in the housing technology in the rural area, with a possibility of replication, tremendous breakthrough is in the offing.

— *Banaras Hindu University*: Banaras Hindu University (BHU) came into existence in 1916 as a teaching and residential University. The University consists of three Institutions - Institute of Medical Sciences, Institute of Technology and Institute of Agricultural Sciences-and 14 Faculties with 121 academic departments and four Interdisciplinary Schools. The University also maintains a constituent Mahila Mahavidyalaya and three School level institutions. Four colleges in the city are admitted to its privileges. It also has a 1000-bedded Modern/Ayurvedic Medicine Hospital. The University has 14,812 students on its rolls. The strength of its teaching and non-teaching staff is 1, 162 and 7,088, respectively. During the current academic session, the University established a Centre for Advanced Studies in Sciences. The University also created the Malaya Centre for Peace Research as an Inter-disciplinary Centre under the Faculty of Social Sciences. Seven endowment funds have been instituted by the University for various scholarships/ medals/cash prizes.

— *Delhi University*: The University of Delhi is a premier university of the country which is known for its high standards in teaching and research and attracts a large number of students not only from all over India but also from several other countries. Established in February 1922 as a unitary and residential university with a nucleus of three colleges, two faculties and about 750 students, it has grown, over the years, into one of the largest universities in the country. At present it has 14 faculties, 82 teaching departments and 78 colleges spread all over Delhi. There are about 2,49,400 students presently enrolled in the University. About 1,31,400 of the students are enrolled in non-formal education programmes offered by the School of Correspondence and Continuing Education, Non-Collegiate Women Education Board and the External Candidates Cell. There are about 337 Professors, 213 Readers, 143 Lecturers and 26

Research Associates making the total strength of 719 of the Faculty of the University. In a special convocation on 13 December 1998, the University conferred Honorary degrees to various eminent persons: Dr Abdul Kalam, Dr R.A. Mashalkar, Dr M.S. Valiathan, Dr John Rawis, Dr Ikeda, Dr Edward Said, Dr Sarup Singh, Dr M.N. Srinivas, Dr Amartya Sen, Sardar Raunaq Singh, Sint. Gangubai Hangal, Ustad Amjad Ali Khan and Prof. K.N. Raj. The University has also accepted in principle, institution of about 13 new courses in various fields. The University has approved the proposal for the institution of scholarships, viz. Dr Virendra B. Mahesh Fellowship and Nupur Mathur Memorial Scholarship in Business Economics.

— *Jamia Millia Islamia*: Jamia Millia islamia (JMI) which had been functioning as a Deemed to be University since 1962 acquired the status of a Central University in December 1988. The University imparts education from the Nursery stage to Post-graduate and Doctorate levels. It has six Faculties and eight Centres (excluding Balak Mata Centres). There has been a constant increase in the number of books and research journals in Dr Zakir Hussain Library of the University. The number of books in the Library rose from 2,61,247 (1996-97) to 2,64,292 (1997-98). The A.J. Kidwai Mass Communication Research Centre of JMI is not only providing training at Post-graduate level in Mass Communication but it is also producing educational material on different educational aspects/ subjects for the UGC, INSAT programme. One live Video Conference was recorded between studios at the Centre and studios in Paris, France. A residential Management Development Programme for University Administrators instituted with the approval and financial support of the UGC provides necessary training to Deputy and Assistant Registrars and equivalent posts enabling them to be eligible for placement in the next grade. The Centre has organised four programmes in 1997-98 and successfully provided training to 84 administrators from all India universities and institutions of higher learning.

— *Aligarh Muslim university* : Aligarh Muslim University (AMU), established in 1920 as a Central University, is one of the premier fully residential academic institutions of the country. The University has 92 Departments/ Institutions/ Centres grouped under 11 Faculties. The University also maintains four Hospitals, six Colleges (including Medical, Dental and Engineering Colleges), two Polytechnics and eight Schools. Admissions to BDS course in Dental College established in 1997-98 have been made during the current academic session, viz. 199899. The University also offers six diploma courses exclusively for women, in the fields of Electronics Engineering, Electronics (TV Technology), Computer Engineering, Costume Design and Garment Technology, Office Assistantship and Secretariat Practice, and General Nursing and Midwifery. Seven new courses namely, B.A/LL.B (five-year integrated course), M.A. (Human Rights), P.G. Diploma (Human Rights), Bachelor of Fine Arts, Master of Fine Arts, B.A. (Hons.) in Communicative English and Master of Journalism and Mass Communication were introduced in the current session. During the year under report, the University has on its roll a total of 18,562 students (including school strength). The total strength of teaching staff of AMU is 1,457 and that of non-teaching staff 5,899. Each Department of the University has a Seminar Library for PG and Research Students. Colleges like J.N. Medical College, A.K. Tibbiya College, Z.H. College of Engineering and Technology and Women's College have separate libraries. Academic Staff College of AMU has organised three Orientation Programmes, nine subject Refresher Courses and three Induction Training Programmes (sponsored by the All India Council for Technical Education). In addition, eight Programmes/ Courses are planned to be organised during the remaining part of the current academic session. With a view to promoting sports and allied activities the University maintains ten clubs. namely, Riding Club, Hockey Club, Tennis Club, Hiking and Mountaineering Club, Swimming Club, Athletic Club, Cricket Club, Football Club, Gymkhana Club and Gymnasium Club. AMU is the only University in India which maintains (a) a Riding Club and (b) a covered swimming pool.

Assam university: Assam University, Silchar was established on 21.1.1994. It is a teaching-cum -affiliating University with its jurisdiction over the districts of Cachar, Karimganj, Karhi, Anglong and Hailakandi in the State of Assam. The University has granted affiliation to 53 colleges. The University has all its departments and offices at Dorgakona where the Government of Assam had allotted 600 acres of land. The University has 24 Departments under 8 schools of studies and in addition, it has 3 centres of studies. The total number of faculty members is 101. The University library has 32,400 volumes and has a subscription of 300 National and International journals. The University library is fully computerised.

— *Babasaheb Bhimrao Ambedkar University*: Babasaheb Bhimrao Ambedkar University, Lucknow was established in 1994. The University was notified as a Central University on 10 January 1996. It aims to provide instructional and research facilities in new and frontier areas of learning and to launch academic programmes in these areas. The University has set up three schools and three centres: School of Ambedkar Studies, School for Information Science and Technology and School for Environmental Studies and Centre for Rural Technology, Centre for Vocational Studies and Centre for Human Rights. The academic programmes in these Schools and Centres have started with a faculty strength of 13 members and 118 students including 54 SC/ST candidates.

— *University of Hyderabad*: The University of Hyderabad, established by an Act of Parliament in 1974, is a premier institution of post-graduate teaching and research in the country. The academic activities of the University are undertaken through its eight Schools of Studies. Besides, the Centre for Distance Education of the University offers post-graduate diplomae in five disciplines. The University has a faculty strength of 215 consisting of 69 Professors, 86 Readers and 60 Lecturers during the year under report. The faculty of the University has obtained research support from several funding agencies. Over 105 such research projects are currently under investigation by the faculty. Some projects for investigation by the faculty have been sponsored by foreign agencies such as Naval Research of USA, Volkswagen Foundation of Germany and Rockefeller Foundation of USA. Several faculty members have won National and

International awards. The University has also entered into a few Memoranda , of Understanding with local industrialists. Several eminent scholars from India and abroad occupied the two prestigious chairs named after Shri Jawaharlal Nehru and Dr Sarvapalli Radhakrishnan.

— Jawaharlal Nehru University: Jawaharlal Nehru University (JNU) came into existence in 1969. It is primarily concerned with Post-graduate Education and Research. The University has seven Schools consisting of 24 Centres of Studies. In addition, it has a separate Centre for Bio-Technology. The strength of its teaching and non-teaching staff is 370 and 1,350, respectively. The total enrolment in the University was 3,892 students with adequate representation of SCs., STs and other backward classes.The Faculty members of the JNU produced 400 publications which include 55 books, contributed 10 chapters to books and 235 research articles in various national and international journals of repute. The Faculty has at present 174 on-going research projects sponsored by various funding agencies. A number of distinguished faculty members received honours/awards from various national and international organisations. .The University library acquired 5,321 volumes of various bound periodicals and newspapers in the year under report. The total collection of books and periodicals now stands at 6,67,993 volumes. The JNU Academic Staff College set up by the UGC to impart refresher courses and orientation training to college and university teachers for their academic development and growth and organised 13 refresher courses during this period.

— *Indira Gandhi National Open University*: Indira Gandhi National Open University (IGNOU) was established in 1985 for introduction and promotion of Open University and distance education system in the educational pattern of the country and for the coordination and the determination of standards in such systems. The major objectives of the IGNOU include widening of access to higher education by providing opportunities to large segments of the population, particularly the disadvantaged groups, organising programmes of continuing education and initiating special programmes of higher education for specific target groups like women, people living in backward regions, hilly areas, etc. The University is offering 43 programmes. During 1998, the total number of students registered for various programmes was 1,63,000. The network of Students Supports Services in 1998 consist of 19 Regional Centres and 346 Study Centres. Three more Regional Centres are likely to be established during 1998-99 at Srinagar Valley, Dehradun and Chandigarh or Jalandhar. The telecast of IGNOU programmes on the Doordarshan Network continued on every Monday, Wednesday and Friday up to September 1998. From October 1998 onwards IGNOU started telecast of its programmes for half an hour a day for six days from Monday to Saturday.

As part of its mandate for training of distance educational personnel, Staff Training and Research Institute in Distance Education (STRIDE) continued to organise workshops. The IGNOU Act was amended in 1997 to allow the university to set up its Study Centre, outside the country with the approval of the Visitor. The Distance Education Council (DEC) will assume the responsibility for development of correspondence education programmes offered by the traditional universities during the Ninth Plan. In the initial phase, the effort will be to transform the programmes into mainstream of distance education programmes. The DEC has finalised guidelines for providing development support to State Open Universities as well as the Directorates of Correspondence Education in the traditional universities.

— *Nagaland University*: Nagaland University was established on 6 September 1994 by an Act of Parliament with headquarters at Lumami. It is an affiliating University with its jurisdiction over the whole of the State of Nagaland. Presently, the University is functioning from its campuses in Kohima, Lumami and Medziphema (School of Agricultural Sciences and Rural Development (SASRD). The University presently has 25 departments located in three campuses with 4 schools of studies. The total number of faculty members is 109. The University has 39 colleges affiliated to it. The University library, Kohima has 27,000 volumes and 139 periodicals /journals. The SASRD Library Campus has 18,000 volumes.

— *North-Eastern Hill University*: The North-Eastern Hill university was established in 1973 at Shillong. It has a campus in Aizwal and a Centre in Tura. The University has 31 Post-graduate Departments and four Centres of Studies under its six Schools of Studies and an Under-graduate College. There are 58 Under-graduate Colleges and eight professional course colleges and North-Eastern Regional Institute of Science and Technology (NERIST) affiliated to it.

The University also has Regional Sophisticated Instrumentation Centre (RSIC). The University has an enrolment of 693 Post-graduate students and 65 research scholars, 19,716 Under-graduate students, and 2,274 professional course students during the year 1998-99. The University Central Library has a collection of 1,61,737 books, 3,60,028 bound periodicals and a subscription of 316 foreign and 366 Indian journals. The Mizoram campus library has a total of 2,621 books and a subscription of 66 journals. The University has conducted various seminars/ conferences on such subjects as 'Role of Microbes in Environmental Protection', 'DNA Damage Repair and Radiation Calcinigenesis', and 'Anthropology and Allied Discipline in the North-East Region'.

— *Pondicherry University*: Pondicherry University, established in 1985 as a teaching-cum-affiliating university, has its jurisdiction over the Union Territory of Pondicherry and Andaman and Nicobar Islands. As enshrined in the Act, Sri Aurobindo School of Eastern and Western Thought, Sri Subramaniya Bharathi School of Tamil Language and Literature have been established and given special attention. Pondicherry being the window of French Culture, French Studies is also given its due importance. The University has six Schools, 16 Departments and 12 Centres and offers one Certificate, two P.G. Diploma and 27 Postgraduate courses, 17 M.Phil, 22 doctoral programmes and five-year integrated Master's Degree programme in two Aisciplines. The University has 22 affiliated institutions of which 13 are located in Pondicherry, three in Karaikal, two in Mahe, one in Yanam and three in Andaman and Nicobar Islands. The total students strength in these institutions is 16,374. The students enrolment in the University is 1257. The University has a faculty strength of 138 experienced teachers, 37 Professors, 42 Readers and 59 Lecturers. There are 566 non-teaching staff. There are five hostels, out of 650 hostel students, 208 are women and 120 are SC/ST students. An innovative credit-based PG programme has been introduced since 1992-93 and this has attracted students from all over India. The credit system enables the students to construct their own curriculum and to complete the PG programme at their own pace. It also helps to develop academic networking with other universities institutions.

Pondicherry University had established the Centre for Pollution Control and Biowaste Energy in 1991 to give a renewed thrust to the University's efforts in providing advanced training, research, and consultancy facilities for regional as well as national benefit. During 1997-98 the Centre was further strengthened in terms of laboratory infrastructure and computational facilities which were procured mainly with the funds generated by the Centre through its industrial consultancy and R&D projects. As a consequence the Centre has taken rapid strides forward and is already beginning to be recognised as one of the foremost institutions of its type in India. The University entered into a Memorandum of Understanding with the University of Rennes-2 (France); Poitiers University, France; University of Technology, Australia; and Marne la Vallee University, France in addition to five MOUs already entered with the IGNOU.The Special Cell started in 1987 took all measures for the welfare of the SC/ST and physically handicapped students. Due reservations for SC/ST and physically handicapped candidates were given in admission as per Government of India orders. Out of the students admitted in the first year nearly 32 per cent teachers were women students. Of the 606 students on roll 84 were SC/ST. The number of women students on roll is 195.

— *Maulana Azad National Urdu University*: Maulana Azad National Urdu University was established at Hyderabad mainly to promote and develop Urdu language and to impart vocational and technical education in Urdu medium through conventional and distance education system. The University Act was passed by the Parliament in 1997 and the University came into existence on 9 January 1998 with the enforcement of the Act. Prof. Mohd. Shamim Jairajpuri and Dr M.S. Siddiqi has been appointed as the first Vice-Chancellor and the first Registrar of the University, respectively, by the President of India in his capacity as the Visitor of the University. The first Executive Council of the University has also been constituted by the Visitor. As a gesture the Government of Andhra Pradesh has allotted 200 acres of land for the University free of cost. The administrative office of the University has been set up at Hyderabad. Regional offices at Delhi, Patna and Bangalore have also been set up. The University organised two symposia to formulate its developmental proposal/layout. During the current academic session, the University has started B.A. course in Urdu medium through distance education mode.

— *Mahatma Gandhi Antarrashtriya Hindi Vishwavidyalaya*: Mahatma Gandhi Antarrashtriya Hindi Vishwavidyalaya Act, 1996 seeking establish the Mahatma Gandhi antarrashtriya Hindi Vishwavidyalaya at Wardha was passed by the Parliament in December 1996. The University has come into existence with effect from 29 December 1997. Dr Ashok Vajpeyi has been appointed as the first Vice-Chancellor by the President of India as the Visitor of the University. Though the University will be located at Wardha, given the international character of the institution and initial preparatory responsibilities, the Vice-Chancellor shall have to function from Delhi for some time during the preparatory phase. The first Executive Council of the University has also been constituted by the President in his capacity as Visitor of the University. The Government of Maharashtra has agreed to allocate land for the University at Wardha.

— *Tezpur University*:Tezpur University is a non-affiliated unitary Central University set up in 1994. Its aim is to offer employment- oriented and interdisciplinary courses, mostly at post-graduate level, to meet the local and regional aspirations and the developmental needs of the region. The University has been offering courses and promoting research in emerging areas in Science and Technology. The total number of students enrolled during the year is 544. The total number of teachers is 67. The University has 11 Departments under four Schools of Studies and six Centres of Studies. The first convocation of the University was held on 10 November 1998 wherein students of six Departments were awarded Post-graduate Degrees and Diplomas. Hon'ble

President of India, the Visitor of the University, was the chief guest to the convocation. An International Conference on Disaster Management was held in April 1998.

— *Indian Institute of Advanced Study*: The Indian Institute of Advanced Study (IIAS), set up in 1965, aims at free and creative enquiry into the fundamental themes and problems of life and thought. It is a residential centre for research and encourages promotion of creative thoughts in selected subjects like Humanities, Indian Culture, Comparative Religion, Social Sciences and Natural Sciences and in other areas as the Institute may from time to time decide. The Institute provides facilities for advanced consultation and collaboration besides exhaustive library and documentation facilities. The IIAS awards fellowships for advanced research every year. The Institute holds three seminars each year on themes of national significance when outstanding scholars and experts are invited to join the members of the academic community of the Institute to examine theoretical issues and contemporary problems. Visiting Professors, both from India and abroad, are invited from time to time to deliver a series of lectures at the Institute.

— *Indian Council of Philosophical Research*: Indian Council of Philosophical Research (ICPR) was set up by the Government to promote research in philosophy and allied disciplines. In order to achieve its aims and objects, the Council awards fellowships, organises seminars, conferences, workshops and refresher courses, provides financial support to organise seminars/workshops, travel grant to scholars to present their papers at conferences/ seminars held aboard, sponsors major and minor projects and brings out publications and a triannual journal Journal of Indian Council of Philosophical Research. The ICPR offered four senior fellowships, 11 general fellowships, 17 junior research fellowships, four residual fellowships and one short-term fellowship during the year under report (up to November 1998).

— *Indian Council of Historical Research*: The Indian Council of Historical Research (ICHR) was established in 1972 with a view to providing funds for historical research and to foster objective and scientific study of history. It has been promoting historical research including the history of art, literature and philosophy and allied subjects such as archaeology, numismatic, epigraphy, and the historical study of manuscripts. The Council awards fellowships, study-cum-travel grants and publication subsidies. It also endeavours to make available source material as well as result of historical research through an ambitious publication programme. It also brings out a journal *The Indian Historical Review* which includes interpretative papers and reviews. It organises seminars and academic conferences and gives financial assistance for travel within and outside the country for conducting historical research. The Council also maintains a large and continuously expanding library for the use of historians and researchers. Documentation services are also provided. The most important function of the ICHR is to provide assistance to scholars/institutions for research and publications. National Fellowships are awarded to eminent historians who wish to work on projects of special historical importance.

— *Indian Council of Social Science Research*: The Indian Council of Social Science Research (ICSSR) was established in 1969 with the objective to support and sponsor purposive and meaningful research in social sciences in India. The Council provides maintenance and development grants to 27 research institutes spread over the entire country. The Council has also established six Regional Centres for identification and development of talent through various programmes. During 1998-99, 130 new research projects are proposed to be sanctioned and 90 reports to be received for projects sanctioned earlier. The Council will continue its Cultural Exchange Programmes (CEPs) with Russia, France, the Netherlands, China, South Korea and Vietnam in addition to new CEPs with Japan and SAARC. The Council has been actively participating in the activities of international organisations like ISSC, UNESCO, AASSREC, etc. Indo-Dutch is one of the important bilateral programmes being implemented by the ICSSR in India and the Netherlands Organisation for International Cooperation in Higher Education in the. Netherlands. The collaborative programme has entered the fourth phase. Funding of the project will be continuing during 1999-2000. The National Social Service Documentation Centre (NASSDOC) provides research information services to social scientists and researchers. It is currently involved in the development of a National Information Network in Social Sciences.The data archives of the Council has been developed as a repository of primary data generated through research studies supported by the Council. It is also proposed to provide guidance and consultancy services in data processing to 60 scholars through 11 institutions. A major new initiative proposed in the Ninth Plan is to set up a network of socio-economic data bankers. The ICSSR has been carrying out surveys of research in different social science disciplines. The first series of surveys in all the disciplines have been published. The Council is updating these surveys every five years.

— *Dr Zakir Hussain Memorial College Trust*: Dr Zakir Hussain Memorial College Trust, Delhi was established In 1973 to take over the responsibility of the management and maintenance of Zakir Hussain College (formerly Delhi College), which is one of the constituents of the University of Delhi. The maintenance expenditure of the college is shared between the UGC and the Trust in the ratio of 95:5. In addition, the UGC provides development grant to the College. The matching contribution of such development expenditure is required to be made by the Trust. Since the Trust has no resources of its own, grants are provided by the Department of Education, MHRD for meeting the above expenditure. Financial assistance is also provided for meeting the administrative expenditure of the Trust.

The Association of Indian Universities (AIU) is a voluntary organisation of Indian universities and is registered under the Societies Registration Act. It is also a forum for university administrators and academics to come together to exchange views and to discuss matters of common concern. It acts as a bureau of information in Higher Education and brings out a number of useful publications, research papers and a weekly journal known as University News. The AIU is substantially financed from the annual subscription of the member universities. The Government of India 'sanctions grants for meeting a part of the maintenance and development expenditure including the Research Cell set up to undertake research activities concerning the university system. The Research Cell undertakes various activities including research studies, workshops, training programmes, question banks, tournament and databases, etc.

Towards a New Higher Education Landscape: Meeting the Equity, Quality and Social Development Imperatives of South Africa in the 21st Century

(Report to the Minister of Education presenting proposals of the Size and Shape Task Team of the Council on Higher Education, South Africa)

INTRODUCTION

This Report to the Minister of Education represents the considered proposals of the Size and Shape Task Team of the Council on Higher Education (CHE) on a new and more effective size and shape of South African higher education.

The members of the Task Team:

— Take as their point of departure, Education White Paper 3: A Programme for the Transformation of Higher Education 1997. It is the goals and purposes that the White Paper advances for higher education, and its core principles and values, such as equity and redress, quality, development, effectiveness and efficiency, that guided the Task Team and inform this Report.

— Have a common commitment to transforming higher education so that it is 'responsive to the needs of students of all ages and the intellectual challenges of the 21st century'.

— Share a passionate belief in the vital importance of higher education to democracy, social justice and the economic and social development of this country.

The Task Team understood its brief as:

> an overarching exercise designed to put strategies into place to ensure that our higher education system is indeed on the road to the 21st century. The restructuring will therefore impact on the system as a whole. There can be no business as usual (Minister of Education, May 2000 press statement).

It believes that it has faithfully conducted such an exercise, within the constraints of time. It is confident that its proposals will enable South African higher education to meet the challenges of the 21st century. That there can be no business as usual is clear in the Task Team's analysis of the state of higher education. The fundamental reconfiguration of the present system advocated by the Task Team proposals will certainly impact on the system as a whole and leave no institution untouched.

Soon after taking office as Minister of Education, Professor Kader Asmal announced his intention to review the institutional landscape of higher education. On 27 July 1999, in his Call to Action, he stated that:

The shape and size of the higher education system cannot be left to chance if we are to realise the vision of a rational, seamless higher education system, responsive to the needs of students of all ages and the intellectual challenges of the 21st century.

The institutional landscape of higher education will be reviewed as a matter of urgency in collaboration with the Council on Higher Education. This landscape was largely dictated by the geo-political imagination of apartheid planners. As our policy documents make clear, it is vital that the mission and location of higher education institutions be re-examined with reference to both the strategic plan for the sector, and the educational needs of local communities and the nation at large in the 21st century.

The Minister subsequently requested the CHE to provide him with advice on the reconfiguration of the higher education system so that it could meet the high-level human resource needs of the country.

In December 1999, the CHE submitted a memorandum, Towards a Framework and Strategy for Reconfiguring the Higher Education System in South Africa. The memorandum made recommendations and proposed the key principles and bases upon which the reconfiguration of the higher education system should take place. The CHE also proposed the establishment of a Task Team to develop the details of a framework and strategies for the reconfiguration of the higher education landscape.

At the launch of the Implementation Programme for the Tirisano Call to Action on 13 January 2000, the Minister made the following announcement:

> ...(Last) month I received an important report from the Council on Higher Education advising me (on) how to approach the challenge of restructuring the higher education system. The memorandum set out, for my consideration, the key principles which should guide the reconfiguration of the higher education system, with a proposal that a task team be established to develop the details of a framework and strategy for this reconfiguration. In principle, I have accepted the recommendations of the CHE. A task team, comprising representatives of the CHE,

> the Department of Education, and other persons knowledgeable about higher education is in process of being set up and will report no later than the end of June 2000.

In late January 2000, the Minister indicated his 'broad agreement with the Council's approach'. He also signaled his expectations of the Task Team. The Task Team had to conduct a considered and far-reaching review that answered the President's question: 'Is higher education, will high education be, a system for the 21st century'? It also had to provide the Minister:

> with a set of concrete proposals on the shape and size of the higher education system and not a set of general principles which serve as guidelines for restructuring. I cannot over-emphasise the importance of the point. Until and unless we reach finality on institutional restructuring, we cannot take action and put in place the steps necessary to ensure the long-term affordability and sustainability of the higher education system. I do not have to spell out the consequences of the latter. It is for this reason that I am committed to taking final decisions on restructuring to the Cabinet by no later than the end of August 2000. I have therefore indicated to the Council that their report must be completed by the end of June 2000.

In a May 2000 press statement, the Minister made it clear that the work of the Task Team was not 'targeted at closing institutions and in particular, historically disadvantaged institutions' - 'on the contrary, the reconfiguration exercise is key to preventing closure of those institutions that are experiencing serious difficulties'. He also indicated that:

> Subsequent to receiving the advice of the CHE, as well as on the basis of ongoing work undertaken by my Department, I will publish a national plan, which will contain my Ministry's comprehensive proposals

> for the shape and size of the higher education system. The plan, which I shall take to Cabinet, will be linked to ongoing processes of institutional planning and to implementation time frameworks.

The Minister reiterated that:

> the national plan will be framed within the broad framework of government policy as outlined in Education White Paper 3: A Programme for the Transformation of Higher Education 1997. The plan will be a break from the past - a past largely dictated by the geo-political imagination of apartheid planners. The plan will also signal a break from the inequalities and inefficiencies which continue to plague the higher education system.

THE CHE TASK TEAM

The CHE Task Team was constituted in early February 2000 and began its work later that month. It met on a number of occasions, supported by a small secretariat. To aid its work, a number of studies were commissioned and various unsolicited reports and papers provided to the Task Team were also examined. It also had full access to the institutional plans of all the universities and technikons and to various reports and databases of the Department of Education.

On 7 April 2000, the Task Team produced a Discussion Document to engage the key constituencies in higher education on reconfiguring higher education. On 17 April 2000, a consultative meeting was held on the Discussion Document. The Task Team took serious note of the concerns expressed in the valuable discussion at the meeting.

The Task team also invited public responses to the document and received more than 60 written responses.

These were analysed and the substantive issues and problems raised by stakeholders were duly considered at various Task Team meetings. There were questions around the compatibility of the Task Team's ideas with the White Paper, the ostensible rigidity of the proposed structure for differentiation, the resources and capacity for institutional reconfiguration, the 'size' of the system, the qualification and degree structure, and the implications of private provision. Concerns were also raised around a national human resource strategy, admissions, research and academic development, and the question of effective national planning or steering. The Task Team has incorporated these concerns, which has strengthened the Report.

The Task Team was aware that during the period of its deliberations, other task groups were investigating the issue of nursing colleges and agricultural colleges. There has also been an investigation into private higher education. The Task Team proposes that the implications of these investigations for the reconfiguration of higher education must be accommodated in national planning.

THE CHE TASK TEAM REPORT

— Seeks to institutionalise the principles and values of the White Paper in order to realise its social and educational goals. The overall objective is the development of a higher education system that delivers effectively and efficiently and is based on equity, quality and excellence; responsiveness; and good governance and management.

— Points to a historic opportunity to reconfigure the higher education system in a principled and imaginative way, more suited to the needs of a democracy and all its citizens in contrast to the irrational and exclusionary imperatives that shaped large parts of the current system.

— Provides a framework and foundation for making the present incoherent, wasteful and unco-ordinated higher education system rational, enabling significant improvements in quality and equity and ensuring that the knowledge and human resource needs of a developing democracy are effectively realised.

— Recommends that the present system should be reconfigured as a differentiated and diverse system so that there can be effective responses from institutions to the varied social needs of the country.

— Recommends that in a new reconfigured system, institutions should have a range of mandates (principal orientations and core foci) and pursue coherent and more explicitly defined educational and social purposes with respect to the production of knowledge and successful graduates.

— Recommends that these mandates define institutions as:

1. Institutions which constitute the bedrock of the higher education system. The orientation and focus of these institutions would be:

   — quality undergraduate programmes;

   — limited postgraduate programmes up to a taught masters level;

   — research related to curriculum, learning and teaching with a view to application.

2. Institutions whose orientation and focus is:

   — quality undergraduate programmes;

   — comprehensive postgraduate taught and research programmes up to the doctoral level;

   — extensive research capabilities across a broad range of areas.

3. Institutions whose orientation and focus is:
   - quality undergraduate programmes;
   - extensive postgraduate taught and research programmes up to the masters level;
   - selective postgraduate taught and research programmes up to the doctoral level;
   - select areas of research (basic, applied, strategic and development).
4. An institution whose orientation and focus is dedicated distance education.
5. Private higher education institutions.
   - Stresses that the Minister must be mindful that under apartheid, institutions designated for black South Africans and the technikons were disadvantaged in different ways. The Task Team's reconfiguration proposals makes possible developmental trajectories for institutions to enable them to undertake specified mandates within a new national framework.
   - Advocates that there should be no closure of institutions but that the absolute number of institutions should be reduced through combination.
   - Argues that combination offers the opportunity for creating a more responsive higher education landscape than that which is a legacy of apartheid, particularly in relation to increasing the participation rates of African and Coloured learners, and mature learners.

— Provides examples of possible combinations for illustrative purposes.

— Strongly recommends that the Minister should investigate the full range of possibilities for combinations, and should also be open to compelling combination possibilities that may emerge from the iterative national planning process.

— Proposes that as part of national planning and the development of a national plan, there should be an iterative process between the Minister and institutions around the reconfiguration of the system, combination and the mandates of institutions.

— Emphasises that the success of reconfiguration will require the setting of nationally negotiated priorities and targets, as well as monitoring and evaluation mechanisms to track progress in their achievement.

— Urges that the current levels of public funding of higher education should be maintained.

— Highlights that without the mobilisation of public, international donor and private sector funds for key strategic interventions, the achievement of a new institutional landscape will not be possible.

A range of proposals and recommendations - around reconfiguring the system, pre-requisites for successful reconfiguration and combination, the process of creating a new differentiated and diverse landscape, distance education, funding and a number of other issues - are also advanced in the Report.

The Task Team considers the Report to be a contribution to the overall activities of national planning, the development of a national plan by the Department of Education and the production of three-year plans by public higher education institutions. Decisions on reconfiguration should become part of the national plan. The proposals on the reconfiguration of the system, on combination and on nationally agreed targets will give a new shape to higher education. The proposals on participation rates, public sector enrolments, increasing access for disadvantaged social groups and mature learners, and on reducing the overall number of institutions will impact on the size of the system.

In brief: Chapter One indicates the goals, values and principles that guided the Report and the key premises that informed the work of the Task Team. It analyses the different problems and shortcomings of the higher education system and the key equity, quality, effectiveness and efficiency challenges that these represent.

Equity is a defining imperative of the Task Team's reconfiguration proposals. The achievement of equity is compromised by inefficiencies, lack of effectiveness, and shortcomings in quality. Equity targets must be established as part of national planning around access to, opportunities within, and outcomes of higher education.

Equity should mean more than access into higher education. It must incorporate equity of opportunity - environments in which learners, through academic support, excellent teaching and mentoring and other initiatives, genuinely have every chance of succeeding. Equity, to be meaningful, is also ensuring that learners have access to quality education, and graduate with the relevant knowledge, competencies, skills and attributes that are required for any occupation and profession.

Finance is required to achieve equity. While finance is a necessary condition it is not a sufficient condition. A coherent framework for the more effective pursuit of equity is also essential. Such a framework must look forward towards the 21st century but also recognise the inequities of the past. It must encompass possibilities of enhancing redress for historically and socially disadvantaged social groups through unhinging institutions from their past and setting them on new roads to development in accordance with social needs. The Task Team's proposals on reconfiguration and combination provide a framework for creating a higher education system that is geared towards delivering equity through the effective functioning of all sectors of the system.

Chapter Two argues the case for public higher education. Higher education has immense potential to contribute to the consolidation of democracy and social justice, and the growth and development of the economy. These contributions are complementary. The enhancement of democracy lays the basis for greater participation in economic and social life. Higher levels of employment and work contribute to political and social stability and the capacity of citizens to exercise and enforce democratic rights and participate effectively in decision-making. The overall well-being of nations is vitally dependent on the contribution of higher education to the social, cultural, political, and economic development of its citizens.

It is also argued that although the costs of higher education are relatively higher than that of school or other levels of education, continued expenditure in higher education is important. Schooling and other levels of education cannot produce the kinds of knowledge or the highly skilled professionals that are necessary for South Africa's successful entry into the arena of globalisation. South Africa's industrial, trade, investment and science and technology policies are predicated on the pursuit of the 'high-road' of development. This 'high-road' depends on investment in human resource development and the availability of high quality graduates.

Chapter Three addresses the critical issue of the diversification and differentiation of the higher education system. It argues the case for a differentiated and diverse system that is also strongly integrated through a wide range of articulation mechanisms. Differentiation allows for specialisation and for the more focused and targeted pursuit of educational and social goals and purposes. The key characteristics that should inform a new system and the range of institutions that should feature in a new reconfigured system are identified.

Chapter Three also deals specifically with articulation as a fundamental requirement of an integrated and co-ordinated system. It comments on the degree structure and, finally, addresses the question of the 'size' of the higher education system.

Chapter Four deals with the change management aspects of creating a reconfigured system and new higher education landscape. It covers the key requirements for successful reconfiguration, the processes of reconfiguration, and the issues of time-frames and funding. It also discusses combination as a means of reducing the absolute number of institutions, its benefits, and the various considerations that should inform the combining of institutions. Examples are provided of possible combinations and, very briefly, the objectives that could be achieved.

The proposals on the reconfiguration of the system, on combination and on nationally agreed targets will give a new shape to higher education. The proposals on participation rates, public sector enrolments, increasing access for disadvantaged social groups and mature learners, and on reducing the overall number of institutions will impact on the size of the system.

A number of fundamental problems and weaknesses afflict the higher education system. The Task Team is united in the view that these problems and weaknesses should not be tolerated any longer. They constitute a serious drain on national resources and undermine government's ability to achieve its set national goals. They also impact negatively on the possibilities for democratic consolidation in the country through not realising the social benefits of higher education for the development of society as a whole. They are testimony for the need to urgently and aggressively reconstruct the system as a whole.

The Task Team is adamant that no public institution should believe that it is exempt from the imperative of system-wide reconfiguration, from the need to change fundamentally, and from contributing to the achievement of a new higher education landscape. No higher education institution can assume that its track record with respect to equity, quality, social responsiveness and effectiveness and efficiency is beyond dispute and self-evident. Much remains to be achieved by all institutions to advance new social goals and to take us beyond the distinctions between historically advantaged and historically disadvantaged.

The Task Team believes that it has effectively discharged its responsibilities in the time available. As requested, it has advanced concrete proposals and has recommended certain issues for further investigation. It is convinced that the problems and weaknesses of the higher education system will not disappear on their own or be overcome by institutions on their own. They must be confronted and resolved in a systemic way. This will require the reconfiguration of the present system and the creation of a new higher education landscape. It will entail extensive, integrated, iterative processes of national planning as well as multiple co-ordinated interventions and initiatives. It will also require political will, sustained commitment and the courage to change at system and institutional level.

CHAPTER I
SOUTH AFRICAN HIGHER EDUCATION: GOALS, PROBLEMS AND CHALLENGES

The higher education system has strengths and immense potential to contribute to the economic and social development needs of South Africa, the Southern African region and the African continent. However, the present system also has a number of fundamental problems and serious weaknesses as a result of its apartheid past and developments during the past decade. These problems and weaknesses severely compromise its ability to effectively and efficiently achieve important national goals and serve various social and educational purposes. The proposals of the Task Team address the fundamental problems and weaknesses of the system. They also identify opportunities for creative and constructive intervention in shaping a system that could yield many more social and educational benefits than currently possible. The key outcomes of the proposal are: making rational the present incoherent, wasteful and unco-ordinated higher education system, enabling significant improvements in quality and equity and ensuring that the knowledge and human resource needs of a developing democracy are effectively realised.

The recommendations of the Task Team point to a historic opportunity to reconfigure the higher education system in a principled and imaginative way, more suited to the needs of a democracy and all its citizens in contrast to the irrational and exclusionary imperatives which shaped large parts of the current system. The country faces a challenge of immense significance in demonstrating the benefits of higher education planning that is informed by the requirements of democracy and socio-economic development. The reconfiguration of higher education must be seen as part of the process of constructing a seamless lifelong learning system that embraces schools, further education, higher education, workplace-based learning and non-formal learning. Such a system should provide ever greater levels of access to learning opportunities across a range of programmes and entry points in a way that forms the critical basis for social justice and economic revitalisation.

This chapter sets out the overall goals that South African higher education must achieve and the principles and values that the system must institutionalise. It then highlights the major problems and weaknesses of the present system and indicates the principal outcomes that must be achieved through the reconfiguration of the higher education institutional landscape.

Goals, principles and values

Higher education must help erode the inherited socially structural inequities and provide opportunities for social advancement through equity of access and opportunity. It must produce, through research, teaching and learning and community service programmes, the knowledge and personpower for national reconstruction and economic and social development to enable South Africa to engage proactively with and participate in a highly competitive global economy. Given the apartheid legacy and the social and developmental challenges, the higher education transformation agenda has to be radical and comprehensive. It also needs to be pursued with particular urgency.

The White Paper of 1997, A Programme for the Transformation of Higher Education, identifies the various, and indeed diverse, social purposes that higher education must serve:

— Attention to the pressing local, regional and national needs of the South African society and to the problems and challenges of the broader African context.

— The mobilisation of human talent and potential through lifelong learning to contribute to the social, economic, cultural and intellectual life of a rapidly changing society.

— Laying the foundations of a critical civil society, with a culture of public debate and tolerance which accommodates differences and competing interests.

— The training and provision of personpower to strengthen this country's enterprises, services and infrastructure. This requires the development of professionals and knowledge workers with globally equivalent skills, but who are socially responsible and conscious of their role in contributing to the national development effort and social transformation.

— The production, acquisition and application of new knowledge: a well-organised, vibrant research and development system which integrates the research and training capacity of higher education with the needs of industry and of social reconstruction.

It also sets various goals for the higher education system and for institutions. These include:

— Increased and broadened participation within higher education to meet personpower needs and advance social equity.

— Co-operative governance of the system, institutions and partnerships.

— Curriculum restructuring and knowledge production which is responsive to societal interests and needs.

— Promotion of quality and quality assurance through accreditation and assessment of programmes.

— Incorporation of higher education programmes and qualifications within a National Qualifications Framework designed to promote articulation, mobility and transferability.

— Improved institutional planning and management and the development of three-year institutional plans.

Especially pertinent is that a key policy goal is the establishment of a national, integrated, co-ordinated and differentiated higher education system.

In meeting its goals and giving effect to its defined purposes, the White Paper is clear and explicit about the principles and values that must be promoted. These are:

— Equity and redress;

— Democratisation;

— Development;

— Quality;

— Effectiveness and efficiency;

— Public accountability;

— Institutional autonomy;

— Academic freedom.

The proposals for the reconfiguration of the higher education system and individual institutions seek to institutionalise these principles and values and to help realise the defined policy goals. The overall objective is the development of a higher education system characterised by quality and excellence, equity, responsiveness and effective and efficient provision, governance and management.

However, with respect to principles it is necessary to address some important issues. Firstly, the apartheid legacy imposes extremely onerous conditions on the process of transformation. The challenges have to be met without becoming paralysed by the legacy of the past. Higher education institutions need to be liberated from such a past to enable them to meet societal goals.

All higher education institutions are products of segregation and apartheid, of the 'geo-political imagination of apartheid planners'. It is also beyond dispute that under apartheid certain higher education institutions experienced a history of disadvantage. Claims for institutional redress on the part of 'historically disadvantaged' institutions must confront the realities of the financial and human resources available to higher education to meet all claims.

The claims for institutional redress must also be balanced against the imperative of social redress for historically disadvantaged groups of people. Social redress and institutional redress are connected, but the former is not reducible to the latter. Students from historically disadvantaged social groups are in large and increasing numbers entering institutions characterised as 'historically advantaged'. The categories of 'historically advantaged' and 'historically disadvantaged' as applied to institutions are becoming less useful for social policy purposes. While planning must take cognisance of the institutional inequities and the distortions of the past, it is vital to look to the future. The 36 public higher education institutions inherited from the past are all South African institutions. They must be embraced as such, must be transformed where necessary and must be put to work for and on behalf of all South Africans.

Secondly, 'quality' and 'standards' are not timeless and invariant. It is unwise and inappropriate to conceive of quality as being attached to a single, a-historical and therefore universal model of a higher education institution. Quality and standards are historically specific and must be related to the objectives of higher education institutions and to educational and broader social purposes. A differentiated system in which institutions have different objectives and which caters for different social and educational purposes will necessarily have a variety of standards requirements that are appropriate to specified objectives and purposes.

At the same time, all institutions must strive for excellence. Government, employers, parents and students must be assured that graduates are able to fulfil the requirements of the various professions and the labour market, to be life-long learners and able to function as critical, culturally enriched and tolerant citizens. Quality and excellence are not in competition with equity/ redress; they are intrinsic to the achievement of meaningful equity and the substantive erosion of an inequitable occupational structure and the current distorted pattern of knowledge production. Quality is also related to the social composition of the students and staff of institutions. Diversity of cultures and economic and social backgrounds enriches the educational experience of both staff and students and constitute one element of excellence in an institution.

Thirdly, in the same way, efficiency and effectiveness in the achievement of missions and goals by higher education institutions are not in competition with quality, equity or democracy. A lack of institutional effectiveness compromises accountability to the public and government in relation to the investment of public resources. The costs of institutional inefficiency are ultimately borne by the public and especially by parents and students from working class and rural poor backgrounds.

It is also necessary to comment on the strategies and policy instruments and mechanisms advocated in the White Paper in relation to the above goals. The White Paper advocates various strategies and policy instruments and mechanisms for achieving the desired goals. For example, with regard to achieving an integrated yet differentiated and diverse higher education landscape, it suggests that steering through government funding, national and institutional planning and quality assurance mechanisms should be used. There have been constraints in the use of these steering instruments over the last few years.

There have been changes in the environment inside and outside higher education. A new political and economic environment has emerged. Policy formation has given way to a focus on the effective realisation of policy goals and efficient and accountable use of public resources. The higher education terrain has changed as a result of how individual institutions have 'read' the White Paper, the nature of the responses of public institutions and the expansion of the private higher education sector. There has been an accelerated incorporation of information and communication technologies in learning and teaching. There have also been difficulties in quickly mobilising human and financial resources for the effective steering and regulation of higher education. Unchecked, recent developments within higher education could result in a system characterised by even greater fragmentation and incoherence and inefficient and ineffective utilisation of resources than previously.

The above changes require us to interrogate whether and how the strategies and policy instruments and mechanisms proposed by the White Paper for effecting the transformation of higher education need to be supplemented and supported by additional measures which could strengthen the planning framework and enable the proposed steering mechanisms like funding and quality assurance to succeed. The full range of strategies and policy instruments and mechanisms must be determined not only by goals and principles but also by concrete conditions, both within society and the higher education arena. It is necessary, therefore, to explore additional strategies and instruments to pursue the achievement of the key policy goal of a national, integrated, co-ordinated and differentiated higher education system.

Premises of the Task Team

A number of premises inform the Report of the Task Team.

1. The Task Team's work is a component of the overall activities of national planning, the development of a national plan by the Department of Education and the production of three-year plans by public higher education institutions. Task Team proposals that are accepted must become part of the national plan. Likewise, the reconfiguration of the system and institutions must be an integral element of iterative national and institutional planning processes.

2. The success of reconfiguration will require creative change management at national and institutional levels. Serious consideration must be given to the instruments, mechanisms, processes and procedures as well as the time-lines and pace of change in relation to available financial and human resources. There is a need for national and central shaping and steering of the system to effect appropriate and timely interventions.

3. The success of reconfiguration will also require the setting of national targets and priorities and a monitoring and evaluation system to track their progress. These targets and priorities will have to be nationally negotiated and agreed, and will need to take into account current realities, available resources and future goals.

4. An adequately funded public higher education system that is committed to excellence and equity and is responsive to societal needs is vital to South Africa's future development. Such a higher education system is a public good.

5. There must be an articulation between economic and social policy and human resource development policy and strategies. In the absence of a human resource development strategy and plan, the Task Team has had to be guided by a synthesis of existing work on this matter. Higher education has a vital role to play in human resource development. There is a need for government to clarify its human resource development strategy in order that the public higher education and training institutions can more adequately align themselves to national priorities. Without a clear human resource development strategy, it is not possible to set meaningful priorities in programme mix and levels.

6. The Constitution and the 1997 Higher Education Act provide for the existence of private higher education. A private sector has the potential to contribute to expanding access and address social and development needs. However, it is necessary to ensure that an adequate regulatory framework is established to promote a harmonious environment for both private and public higher education. Such a framework must impose obligations on private higher education to facilitate the goal of a national, integrated and co-ordinated higher education system.

7. Strong linkages between further education and training and higher education and training systems are essential to generate mutual benefits for both systems and institutions and the country as a whole and appropriate initiatives to strengthen linkages must be vigorously pursued.

8. The orderly reconfiguration and development of higher education may require a greater direction from the Department of Education around certain initiatives and activities of higher education institutions. Such initiatives may include large new capital investment initiatives, the introduction of new programmes, the closure of programmes and departments, new public-private partnerships and the establishment of new satellite campuses and tuition centres.

9. The reconfiguration of the system and institutions will have major financial and human resource implications. Public and donor funds must be mobilised to support national structures and institutions to develop capacities congruent with achieving the desired reconfiguration and to support priorities and strategic initiatives. The availability of adequate resources will unavoidably shape the

trajectory, dynamism and pace of reconfiguration. What is also clear is that the setting of priorities for the utilisation of funds as well as appropriate fiscal discipline will have to be a strong feature of the new system.

10. There is some public scepticism around the value, worth and contribution of public higher education. The contribution of higher education is not self-evident and it is imperative to state the case for public higher education. Further, it is necessary for higher education to both signal a clear and explicit commitment to pursue the general and specific goals delineated in the White Paper. Such a commitment is a pre-condition for a case for additional funds for higher education and more specifically for reconfiguration and development.

Key problems

A number of conditions and developments within higher education represent fundamental challenges to the system and major obstacles to the achievement of policy goals. The system and individual institutions manifest two different though connected kinds of problems and weaknesses. These can be loosely characterised as 'structural' (fundamental, long-standing, contextual) and 'conjunctural' (immediate, contextual). Structural problems include:

1. The geographic location of institutions which was based on ideological and political considerations rather than rational and coherent planning. This results in fragmentation and unnecessary duplication.
2. The continued and even increasing fragmentation of the system. The higher education system still does

> not function in the co-ordinated way envisaged by the White Paper. Neither the existing planning instruments nor the institutions have produced meaningful co-ordination or collaboration. There are only few and limited examples of successful co-operative initiatives and programmes between institutions. Many of the features of apartheid fragmentation continue within the system and between institutions. Excessively competitive behaviour and practices increasingly abound with potentially damaging effects on other institutions, especially those in more rural areas. Public universities and technikons appear to regard their immediate neighbours and other public institutions more as market competitors rather than as colleagues striving towards a unified and co-ordinated higher education system. This is inevitable in a context of falling enrolments and the absence of a clear, explicit and comprehensive national planning framework.

The competition among public providers is particularly evident where traditional contact institutions have embarked on large-scale distance provision. There are now over 39,000 students in such arrangements, mostly at historically Afrikaans-medium universities. The full time equivalent (FTE) number is, however, uncertain given differences in the manner in which institutions report such enrolments. This increase in distance provision has resulted, without any national planning, in the establishment of learning centres in various cities and towns (as support bases for students). The establishment of satellite campuses by some institutions has also been on the increase. These are partial replicas of the main campuses offering daily contact tuition, library facilities, etc. It is also evident that there are growing instances of 'programme creep' - historical types of institutions (universities, technikons, colleges) beginning to offer programmes and qualifications that were traditionally offered by other institutional types.

Some of the changes may be positive. However, they occur mainly as individualised initiatives by institutions, frequently with no or little reference to real socio-economic and educational needs and to the programme offerings of neighbouring institutions. The absence of well-established and optimally functioning accreditation and quality assurance mechanisms creates major concerns about the quality of teaching and learning. The major dangers are: lack of institutional focus and mission incoherence; rampant and even destructive competition in which historically advantaged institutions could reinforce their inherited privileges; unwarranted duplication of activities and programmes; exclusive focus on only 'paying' programmes; excessive marketisation and commodification with little attention to social and educational goals; and insufficient attention to quality. All of this could ultimately hamper the achievement of a national, integrated, co-ordinated and differentiated higher education system, a key goal of the White Paper.

3. There are major inefficiencies related to student throughput rates, graduation rates, student dropouts, student repetition and the retention of failing students, and unit costs across the system.

South African universities and technikons produced about 75 000 graduates and diplomates in 1998 on a head count enrolment base of 600 000 students (350 000 in contact programmes and 250 000 in distance programmes). If the system had achieved reasonable throughput rates of 20% for contact programmes and 12% for distance programmes, then at least 100 000 graduates/diplomates would have been produced by the higher education system in 1998. The inefficiency of the system resulted in South Africa producing 25 000 fewer graduates/diplomates in 1998.

Unacceptably large numbers and proportions of students drop out of the system each year. This is particularly true in the case of first-time entering undergraduates, that is students who had not previously been registered at a higher education institution. The system's intake of first-time entering undergraduates has averaged about 120 000 for the past few years. At least 30 000 (25%) of these new undergraduate students drop out of universities or technikons at the end of their first year of study. The total number of students that drop out of South African universities and technikons is at least 100 000 students per year, out of an enrolment total of about 600 000 students.

Another major aspect of inefficiency in the system is the retention of failing students in the system. A number of institutions report poor success rates by course (averages of 70% and below), low graduation rates (often 15% or below), and yet record no academic exclusions. This means that their enrolment (and subsidy student) totals are inflated by repeating students who have little or no prospect of completing their studies. Of course, such prospects are not unrelated to whether there are appropriate academic support and development initiatives at institutions.

Finally, costs per enrolled student and per graduate/ diplomate vary widely across programmes and institutions in the higher education system. These variations are often the result of low student enrolments in specialised courses and programmes, unwillingness of institutions to co-operate in the offering of expensive programmes and poor student success and throughput rates.

4. There are skewed patterns of distribution of students in the various fields of study - Science, Engineering and Technology (SET), Business and Commerce, and the Humanities and Education.

In terms of national development needs, there is a greater concentration of students in the humanities and education fields relative to other fields. In 1999 about 15% of all students in universities and technikons were following teacher training programmes and about 35% other humanities programmes. About 25% of students were enrolled in programmes in business and management studies, with a further 25% in the broad fields of life and physical sciences, engineering, computer science, all the health sciences, and in various fields of applied technology. It is important that a balance that is appropriate to the needs of a developing country exists in the distribution of students across the different fields.

These enrolment patterns are displayed among graduates and diplomates. Of some 75 000 graduates/diplomates, 25 000 leave with qualifications in the broad humanities, 10 000 with teaching qualifications (most of which are upgrading of qualifications of teachers already in service) and 20 000 with qualifications in business (including office administration), accountancy, and management. Only 20 000 graduate in fields related to science, engineering and technology. These proportions may not be appropriate for the development challenges that face South Africa. However, the crucial issue is not only the field of graduation but also the quality of graduates.

5. The distribution of students in the various levels and fields of study - SET, Business and Commerce, and Humanities and Education - and at certain institutions is skewed in terms of race and gender.

Gender equity improved in higher education enrolments between 1993 and 1999. Whereas in 1993, 43% of students were female, their proportion increased to 52% in 1999. This change, however, masks inequities in the distribution of female students across academic programmes as well as at higher levels of post-graduate training. Female students tend to be clustered in the humanities and, in particular, teacher education programmes. They remain seriously under-represented in science, engineering and technology and in business and management. These are programmes that produce higher levels of private benefits to successful graduates than those in education and in the humanities.

Black, and in particular African, student enrolments also increased rapidly between 1993 and 1999. Compared to 40% in 1993, 59% of all students in universities and technikons in 1999 were African. Concomitantly, the representation of white students in the higher education system fell from 47% in 1993 to 29% in 1999. The rapid increase in African students, however, masks an inequity similar to that of female students. Large proportions of African students were in 1999 enrolled in distance education programmes, most of which were humanities and teacher-upgrade programmes. The numbers and proportions of African students in programmes in science, engineering and technology and in business/ management remained low in 1999. Post-graduate enrolments across most fields are also extremely low. A further worrying trend is that at historically Afrikaans-medium universities, the predominant form of incorporation of African students has been through the enrolment of distance students who are seldom seen on campus.

6. Academic and administrative staff (in many fields and disciplines and at different levels) also display extremely poor patterns of race and gender representation and distribution.

The academic and senior administrative staff complements of universities and technikons remain highly inequitable. All institutions have academic staff and senior administrative bodies that are dominated by males. In academic staff bodies this is particularly true of the higher ranks of professor and associate professor. The historically white universities and technikons, including those that have experienced rapid changes in the racial composition of their student bodies, continue to have academic and senior administrative staff bodies that are dominated by whites.

7. Most institutions have extremely low research outputs and even these institutions that demonstrate a higher ratio of research outputs relative to other institutions have uneven levels of outputs.

Data available indicates that the research outputs of the higher education system have declined since 1994, thus compromising the research and development agenda of the country. In 1998, about 65% of all publications recognised for subsidy purposes were produced by only six of the 21 universities. These same six institutions also produce close to 70% of South Africa's total masters and doctoral graduates. The Task Team acknowledges that the technikons initially were not expected to conduct research and produce high-level graduates and that historically black universities were not designed as knowledge-producing institutions.

These structural characteristics of the higher education system undermine cost-effectiveness and efficiency, and also equity. They also generate the kind of differentiation that is neither desirable, sustainable or equitable. The conjunctural problems of the system include:

1. The decline in student enrolments within the public higher education sector. The increased enrolments predicted by the National Commission on Higher Education have not materialised. Indeed, there have been dramatic declines at many institutions. A

serious decline in the retention rates of students from the first to succeeding years of study has compounded the problem. The overall participation rate has remained static and is estimated for 1999 at 15% for the age group 20-24. This is low for a country striving to become competitive in the global knowledge-based economy.

Student enrolments have not grown for a number of reasons. The first is the failure of the secondary school system to produce sufficient numbers of qualified school-leavers to meet the intake targets of the higher education system. The second is the failure of the public higher education system to 'sell itself' to those school-leavers and mature students moving into the private higher and further education sectors. Third, is the failure of public higher education to retain all students until they graduate.

2. The possible crippling effects on the ability of several institutions to continue to fund their activities because of the relationship between enrolments and funding as well as their inability to attract more diverse sources of funding. The inability of many poor students to pay fees, as well as the institutions' lack of capacity to collect fees, have resulted in increases in student debt.

A number of institutions that have experienced declining student enrolments and/or institutional debt during recent years - essentially the historically black universities and the two traditional distance institutions - could find themselves under severe financial and other pressures. Declining enrolments could possibly reduce the subsidies of individual historically black universities by between 11% and 52%, with an average loss of 23%. There is also the prospect of the higher education system as a whole suffering a loss of 6% of its current allocation in government funding in the near future.

A new funding framework has yet to be finalised. This framework will only distribute funds in a different way and will not necessarily inject any increased funds into the system. The challenge is not simply the formulation and technical implementation of a 'goal orientated new funding system' as proposed by the White Paper. A new funding system has to be linked to the substantive achievement of an accessible, sustainable, robust new higher education landscape. The issue of institutional redress funding also has to be approached within such an overall context.

3. There has been a tremendous increase in private higher education institutions. These mainly take the form of small single-purpose providers. They include local institutions that operate independently or in partnership with local public or overseas public and private institutions, and a number of overseas private and public institutions. As yet, there are no accurate figures for FTE enrolments within the private sector. Private institutions that contribute to the diversification of the higher education system could be sources of innovation. However, they are presently inadequately regulated in terms of registration, accreditation and quality assurance. This raises concerns around quality, the effective protection of learners and possible adverse effects on the public higher education system.

4. Many institutions experience fragile governance capacity (council, management and administration, students) and, at some, the persistence of crises.

The 1997 White Paper introduced institutional governance based on co-operative governance. Co-operative governance has been severely tested at many institutions, where 'agreement in principle' has not always translated into 'unity in practice'. Competing and sometimes irreconcilable claims and interests have led to institutional paralysis and/or loss of coherence and direction at various institutions.

A complex of conditions has given rise to weak and/or inadequate governance and management. The problems at these institutions go well beyond episodic student protests and relate fundamentally to institutional leadership, legitimate authority and management. Yet the principle of co-operative governance and the inclusion of different stakeholders in the new institutional governance arrangements holds real and potential value for higher education institutions and society at large.

The Department of Education recognises that in the new environment education and training initiatives to improve effective governance, including leadership and management and student capacity development programmes, are a necessity. The small number of people available and able to provide national and institutional leadership also has to be increased. Capacity development needs of institutions are quite varied. They range from more conventional and very specific interventions to augment the already existing skills and capacity to the need for multi-skilled institutional support teams to help the leadership of an institution to stabilise, focus and re-direct the institution. It is also evident that the need for training is not restricted to institutional managers and administrators but also extends to members of councils and student leaders.

5. The current higher education information systems are sorely inadequate, especially in relation to information on finance matters. Further, many institutions lack the capacity to provide and process basic data and information. Many have very limited or no culture of reflective institutional research. A much more responsive and modern information system that provides

policy relevant 'real time' data on students and staff is essential to steering in the public and private higher education arenas. The development of an effective Higher Education Management Information System and institutional research are essential. In this regard, a new system is in the process of being developed. The student module has already been implemented and the staff module will be implemented in 2001.

The problems and weaknesses of the higher education system are extensive and varied. They will not disappear on their own or be overcome by institutions on their own. They must be confronted at a national level and addressed with vigour. The Task Team's proposals for reconfiguring the system and institutions cannot and will not immediately solve all the structural and conjunctural problems that afflict the system and institutions. This will require extensive, integrated, iterative national planning as well as multiple co-ordinated interventions and initiatives. The proposals will, however, provide a more rational, focused, effective and efficient framework and basis for overcoming the problems over a period of time.

The systemic problem of the higher education system is its overall coherence, rationality and appropriateness in relation to socio-economic development needs. It also relates to the size of the system (overall enrolments, participation rates and numbers of institutions), the shape of the system (the nature of institutions, their mandates and focus, the levels and range of their programme offerings, their field/disciplinary orientations) and modes of educational delivery (contact, distance).

The key policy objective that must define the overall capacity (size) of the higher education system is the need to develop the high level and varied intellectual and conceptual knowledge, abilities and skills needed to meet the local, regional, national and international requirements of a developing democracy. These capabilities must not be confined to simply economic goals but must address the needs of social, intellectual and cultural development.

This includes intellectual and conceptual knowledge and skills at the levels of knowledge production and dissemination as well as ongoing development of professionals at different levels, for different economic and social sectors, in different fields and disciplines and through different educational and pedagogic modes (shape).

Key Challenges

The above basket of conjunctural and structural problems translate into a number of critical challenges which provide an agenda of tasks as well as a set of targets for achievement and monitoring in the reconstruction of higher education. The targets will have to be continuously reviewed in the light of changing circumstances and needs. The challenges can be grouped under three headings: effectiveness challenges, efficiency challenges and equity challenges.

Effectiveness challenges

The effectiveness of the higher education system in delivering the objectives of the White Paper can be judged in a number of areas. For example, the production of 25 000 fewer graduates in 1998 seriously impacts on the labour market where graduates are 30% more likely to be employed than school-leavers. The reconfiguration of higher education is faced with the challenge of increasing the absolute number of graduates and diplomates to address the shortage of high-level skills on the labour market. In this regard, the accelerated construction of appropriate programme mixes which are responsive to the growth and development needs of the country as well as to individual needs for employment is also urgent, particularly to increase the number of learners in SET fields. The dangers posed to the knowledge needs of society and the economy by low and declining numbers of research outputs also needs to be addressed by measures aimed at increasing the numbers of researchers as well as research outputs from higher education institutions.

Efficiency challenges

Efficiency challenges are often closely tied to quality measures as well as sound planning measures both at institutional and system levels. For example, appropriate quality mechanisms will have to be put in place to reduce repeater, drop-out and failure rates of students so that institutions can discharge their education and training missions and responsibilities. Planning targets will make it possible for institutions to meet the needs of learners, industry and society at large as well as to produce economies of scale through collaboration and rationalisation. Greater complimentarity between public and private provision will also be effected through increasing the capacity of public institutions to improve the quality of their provision and remain institutions of choice for learners.

One particular challenge that will require explicit attention by all higher education providers is the development of information and communications technologies. The rapid growth and convergence in functionality of these technologies over the last few years is being harnessed by a growing number of higher education systems and organisations around the world. Information and communication technology is allowing for exponential increases in the transfer of data through increasingly globalised communication systems. Information and communication technology networks have significantly expanded the potential for organisations to expand their sphere of operations and influence beyond their traditional geographical boundaries. It is expanding the range of options available to education planners with respect to teaching and learning strategies, design and combinations, and administering and managing education.

It is also diminishing barriers to entry of potential competitors to higher education institutions by reducing the importance of geographical distance as a barrier, the overhead and logistical requirements of running education programmes and research agencies, and by expanding cheap access to information resources. In order to integrate information and communication technology applications successfully into higher education, planners will need to develop a clear vision of how their strengths can be harnessed and their weaknesses overcome.

Equity challenges

Given the legacy of exclusion in our country, one of the most critical challenges facing the reconfiguration of higher education is responding appropriately to the equity challenges of the country. Increasing the race, gender and social class distribution of students in various fields and levels of study, improving the racial and gender representivity of staff and ensuring financial access for poor students are all issues that have to be addressed. Equity targets will have to be set and monitored for all programmes and for student and staff equity. Such targets should apply across all other effectiveness and efficiency targets.

Chapter Two makes the argument for the higher education system increasingly to create opportunities for continuing and lifelong learning. Already many traditionally 'contact' institutions are seeing a shift in their student bodies towards older and employed students and often towards their own graduates returning to pursue further studies. Institutions need to provide programmes that do not necessarily require regular attendance of lectures at a central venue at set times and to utilise a range of more flexible delivery strategies.

Outcomes of this Reconfiguration Exercise

The reconfiguration of the system and institutions must lead to a more rational landscape for the investment of resources to pursue excellence and equity. This includes a much more clearly specified range of institutional mandates that encourages institutions to have coherent and more defined purposes in their production of knowledge and graduates.

A more rational landscape for higher education would promote the distribution of the goals and objectives of the White Paper across the entire system. While the system would still have uneven capacities, it would have a clearer and more targeted set of objectives for the investment of resources to strengthen quality and equity. This targeted approach to equity would have to be within a tougher accountability regime for performance and sanctions for non-performance.

A more rational landscape for higher education will provide a more focused framework for innovation.

Innovation in teaching and learning, in research and in community service is more likely through a concentration of resources and attention on niche areas - centres of excellence grounded in real intellectual and physical capabilities - rather than across all areas within the system.

The current exercise must provide an acknowledged framework for competition as well as collaboration within the public sector as well as between the public and private higher education providers. Competition within a properly regulated system enhances quality.

South Africa cannot afford to continue with the incoherent, wasteful and uncoordinated system inherited from the past. It must confront what is required by a developing country with respect to knowledge, human resource and service needs and take decisive action to reconfigure the higher education system.

Differentiation and diversity in higher education is a characteristic of most national systems of higher education. A differentiated and diverse landscape should be based on the levels and kinds of programmes offered, the teaching and research capabilities of institutions, the human and physical resources of institutions, the qualifications of staff and other features.

In South Africa, differentiation has been either along socially unacceptable lines of 'race' and 'ethnic' origins or along essentially horizontal lines. Differentiation has been accompanied by disadvantage and used to maintain white domination and privilege. However, this history should not obscure the immense contribution that a new differentiated and diverse higher education system can make to socio-economic and educational objectives.

A number of fundamental problems and weaknesses afflict the higher education system. Such problems and weaknesses should not be tolerated. They constitute a serious drain on national resources and undermine government's ability to achieve its set national goals. They also impact negatively on the possibilities for democratic consolidation in the country through not realising the social benefits of higher education for the development of society as a whole. They are testimony for the need to urgently and aggressively reconstruct the system as a whole. The problems and weaknesses must be resolved in a systemic way. They require system-wide and fundamental interventions to transform higher education. They will also require political will and the sustained commitment and involvement of key role players across the system.

This Task Team begins with the stated national goals of equity and development. This must lead to the development of institutions collectively focused on and oriented towards such national goals. Next are the principal social and educational purposes of institutions, their appropriate educational and organisational characteristics and their outcomes. The key goal is the pursuit of excellence and equity by every institution and the improvement of quality of output of graduates. Creative change management is critical to successful transformation.

A key premise of the Task Team is that in the public domain the contribution of higher education is not self-evident. It is imperative to state the case for public higher education. The next chapter addresses itself to this issue.

CHAPTER 2

THE CASE FOR HIGHER EDUCATION: DEMOCRACY, KNOWLEDGE AND SKILLS

The South African government has committed itself to a better life for all. Already some important improvements in the quality of life and the collective well-being of South Africans have taken place. Much remains to be done and ongoing social and economic transformation remains South Africa's central challenge. The long history of inequality, injustice and oppression continues to present an enormous challenge to the goals of societal reconstruction and development.

Dramatic and far-reaching improvements in the quality of outcomes throughout the educational system are a crucial part of solving the complex problems arising from South Africa's past. Higher education itself has a vital role in producing the knowledge, generating the socially committed graduates and providing various services for enabling this country to pursue social equity, justice and higher standards of living for all and contributing to the revitalisation of the African continent. A monumental effort is required by the government, educators and by society as a whole to address our challenges with creativity, courage and determination.

The Task Team is mindful of the demands on higher education to be responsive, play a developmental role and be publicly accountable. The demand for public accountability is a necessary and legitimate demand in respect of the use of scarce public resources. Valuable work is being done by many higher education institutions. However, there must be greater levels of responsiveness and accountability within the overall system, and higher levels of trust in higher education and between higher education and the government and public.

The lack of trust in higher education is the result of a number of factors. There is a perception that institutions have in various ways remained largely unchanged from their apartheid past. There is also concern about the quality of the outputs of institutions.

Numerous inefficiencies plague the system. Various institutions evince governance and financial problems, inadequate financial systems, the unwarranted duplication of programmes and the lack of optimal use of infrastructure and human resources.

These problems of trust and accountability occur in a new context of the entry of private higher education institutions and the erosion of the historical monopoly enjoyed by public higher education institutions. If they are to maintain their pre-eminent position within South African higher education, public institutions will have to earn the status of being institutions of first choice for students.

Higher education, and public higher education especially, has immense potential to contribute to the consolidation of democracy and social justice, and the growth and development of the economy, despite the problems and challenges it faces. These contributions are complementary. The enhancement of democracy lays the basis for greater participation in economic and social life more generally. Higher levels of employment and work contribute to political and social stability and the capacity of citizen to exercise and enforce democratic rights and participate effectively in decision-making. The overall well-being of nations is vitally dependent on the contribution of higher education to the social, cultural, political and economic development of its citizens.

Higher Education, Democracy and Social Justice

Higher education contributes to the enhancement of democracy in many ways. It fosters open and critical intellectual debate, contributes to a vibrant and engaged civil society and increases the possibility of participating in decision-making. Through creating the opportunity for social advancement it also enhances equity and social justice.

The role of higher education in the defence and advancement of democracy is closely related to promoting good citizenship, a function that is accorded to it in the White Paper of 1997. Such a role is also intrinsically related to higher education's ability to deliver programmes that are essential to the promotion of a critical citizenry, and to ensure that the higher education system is firmly rooted within South African society and its particular development challenges.

Higher education can play an important role in supporting social policy development and monitoring and evaluating the implementation of policy. In this way it contributes to society by engaging with the actual problems and challenges of social reconstruction and development as well as by functioning as a social critic. This ability is essential to the long-term role of enhancing society's capacity to consolidate democracy and promote prosperity. The rich tradition of social dialogue and tripartism can also benefit significantly from an effective higher education system through its research, critical thinking and community service functions.

President Mbeki has on a number of occasions referred to the role of higher education in society, and especially in emerging democracies such as South Africa. He considers it essential to the stimulation of critical discussion, engagement with social policies and to the reinvigoration of the African continent. The African Renaissance is inconceivable without knowledge and a critical mass of intellectuals being produced or enriched by higher education institutions.

The role of higher education is to develop greater complementarity between the economic and humanising goals of society. Both these goals are of critical importance to the survival and sustainability of nations, and to their ability to participate effectively in a competitive global arena and to meet the needs of citizens.

Democracy is also essential to the evolution of a learning society. Such a society engages broad social layers of its population in the process of learning and promotes tolerance for differing viewpoints. Democratic learning processes engage wide layers of society in the resolution of its problems and rely on the collective experience and wisdom of communities. Democracy creates the best environment for the achievement of a better life for all and democratic societies have a better chance to sustain and renew themselves.

The value and legitimacy of the higher education system in South Africa will also be judged by the extent to which it provides greater access and opportunity for black, and especially African and Coloured, South Africans, women and other socially disadvantaged groups. The higher education system is a potentially powerful agent to enhance the life opportunities of increasing numbers in society over time. High quality, equitable higher education promotes social mobility and the well-being of larger social constituencies, and thereby increases the stability of such a society.

Some success has already been achieved towards the goals of equity and social redress through developments in higher education in South Africa. In terms of 'race' and gender the student body has become much more representative since 1994. In 1999, 52% of students in universities and technikons were female, compared to 43% in 1993. In 1999, 59% of all students in universities and technikons were African and only 29% white, compared to 40% African students and 47% white students in 1993. These changes in student composition within such a short period are unparalleled in the world and constitute a promising platform for greater equity1.

The expansion of access to, and equality of opportunity within, higher and further education for historically and socially disadvantaged groups is essential to long-term development. Equity and access must also reflect greater participation by groups not traditionally well represented in higher education. These include students from working class and rural backgrounds and adults who possess work-related knowledge. The extent to which equity and access are actively promoted or frustrated will determine the nature and extent of social and class stratification and have a direct bearing on the nature of South Africa's democracy, labour market and social stability.

Higher education has private individual and public social benefits. The former relate to enhanced employment possibilities, better salaries and benefits, improved working conditions, improved health and quality of life and greater capacity to participate in policy and decision-making. These private gains also generate public (social) gains such as higher employment rates, higher savings, increased contributions to national revenue and incomes, greater workforce flexibility, a decreased reliance on government financial support and more active citizenship.

Recent studies suggest that in South Africa in 1996, only 2.9% of graduates were unemployed and looking for work2. This is a remarkably low percentage. Unemployment rates below 3% are regarded as full employment since 2-3% of any cohort is not employable due to physical or psycho-social problems. The HSRC graduate study further reported that more than 80% of all graduates, irrespective of field of study, perceived higher education to be of great benefit to them. This is demonstrated by the huge differences in employability and in the income of graduates relative to non-graduates.

In most developing countries, especially on the African continent, access to higher education has continued to be limited to a relatively small social stratum, which has sometimes used authoritarian forms of government to defend its privileged position. In South Africa the social and political challenge is to avoid excessively polarising society by closing off avenues of social advancement - indeed, our challenge is to significantly increase access.

Higher Education, Economic Growth and Development

Studies on the relationship between knowledge production and economic and social development have demonstrated the critical importance of the creation of new knowledge. The growth of knowledge, enhanced by the wider diffusion of information and communication technologies, has been the catalyst for high levels of social and economic development in regions such as the Pacific Rim over the last two decades.

The growth of capital in the global economy is increasingly dependent on knowledge based on a range of disciplines in the humanities, commerce and the social and natural sciences, and on information and communication technologies. The integration of knowledge is necessary to deal with the complex socio-economic problems of modern societies. The increasing generation and accessing of knowledge has led to what is often referred to as the 'knowledge society', promoted in the main by higher education institutions. Castells asserts that 'if knowledge is the electricity of the new informational international economy, then institutions of higher education are the power sources on which a new development process must rely'1. Such knowledge production is especially important for developing countries where the return on investment in higher education is much higher. In South Africa a considerable proportion of intellectuals and knowledge production, dissemination and application is located in higher education institutions. The development of a knowledge society could contribute significantly to managing and mediating the impact of globalisation.

A central feature of South Africa's economic policy is meeting the challenge of international competitiveness. An inability to compete will increasingly marginalise the South African economy, have profound effects on its rate of growth and consequences for the social well-being and stability of South African society. The acquisition of knowledge and access to new knowledge and technology creates new global power relations. Those countries that cannot gain access to knowledge and information technologies will continue to be dominated by countries that can adapt to its demands. Unequal access to knowledge and power reinforces inequality both globally and within countries. In the words of Brazilian President Fernando Cardoso, these countries will 'not even be considered worth the trouble of exploitation, they will become inconsequential, of no interest to the developing globalised economy'. Castells warns that the 'systematic logic of the new global economy does not have much of a role for the majority of the African population in the newest international division of labour...The experience of Africa's transition into the new global economy is that 'structural irrelevance' is a more threatening condition than dependency'.

The South African labour market has been undergoing major restructuring. Increasingly capital- and knowledge-intensive production and services have created a growing demand for skilled professionals in the scientific, technological, technical, and business fields. Professional and managerial occupations have been growing at 5% per annum. It is estimated that their share of total employment will increase from 15.2% in 1997 to 22% by 2002.

From an economic perspective, the private and public returns on many higher education programmes are, at present, greater than other levels of the education system. The availability of skills in the sciences and the technological, technical and business fields is a precondition for competitive success in the production of a wide range of internationally traded goods. The manufacturing, processing and service sectors, which will have a dominant impact upon the country's economic future, will depend much more on the knowledge produced and applied in and by higher education institutions. This is not so in the primary sectors, where South African output and employment has, in recent years, been stagnant or in decline.

It has been argued that international competitiveness could be achieved via short-term steps such as downsizing, privatising, retrenching, slashing of budgets and deficit reduction (also known as the 'low road'). The government's avowed policy is instead to pursue the 'high-road' in its industrial, science and technology, trade, investment and other strategies. This requires the expansion and improvement of higher education to alleviate one of the major present constraints on economic expansion: the shortage of good quality high-level skills. Such expansion and improvement would promote the possibility of jobs for many less skilled and unskilled workers, and a net improvement of economic welfare and equity could be the likely result.

As the share of intellectual value-added-in economic processes continues to grow, the ability to think abstractly will be increasingly important across all professions. Educational experience should span the natural and human sciences and promote the integration of knowledge. The resolution of many developmental problems is dependent on enquiry that is inter- and multi- disciplinary. The knowledge and adaptability and flexibility of skills acquired through life-long learning can enable graduates in developing democracies to operate in diverse social settings and develop complex notions of identity and citizenship. Educational systems that are responsive to social needs and the development challenges are much more likely to be vibrant. Overall, higher education contributes to social and economic development by increasing the level of cognitive skills throughout the society.

The process of democratic transformation and globalisation has placed new demands on the state and on the public service. The development of an honest, efficient, effective and innovative public service is crucial to overcoming the legacy of apartheid. The ambitious social transformation agenda of the reconstruction and development programme can only be tackled through a professional and skilled bureaucracy. Higher education can play a major role in generating the high and medium-level conceptual, policy development, planning and implementation capacities and managerial, administrative and financial competencies and skills that are needed in the public sector.

Higher education also has a crucial role to play in improving the quality of schooling, health care, welfare services and other public services at national, provincial and local levels. This requires more active promotion of continuing education and the upgrading of professional knowledge and technical skills, and creating flexible opportunities for life-long learning for practicing education, health, social services and other public sector personnel. It also requires thoughtful applied and strategic research around key social policy issues and the concrete problems of social reconstruction and development. Such research and the upgrading, consolidation and continuous enhancement of the knowledge, competencies and skills of public sector personnel is necessary for innovation, improved social delivery and development. Giving effect to life-long learning will require concentrated effort, the development of flexible continuing and adult education programmes and support and resources for such work.

Higher education is critical to the resolution of many of the unique and complex problems and challenges that face South Africa and Africa as a whole. These problems require solutions that take into account the African context. While the ability to access and apply knowledge and technologies is extremely important, the solution to many problems lies in the generation and application of knowledge and technologies appropriate to the peculiar conditions of the continent. The African renaissance will not be possible without higher education producing sensitive and committed intellectuals, scholars, writers, dramatists, artists, musicians and critics.

A short-term priority and a long-term policy imperative are the development of socially committed institutions and individuals with the critical intellectual capabilities to produce, disseminate and apply knowledge and technology. Reconstruction and development depends on producing well-educated and trained graduates with a range of competencies and skills. Without investment in human resource development and expanding opportunities for both young and adult learners, sustainable growth and socio-economic development will be difficult. John Douglass writes: 'As the global economy becomes more competitive, those states and nations that invest the most time and energy in expanding and nurturing their higher education systems, will likely be the big winners of tomorrow.

The Task Team acknowledges the higher costs of higher education compared to lower levels of education. This is true of all higher education systems. Especially in circumstances where the school system is in great need of resources to enhance quality, the relative costs of higher education affects the choices made by government in the allocation of limited resources. The case for greater investment in higher education is not made on the grounds of equity and redress alone, although these are extremely important goals in their own rights.

The critical value of higher education to society lies in its ability to provide graduates with intellectual capacities and skills that can both enrich society and enhance its development considerably. This is dependent on higher education's ability to develop higher levels of intellectual rigour, a high level of analytical capacity, self-motivation, independence of thought, basic research skills and a capacity and mental aptitude for innovation. These attributes, delivered by a well functioning higher education system, cannot be achieved at lower levels of schooling. Yet they are crucial since they contribute a quality of public and professional leadership at all levels of society, which is essential to social development and social justice.

It is important that all those who meet the educational requirement for access to higher education, and who seek to enter the system, have access to higher education. The Task Team, however, regrettably concludes that the higher education system in South Africa, as in many other developing countries, will not in the immediate future be a sufficiently mass system in the sense of most of the 20-24 age-group and large numbers of adult learners being enrolled for higher education programmes. Currently, the provision of such higher education is too expensive. Even if students were available in sufficient numbers, the rate of expansion entailed would strain and undermine the quality of institutions.

The Task Team has little doubt that a greater participation level than the present 15% for the age group 20-24 should be pursued (see chapter 3). The proportion of graduates in the population as a whole is presently lower than in countries at a comparable level of per capita income. The benefits arising from quality improvement and an expansion of provision would be palpable, and well worth the costs entailed - including the opportunity costs implied for other parts of the education system.

No country has succeeded in generating sustainable socio-economic development without long-term investment in human resource development. South Africa's success depends on investment in its human resources. An equitable, good quality, efficient higher education system has a major role to play in producing the required high-level human resources. The successful pursuit of South Africa's reconstruction and development programme and the society's embrace of the high road of development demand the engagement of a highly responsive and responsible higher education system.

The current system has numerous shortcomings that were highlighted in the previous chapter. Far-reaching changes in higher education are overdue, urgent and unavoidable. The failure to undertake such changes could have unfortunate consequences for the public higher education system and choke its potential as a powerful 'engine of national development'.

The reconfiguration of the system and institutions should occur without over-zealous intervention or excessive regulation by government. At the same time, inappropriate and defensive appeals to institutional autonomy and academic freedom in the face of the imperative of reconfiguring higher education to meet socio-economic goals should also be avoided. The autonomy of institutions has to be reconciled with the need to account for the use of public resources. The right to pursue intellectual and academic goals has to be exercised within the framework of complementary social goals.

The reconstruction of higher education will require resources and time. The Task Team believes that present levels of funding must be sustained, at least in the next few years. In addition, donor funds must be mobilised for strategic interventions towards the reconfiguration of the system and the achievement of quality, equity, and efficiency in higher education.

CHAPTER 3

RECONFIGURING HIGHER EDUCATION: TOWARDS DIFFERENTIATION AND DIVERSITY WITHIN AN INTEGRATED AND CO-ORDINATED NATIONAL SYSTEM

The higher education institutions that were inherited by democratic South Africa have their roots in an apartheid social order. Some institutions unreservedly served the apartheid government's goals and policies. Others protested against racism and the creation of racial and ethnic institutions. Yet other institutions challenged and actively resisted the social purposes that were defined for them by apartheid planners and attempted to elaborate new purposes linked to democracy and social justice. In a number of areas, the higher education system developed real strengths, whether in relation to knowledge production and application, co-operative education or producing graduates that compare with the best in the world. However, overall, the inherited system is not effectively responding to the new needs of the country and it is essential to reconfigure it to serve the new democracy.

The country requires institutions with particular social mandates and a diversity of institutions with different and distinct missions. The heart of the system must be well-resourced high-quality predominantly undergraduate teaching institutions oriented towards the production of graduates with the knowledge, competencies and skills to contribute to the economic and social development of the country. Institutions with this mandate must constitute the bedrock of the higher education system. Excellence and the quality of the graduates of these institutions will fundamentally determine whether South Africa will grow, develop and create a better quality of life for all its people.

South Africa will not be unique in reconfiguring and reconstructing its higher education landscape. Higher educational reform and the re-organisation of higher education systems have occurred and continue to occur in countries throughout the world. Impetus for reorganisation arises from significant changes in national conditions and/or momentous world-wide changes that impact on the economy, labour market and society more generally and have major implications for the requisite knowledge, competencies and skills base of graduates and the production and application of knowledge.

The role of the nation state in creating an innovative society is crucial to the well being of citizens in the information age1. There is overwhelming evidence that in developing integrated market economies, the strategic role and interventions of the state must balance market forces. Such interventions must establish the institutional, infra-structural and interlocking policies and instruments that are needed to underpin both equitable social development and successful incorporation into the global economy.

A number of government departments are contributing to an institutional and policy environment to facilitate growth and development through cross-sectoral state policy co-ordination, partnerships and co-operation. The Department of Trade and Industry (DTI) is implementing policies to simultaneously stimulate export-led growth and opportunities for labour intensive growth and marginalised small, medium and micro enterprise. The Department of Labour has introduced an ambitious Skills Development Programme which, through the establishment of Sector Education and Training Authorities (SETA), seeks to enhance skills development through education and training. The Department of Education has advanced policies that emphasise institutional 'responsiveness' and 'relevance' to local economic and social needs. The Department of Arts, Culture, Science and Technology (DACST) is building a National Innovation System (NIS). The Presidency, together with the Departments of Labour and Education, is focusing on the development of a national human resource strategy. Higher education must participate in, respond to and ultimately help give effect to the development of an integrated and co-ordinated human resource development strategy.

Chapter Two made the case for higher education as a potentially powerful contributor to, and necessary condition for, achieving the goals of social equity, economic and social development and democracy. The national system must respond to the requirements of a society emerging from a long history of structural inequality and underdevelopment. It must respond to the challenges of social, economic and cultural development and encompass development across a broad range of areas of knowledge1. Higher education's primary role is to develop the intellectual and skills capabilities of our society to address and resolve the range of economic (including labour market), social, cultural, political and other challenges faced by society. It must do so at a national, regional and local level as well as contribute to the development of the continent. Higher education must also play a central role in meeting the difficult realities of international competition under the new conditions of globalisation.

Internally, the higher education system must strive to achieve equity and aspire to excellence, which is essential to the achievement of meaningful equity. It must also be committed to achieving significant improvements in the quality of higher education teaching and learning, research, community service and innovation.

There are many positive features of the South African higher education system—widespread commitment to equity and excellence and improvements in quality, innovative programmes and learning and teaching, quality of research outputs etc.

Reform and innovation are continuous processes. Changing environments—national and international, internal and external to higher education - require timely and flexible institutional responses. While the White Paper provides a powerful and robust framework for the transformation of higher education, it did not, and could not, anticipate a number of conditions and developments. These include:

— Institutional responses that exacerbate the inherited fragmentation and incoherence of the system and the inefficient and ineffective utilisation of resources.

- — Competition between public institutions around programme offerings and student enrolments which overshadows co-operation and leads towards homogeneity and sameness in an environment of declining enrolments.
- — The rapid incorporation of information and communication technologies within higher education.
- — The pace of change in instructional modes at various institutions.
- — Weaknesses and capacity problems in national and institutional planning processes which in the short term compromise the efficacy of these instruments to steer and regulate higher education.
- — Inadequate senior and middle-level management capacities within the system.
- — The diversification of funding and sources of revenue and the extent to which state funding could become an increasingly limited instrument for steering and regulation of higher education.
- — The difficulties in establishing effective accreditation and quality assurance mechanisms in the short term.
- — The excessive marketisation and commercialisation of higher education.
- — The decline in students with matric exemptions.
- — The lack of adequate regulation of private higher education which could have adverse consequences for a vibrant public higher education sector.

These conditions threaten important policy goals and require an immediate response. South Africa cannot continue to function on the basis of an inefficient, fragmented and unplanned set of institutional roles. No single institution has the capability to achieve all that is expected of higher education as a system. The White Paper calls for a coherent, co-ordinated and integrated national higher education system that is simultaneously differentiated and characterised by diversity. This is no contradiction. A coherent, co-ordinated and integrated national system need not be a uniform system. Indeed, uniformity in South Africa's circumstances is highly undesirable.

The Case for Differentiation and Diversity

The terms 'differentiation' and 'diversity', as employed by the Task Team, are both distinct and connected. 'Differentiation' is used to refer to the social and educational mandates of institutions. The mandates orient institutions to meet economic and social goals by focusing on programmes at particular levels of the qualification structure and on particular kinds of research and community service. Qualitative and quantitative criteria (minimum student Full-time Equivalents [FTEs], minimum enrolments in broad fields, staff qualifications and research output, etc.) underpin the mandates of institutions. 'Diversity' is used with reference to the specific missions of individual institutions. Differentiation and diversity are connected in that mandates provide the overall national framework within which individual institutions pursue specific institutional missions. To ensure diversity, the missions of individual institutions must be varied.

The goal is a differentiated and diverse but also integrated and co-ordinated system. Articulation between institutions with different mandates and different missions to ensure student and staff mobility, enable teaching and research collaboration and promote partnerships must be an integral feature of the new reconfigured system. Mechanisms for articulation cannot be voluntary in nature and only depend on the goodwill of individual institutions, administrators and academics. They must be a structural feature of the new system.

Differentiation and diversity are necessary for a number of reasons. First, nothing is gained through a homogenous and uniform system in which all institutions have exactly the same mandates and missions and seek to be the same in all respects. Nor does homogeneity and aspirations to sameness result in institutional equality. Second, a differentiated and diverse system will over time enable certain critical outcomes that are strongly related to achieving quality higher education, ensuring more meaningful equity for historically disadvantaged students, enhancing the efficiency and effectiveness of the system, and meeting development needs of society. These critical outcomes would be:

1. Achieving a more rational landscape than the incoherent, wasteful and uncoordinated higher education system inherited from the past by defining overall mandates for institutions within which diversity is encouraged through explicit, clear and coherent institution-specific missions. Such a new landscape would enhance the investment of public resources to deliver quality and equity.

One definition of quality in higher education is fitness for purpose in the context of missions. This would enable the quality assurance system to make better judgements about institutional fitness for purpose as a result of the clearer demarcation of institutional purpose in place of the diffuse spread of purposes across institutions.

2. Goals and objectives of higher education can exist in a distributed way across the entire system to enable a more appropriate allocation of resources in a rational landscape for higher education.

One example illustrates this. At the moment the goal of providing market-responsive training receives more explicit attention than the goal of contributing to cultural and civic life. This is squeezing out the humanities, particularly at historically disadvantaged institutions. A reconfiguration would create legitimate spaces and support for knowledge disciplines and fields in the humanities and social sciences threatened by parochial and crude interpretations of what the market requires. Informed business and union leaders suggest that with respect to employment the field of study is only one consideration. A key consideration is the quality of the graduate.

3. After an iterative process between the Department of Education and individual institutions, the range and level of programmes and qualifications that an institution should offer through focused institutional mandates and specific missions must be identified. This would concentrate attention, energy and resources on a more limited range of purposes and outcomes. It will also enable the more effective and efficient utilisation of physical and human resources.

Quality assurance can then target programme improvement in a strategic way within single or across multiple institutions. Given limited financial resources and the small number of academics with advanced qualifications and research experience, it makes little sense from a quality assurance point of view to have all higher education institutions offering, for example, doctoral level (or perhaps, even masters level) studies in all fields.

4. The prospects of increasing overall participation levels in higher education will be greater since a diverse system in which institutions orient themselves towards different social and educational

needs and purposes will enable different and more flexible criteria for admission. This will also provide much greater levels of access to school-leavers and mature learners.

Active policies are needed to develop a more diverse student profile at every institution. The student population should be consciously drawn from diverse backgrounds defined by 'race', socio-economic origins, gender, age and other social characteristics. There are good educational and social reasons for such policies of 'constituting the class'. It also provides practical ways to address the equity of access challenge for higher education institutions. Institutions should be required to incorporate into their planning quantitative targets to ensure adequate representation of African students, women and students from working class and rural poor backgrounds. In addition, consideration should be given to including a target for international students, particularly from the African continent.

5. Providing a focused framework for knowledge production and application and innovation is better achieved in a reconfigured and rational landscape for higher education. Innovation in teaching and learning, research and community service will occur through a concentration of resources and attention on niche areas rather than across all areas within the system. The quality assurance system cannot be satisfied with minimum standards only. It must also facilitate the excellence that will yield innovation as well.

6. It will provide for and encourage different modes of teaching, learning and assessment. At the same time it will also establish the parameters - possibilities and limitations - of different modes of delivery (different forms of contact and distance) for different

institutional focuses. This will help to address the unregulated and unfortunate manner in which institutions are currently establishing satellite campuses and tuition centres and moving into the distance education arena.

7. It will provide an acknowledged framework for competition as well as collaboration within the public sector, as well as between the public and private higher education providers. Some types and levels of competition can enhance quality. Unrestricted competition, however, could damage public institutions and programmes whose capacity is being strengthened within a reconfigured system.

Perceptions and uninformed notions will exist about the social and educational status, excellence and quality of institutions with different mandates and different specific missions. These must be vigorously addressed. The purpose of differentiation and diversity is to ensure a range of institutions, institutional programmes and capabilities appropriate to national need.

Differentiation and diversity must not undermine the development of an integrated and 'seamless' national system. There must be continuities, permeability and articulation between institutions regardless of individual missions and effective mechanisms to overcome barriers to articulation. Mechanisms to ensure student mobility and staff collaboration and mobility between institutions must be put in place so that life-long learning and horizontal and vertical mobility are all enhanced. Focused projects that enable learning that has occurred in non-formal contexts to be considered for entrance to higher education programmes - for example through 'Recognition of Prior Learning' - should be promoted. The system of accreditation and quality assurance, the national qualification structure and national planning processes must reinforce articulation.The extent to which the higher education system will evince high levels of diversity and differentiation to serve South Africa's diverse needs is dependent on policy intervention and effective steering. It will not occur on its own or through the 'market'.

Institutional Types Based on Orientation and Focus

A range of institutions with different institutional mandates based on different orientations and foci are necessary to achieve the diversity of social and educational goals, purposes, roles and outcomes. Institutional mandates provide a framework for individual institutions to formulate the specific institutional missions and strategies that would ensure diversity.

This section sets out the key characteristics that should define institutions with different mandates. Institutions are further described on the basis of orientation and foci.

Key Characteristics of Public Higher Education

Multi-purpose institutions

The knowledge economy and complex societal problems require inter-disciplinary and multi-disciplinary knowledge production and graduates that possess a range of competencies and skills. The production of graduates as critical citizens vital to a democratic society also requires education and training that is not narrow but spans and incorporates various disciplines and fields. Public higher education institutions should be multi-purpose institutions and offer broad-based higher education to achieve the goals set for higher education. Programmes should not be concentrated in only one or two broad areas of study. This would enable institutions to accommodate newly developing areas of study, which in many cases arise from the combination of existing knowledge areas, more easily in their learning programmes.

Single purpose institutions generally tend to be expensive and unable to subsidise expensive programmes. A large number of single-purpose institutions would also not be appropriate given the already existing inadequacies in higher education management capacities and skills.

The academic and economic viability of institutions

Higher education institutions are primarily concerned with advanced levels of learning. The principal aim normally is to develop increasing levels of intellectual maturity in learners to enable them to contribute to the creation of new knowledge and to new applications of knowledge. To meet this and other higher educational goals, as well as for reasons of economic viability, institutions should have a minimum operational basis. This is usually expressed in terms of the size of institutions, using the measure of the number of FTE enrolled students. Academic viability as a multi-purpose institution requires that student enrolments in public institutions should not be concentrated in a single broad area of study but should be spread over a number of broad areas of study. In South Africa it has proved useful to distinguish between the following broad areas of study: Humanities and Social Sciences (including Education), Business and Commerce, and Natural Sciences, Engineering and Technology (SET). This is expressed as the shape of institutions.

Distance education institutions do not generally offer many learning programmes in engineering and the natural and health sciences due to the intensive laboratory/practical components associated with such study. Typically, distance education student enrolments would be concentrated in the Social Sciences, Humanities, Education and Business and Commerce. Special consideration would have to be given to these institutions in applying this criterion.

Some countries have expressed the characteristics concerning academic and economic viability quantitatively. In Australia, for example, institutions were required to make applications to join the unified national system (UNS) and qualify for federal funding on the basis of Equivalent Full-time Student Units (EFTUs). The required institutional size for membership of the UNS was 2000 EFTUs. The required institutional size to have a broad teaching profile with funding for some research activity was 5000 EFTUs. The required institutional size for comprehensive involvement in teaching and research was 8000 EFTUs.

In 1994, the Higher Education Quality Council of the United Kingdom established various quantitative criteria for institutions to be recognised as universities. These included a higher education student enrolment of at least 4000 FTEs, an enrolment of at least 3000 FTEs on degree level courses, and an enrolment of at least 300 FTEs in degree level programmes in each of five different academic subject categories. In South Africa, the Minister of Education recently determined that colleges of education with a student enrolment of less than 2000 FTEs would have to be incorporated into a university or technikon.

Research involvement of institutions

A goal of higher education is to contribute to the creation, dissemination and evaluation of new knowledge and to contribute towards finding new applications of knowledge. This is normally achieved through high-level intellectual enquiry and research. The generation of new knowledge and its evaluation is an activity subject to national and international norms and standards through the generally accepted mechanism of peer review. Involvement in research therefore makes heavy demands on higher education institutions with respect to the qualifications and quality of staff, research infrastructure, the quality and availability of post-graduate students, the quantity and quality of research outputs, etc. These requirements make it impossible for South Africa to sustain an adequately resourced extensive and high-level research capability and involvement at every higher education institution on an efficient and effective basis.

High-level research requires appropriately qualified staff. The ability of institutions to conduct high-level research is usually measured by the number of staff possessing doctorates - the doctorate serving as an indicator of being able to conduct independent research and supervise high-level research. The guidelines of the Australian Vice Chancellors Association (AVCC) state that to operate as a university, at least 25% of all academic staff should have a relevant doctorate and some research experience. An institution's high-level research ability is generally also measured in terms of the refereed research outputs of its academic staff members. The AVCC suggests an average of 0.5 refereed publications per annum per FTE academic staff member. Since research in higher education institutions also draws on post-graduate students, extensive and high-level research involvement would also require a sufficient FTE student enrolment at the masters and doctor's degree levels. In both the Australian and New Zealand systems, benchmark levels are set for such postgraduate enrolments.

It is useful to draw on the characteristics noted above. With appropriate modifications that are sensitive to conditions of the present South African higher education institutional landscape, they are used later in proposing what should be the key features that characterise institutions with different mandates. The question of the characteristics that should be used for social and educational reasons to promote the development of certain historically disadvantaged institutions is addressed in the following chapter.

Orientation and Focus

Having made the argument for differentiation and diversity, the Task Team recognises that there are two outcomes that must be avoided. The first is to spread all the purposes and functions of higher education so widely that the higher education system becomes characterised by homogeneity rather than differentiation and diversity. The second outcome is creating a new landscape that is, or is perceived as, characterised by 'poor quality' and 'high quality' institutions. A new differentiated system cannot produce ghetto and privileged institutions and also reproduce the apartheid institutional configuration.

The Task Team proposes that over a period of time and through an iterative process within the framework of the national and institutional planning processes, the country should strive to achieve institutions with the following broad mandates, predicated on principal orientation and core focus.

Institutions which constitute the bedrock of the higher education system

The future political, economic and social well-being of South Africa is crucially dependent on the quality of the first degrees and diplomas of graduates. To this effect, the country critically requires as the bedrock of its higher education system institutions that are dedicated to predominantly undergraduate teaching. Such institutions should constitute the foundation of the higher education system and also the great majority of institutions in South Africa. They should be well-resourced to undertake their vital responsibility of providing undergraduate programmes of high quality to the great majority of learners in the system and producing graduates with the knowledge, competencies and skills needed for economic and social development.

Institutions that focus on excellence in undergraduate teaching programmes are fundamental to any prosperous society but are also critical to the transformation of the current higher education system. They are crucial in ensuring equity and redress through increasing and widening participation based on appropriate admission requirements and quality and standards. Since these institutions will face the challenge of providing not simply access but also equity of opportunity on a large scale, they will have to be provided with resources to address the specific needs of under-prepared students through academic support and development initiatives.

The geographic location of these institutions must ensure that learners from both urban and rural areas are able to access higher education provision. Unlike under apartheid, when the remote rural location of some institutions imposed various limitations, location must now be put to use to strengthen equity and to contribute to both urban and rural development needs through appropriate community service programmes.

Such institutions would function as multi-purpose institutions operating across a broad range of learning areas. They should achieve pre-eminence in various undergraduate programmes, particularly those that are for specific professions and career-oriented. The vital role that the current technikons play in co-operative education and producing technically competent and skilled diplomates in a range of science, engineering and technology fields should be expanded and enhanced. In cases where institutions apply the practice of co-operative education, this should be valued and adequately resourced.

These institutions should also offer limited postgraduate programmes up to a taught masters level in alignment with their capabilities and institutional missions. Excellence in undergraduate learning and teaching would provide graduates access to the more extensive range of postgraduate teaching and research programmes of institutions with different mandates.

Institutional research focus should be largely on improving curriculum, learning and teaching and enhancing the quality of graduates. Academics with research capabilities will continue to have access to research funding through the science councils. Collaborative research relationships with academics from other institutions must be facilitated. In essence, the orientation and focus of such multi-purpose institutions would be, in alignment with the institutional mission, the provision of:

— Quality undergraduate programmes.

— Limited postgraduate programmes up to a taught masters level.

— Research related to curriculum, learning and teaching with a view to application.

'Constituting the class' in these institutions will entail special attention to the 'race' and gender of students, access for learners with disabilities and from working class and rural poor backgrounds, the incorporation of continuing education students and mature learners through flexible entry requirements, including the 'Recognition of Prior Learning'. Institutions with this orientation and focus must be encouraged to build strong links with the schooling system, further education and training institutions and the world of work. Equity of access and opportunity depends on working with schools and other institutions to ensure greater levels of academic preparedness on the part of learners for the demands of higher education and training.

Innovative partnerships with further education and training institutions could contribute to building a high quality SET sector and enable more students to enter higher education. They should be encouraged to give special attention to facilitating access for learners through recognition of prior learning initiatives and continuing education programmes. There should be a consolidation of the links that presently exist between the technikons and business and industry to ensure responsiveness to economic needs. There should also be a focus on local and regional development needs through partnerships with local and provincial governments, communities and trade unions.

In view of the earlier arguments concerning the academic and economic viability of institutions, institutions with such an orientation and focus should consist of at least 4000 FTEs. In addition, student enrolments should be spread over the three broad fields of study: humanities and the social sciences, commerce and SET and should not be highly concentrated in only one or two of these broad areas of study. Institutions wishing to have a strong technological learning orientation would need to have a minimum of 25% student enrolments in SET.

Many countries have institutions which play the role described above with distinction. Such institutions are regarded as highly prestigious in their own right because of their critically important contribution to meeting particular social and educational objectives.

Since these institutions are fundamental to the social needs of the country, they must be accorded their proper social value and their contributions duly acknowledged. To enable them to discharge their important social responsibilities they must be provided with the necessary resources to undertake academic support and development activities, promote quality improvements, reward excellence in teaching and become institutions of first choice for the vast majority of learners.

Comprehensive postgraduate and research institutions

Multi-purpose institutions with this mandate would, in terms of their orientation and focus, provide both undergraduate programmes as well as a comprehensive range of quality taught and research postgraduate programmes. Their social value would be to produce high-level graduates and knowledge producers and to ensure that in an environment of high levels of international competition between countries, South Africa maintains an appropriate degree of high-level research capabilities related to the production and application of new knowledge and technologies. At the same time, the capabilities must also be turned towards an engagement with the concrete economic and social development problems of South Africa, the Southern African region and the African continent.

No countries can institutionalise postgraduate teaching and high-level research in a comprehensive way in every one of its higher education institutions. The constraints of available human and financial resources preclude this and permit the development of only a limited number of institutions with such a mandate. There would need to be dedicated funding for postgraduate teaching and research. However, this will not necessarily be across the board for it cannot be assumed that postgraduate teaching and research capabilities will exist in every field and discipline at every institution. Institutions will be subject to accreditation processes and quality assurance procedures to access public funding.

In essence, the mandate of such multi-purpose institutions would be, in alignment with the institutional mission, the provision of:

— Quality undergraduate programmes.

— Comprehensive postgraduate taught and research programmes up to the doctoral level.

— Extensive research capabilities (basic, applied, strategic and developmental) across a broad range of areas.

In producing new generations of high-level knowledge producers of national and international standing, these institutions must be fully cognisant of the inherited social relations of knowledge production in South Africa that results in knowledge production being the preserve primarily of white and male South Africans. They must be held tightly accountable in ensuring that this pattern of knowledge production is eroded and transformed in all disciplines and fields through high-level education and training opportunities to expanding numbers of black and women South Africans.

In collectively offering a comprehensive range of taught and research postgraduate programmes, these institutions must also ensure that they produce increasing numbers of high-level black and women graduates that are equipped to occupy positions in the public and private sectors and academic positions in higher education institutions. Thus, they have the social responsibility of contributing to transforming the inequitable predominance of white and male South African as academics in research and development establishments and at senior levels in the private and public sectors.

Constituting the class will be a special challenge of these institutions if they are not to become the preserves of solely white and Indian students and students from upper middle-class and wealthy backgrounds. Serious attention will need to be given to access and opportunities for African and Coloured students, students from working class and rural poor families and adult learners.

Until conditions in schooling are considerably improved, these institutions will require resources for academic support and development initiatives in key fields, particularly in the broad areas of Natural Science, Engineering and Technology and Business and Commerce. They should also be encouraged to seek donor and private sector support in this regard.

These institutions have, especially at postgraduate levels, the potential to attract greater numbers of international students, particularly from sub-Saharan Africa and parts of Asia. The appropriate infrastructure should be put into place to promote the internationalisation of the student body. Such a process would be the yeast to enhance excellence in higher education as well as to mobilise extra resources. Long-term relationships promoted through higher education contact have proved to be invaluable in promoting life-long intellectual, social and economic collaboration.

To realise their potential and become integral elements of the national innovation system, such institutions would need to pursue strong partnerships with the science councils, private sector research and development establishments, industry, and continental and international academic and research institutions. Dense networks should be created through which there could be flows of academics, researchers and postgraduate students between higher education and other institutions. This would also enhance the potential of higher education institutions to contribute to the ongoing development of practising professionals.

These institutions must not be permitted to exist as islands with no connection to institutions with other mandates. Articulation mechanisms must enable students with the requisite qualifications from institutions with alternative mandates to enter these institutions. There should be funding incentives to promote research collaboration with academics from institutions with other mandates. Finally, academics based at institutions with different mandates that have recognised specialist expertise in particular disciplines and fields should have the opportunity for collaboration through research funds awarded on merit to them as individuals.

Diversity would be encouraged to obviate homogeneity. This should be reflected in specific institutional missions, undergraduate programme offerings, taught and research postgraduate offerings up to the doctoral level, a variety of community service and linkages with the external environment.

To ensure the academic and economic viability of these institutions, they should consist of at least 8 000 FTEs. In addition, student enrolments should be spread over the three broad fields of study in the following way: a minimum of 15% enrolments in Humanities and the

Social Sciences, 10% in Commerce and 25% in SET. Institutions wishing to have a strong technological learning orientation and be regarded as technological higher education institutions would need to have 50% of their enrolments in SET.

To achieve the research-related goals, a minimum of 10% of FTE enrolments should be at the masters and doctoral level. At least 40% of academic staff should have relevant doctorates. In addition, average annual research outputs per academic staff member should, in terms of the Department of Education's research output system, be not less than 0.5 units.

Extensive masters and selective doctoral institutions

Multi-purpose institutions with this mandate would, in terms of their orientation and focus, provide both quality undergraduate programmes, an extensive range of postgraduate programmes up to the masters level and selective doctoral programmes.

In essence, the orientation and focus of these multi-purpose institutions would be, in alignment with the institutional mission, the provision of:

— Quality undergraduate programmes.

— Extensive postgraduate taught and research programmes up to the masters level.

— Selective postgraduate taught and research programmes up to the doctoral level.

— Select areas of research (basic, applied, strategic and development).

A limited number of institutions with such an orientation and focus are necessary to prevent the overall system from becoming excessively rigid and to provide necessary flexibility. These institutions would share social purposes and roles and, thus, various characteristics with the institutions whose mandates have been defined above. For example, in common with institutions with mandates to function as predominantly undergraduate teaching institutions, academics with research capabilities at these institutions must continue to have access to research funding through the science councils and must be enabled to enter into collaborative relationships with academics from other institutions. Similarly, in common with institutions with mandates to function as comprehensive predominantly postgraduate institutions, there must be articulation mechanisms to enable students with the requisite qualifications from institutions with alternative mandates to enter these institutions. Moreover, funding incentives should exist to promote research collaboration with academics from institutions with other mandates.

However, in contrast with institutions with mandates to function as comprehensive postgraduate institutions, the responsibilities of these institutions, with respect to knowledge production, production of high-level knowledge producers and graduates for the academic and other professions, would be more limited in scope.

For reasons related to the academic and economic viability of these institutions, they should consist of at least 6000 FTEs. In addition, student enrolments should be spread over the three broad fields of study in the following way: 25% in the Humanities and the Social Sciences, 10% in Commerce and 15% in SET. Institutions wishing to have a strong technological learning orientation would have to have 30% of their student enrolments in SET.

In order to achieve the research related goals a minimum of 5% of FTE enrolments should be at the masters and doctoral level while at least 20% of academic staff should have doctorates. In addition, average annual research outputs per academic staff member should, in terms of the Department of Education's research output system, not be less than 0.20 units.

There would need to be a diversity in specific institutional missions, undergraduate programme offerings, taught and research postgraduate offerings up to the masters level, selective doctoral level programmes, basic and applied research, and community service and linkages with the external environment. This would obviate homogeneity. 'Constituting the class' at these institutions would entail considerations of a similar nature to that of institutions with comprehensive postgraduate mandates.

Distance education provision

There is debate around the usefulness of depicting provision as 'contact' and 'distance' and the dichotomy between 'contact' and 'distance' as modes of education delivery. It is suggested that while historically the distinction was useful and facilitated the establishment of innovative responses to education problems, it has outlived its usefulness. Reference is made to the wide diversity of practices within institutions that challenges the traditional dichotomy of 'distance' and 'contact' education. It is also argued that South Africa's traditionally contact institutions now evince a growing diversity of education - telematic education, flexible learning, reduced contact and mixed mode - that are all clustered under the catch-all phrase of 'distance' education.

Although these new initiatives all utilise 'distance' education strategies, it is difficult to categorise them as either 'contact' or 'distance' programmes. There could be a need to introduce the notion of a continuum of education provision for planning purposes. This continuum would have as two poles, provision purely at a distance and provision that is solely face-to-face. In reality, all education provision could increasingly exist somewhere on this continuum. The crucial issue is the nature of learning, and the social and educational value of a programme's content.

These developments are also related to the exponential growth of information and communication technologies, which have created opportunities for a variety of educational delivery strategies. These technologies should be harnessed to improve the quality, flexibility and cost effectiveness of provision. However, while these developments are largely positive, there are negative features that require some regulation. At the same time the costs of the new technologies should not be underestimated and their value must not be overstated.

Most of the programmes at traditionally contact institutions that make extensive use of distance education strategies are aimed at relatively small numbers of post-graduate students. This sometimes makes them expensive. Ways need to be explored of stimulating cooperation across these programmes especially where significant resources are needed for programme design and development. The large-scale programmes, which often achieve economies of scale, are in general confined to very few educational sectors, most notably nursing and teacher education.

In recent years, some institutions appear to have embarked on large-scale distance programmes primarily for financial gain. This has generated concern about the quality of provision. Some of these programmes do not appear to relate to the social or education goals of the country. Appropriate measures are now required that allow institutions to respond imaginatively to new demands and make use of innovative teaching and learning strategies, but at the same time ensure quality programmes and dispense with unnecessary duplication and inefficient use of precious resources.

The Task Team recognises that the current moratorium on the introduction of new distance education programmes by contact institutions which was imposed by the Minister has created uncertainty and has made institutional planning difficult. It therefore recommends that the Minister should lift the moratorium. However, the lifting of the moratorium should be linked to the development of a clear policy directive, including conditions and criteria, for the continued provision of large-scale distance education programmes by traditionally contact institutions. For example, the Department of Education could stipulate that to introduce any large-scale (say, more than 500 enrolments) distance learning programmes, institutions should prove that there is a demonstrated need for such a programme and that appropriate quality assurance mechanisms are in place. The Task Team recommends that the Higher Education Quality Committee (HEQC) give priority to the quality assurance of such large-scale predominately distance programmes.

The rationale for supporting South Africa's dedicated distance education provision remains. The Task Team is of the view that a single predominantly dedicated distance institution that provides innovative and quality programmes, especially at undergraduate level, is required for the country. The opportunities that the present distance education institutions have created for students in Africa and other part of the world must be maintained and expanded.

As a multi-purpose institution, a dedicated distance education institution would, in alignment with its institutional mission, provide:

— Quality undergraduate programmes of a predominantly distance nature.

— Extensive taught and research postgraduate programmes of a predominantly distance nature up to the masters level.

— Select taught and research postgraduate programmes of a predominantly distance nature up to the doctoral level.

The Task Team advises that the Minister should establish a Working Group to investigate integrating the current dedicated distance education institutions in South Africa and to provide recommendations by the end of June 2001.

Private higher education

The South African Constitution and the Higher Education Act of 1997 provide for private higher education. Appropriate legislation and regulations would enable private institutions to contribute to providing access to higher education of quality and to meet development needs, on their own or in responsible partnerships with South African public institutions. The accreditation and registration of providers will enhance quality provision and protect students.

The extensive demand for accreditation and registration as higher education providers has taxed the relatively new public bodies charged with these responsibilities. A crucial issue is the definition of 'provider'. The Task Team welcomes the proposed amendments to the Higher Education Act relating to private higher education. It also welcomes the impending issuing of regulations around the registration of private providers and future regulations around accreditation, once the HEQC is operational.

The numerous public institution-private institution partnerships have posed challenges with respect to accreditation of programmes and the registration of private providers. Some partnerships could have possible detrimental effects on other public institutions. The Task Team recommends that the moratorium that has been in place as of early 2000 with respect to new public-private partnerships should remain in place until investigations have been completed.

Private providers will in the main be single-purpose institutions. While they should be accredited and registered as such, it must be noted that a concentration by private providers on programmes with high economic returns could damage public institutions.

Private providers seeking to function as multi-purpose institutions with the mandates defined in 1), 2) and 3) above should be required to meet the set criteria for these institutions and also fulfil their social purposes, roles and goals. It is important that any measures applied to public institutions to ensure achievement of overall social and educational goals do not disadvantage public institutions vis-^-vis private institutions.

The proposed institutional landscape is essential to meet the socio-economic needs of South Africa. It enables institutions to focus on particular challenges and address specific needs. At the same time, higher education should also be able to deal with special needs and accommodate changes in the economic and social environment. Planning should be responsive to innovative ideas and initiatives that seek to extend access to higher education and equity, and make a meaningful contribution to economic and social development.

Apartheid generated a historical geography of higher education that resulted in an excessive concentration of institutions and provision in certain areas of the country and an absence of readily accessible contact provision in other areas. In view of this, the Task Team encourages the Minister to consider creative initiatives that may be advanced to accommodate needs in particular regions of the country, as may be the case with the Northern Cape and Mpumulanga provinces. The sustainability of new initiatives must be thoroughly investigated. Moreover, there should be no accession to any claims for provincial competencies in the area of higher education. In the interests of coherent and rational planning, higher education is and must remain an exclusively national competency.

Finally, a question posed in the Task Team was the terms that should be employed to designate institutions in a reconfigured system. The Task Team is of the view that all multi-purpose public and private institutions that satisfy the characteristics of at least 'bedrock' institutions should be permitted to use the term 'university' and qualifying terms appropriate to their missions.

Single purpose higher education institutions should be restricted to using the term 'college', or other relevant term, and qualifying terms appropriate to their missions. Institutions seeking to refer to themselves as 'technological universities' must meet the additional criterion of certain minimum student enrolments in the SET area of study.

Articulation

While differentiation and diversity must be a principal feature of a reconfigured higher education system, articulation mechanisms must exist to ensure that the system is also highly integrated. Indeed, the success of a differentiated and diverse system is dependent on structural integration. Articulation mechanisms cannot be of a solely voluntary and goodwill nature and dependent entirely on institutional partnerships. Articulation between institutions must be embedded features of, and must permeate, the entire system so that continuing education, life-long learning, horizontal and vertical mobility are all enhanced. The system of accreditation and quality assurance, the national qualification structure and national planning processes must overcome barriers and reinforce articulation.

Articulation must enable the horizontal and vertical mobility of students between institutions with different missions and mandates. It must also enable staff mobility for the purposes of teaching and research. Thus, academics that have recognised specialist expertise in particular disciplines and fields should have opportunities to teach and supervise students of, and at, other institutions. There should also be funding incentives to promote research collaboration between academics from institutions with different missions and mandates.

Not only must there be articulation within the higher education system but also between this system and schooling, further education and training, the world of work and other social sectors. Appropriate admission requirements and programme development should be pursued to enable access of adult and mature learners. Healthy partnerships should exist between higher education institutions and the Sector Education and Training Authorities (SETAs) to provide programmes that respond to the skills development needs of the country. As noted, institutions should also pursue strong partnerships with the science councils, private sector research and development establishments, industry, civil society institutions, local, provincial and national development structures and international academic and research institutions. Dense networks should be created through which there could be flows of knowledge and personnel between higher education and other institutions.

The Degree Structure

It is necessary to re-examine the current academic policy and qualification structure to ensure quality and equity and the overall integration of the system and to orient higher education to the changing knowledge environment.

Certain qualifications, such as the current traditional three-year degree programmes, could have limitations in responding to changing educational and socio-economic needs. In some disciplines, the three-year degree is being

questioned as an adequate terminal qualification for professional purposes. It is suggested that such qualifications do not provide an adequate foundation for the development of generic skills. Three years also makes it difficult for programme planners to reconcile the demands of outcomes based learning with the constraints imposed by available time.

In addition, the phenomenon of high attrition and problems in throughput and graduation rates are being ascribed partly to the nature of the three-year degree.

The Task Team proposes that provision should be made for the introduction of a four-year first bachelor's degree. The first two years of the four-year first bachelor's degree could provide for the development of required generic and foundation skills and include some broad discipline and multi-discipline based knowledge.

Years three and four of the degree could include a strong emphasis on single discipline and multi-discipline based specialisation, including an introduction to elementary forms of investigation and research methodology. The implication of and the relation between the four-year degree and the existing Honours qualification would need to be examined.

The desirability and feasibility of the four-year degree being established in a two-year plus two-year curriculum structure should be investigated. It has been suggested that a number of initial two-year programmes leading to an associate bachelor's degree could be developed which would have relevance for the world of work. Some learners may wish to exit with a qualification after two years of study. Others could opt to continue with the third and fourth specialisation years of the four-year bachelor's degree.

The extent to which a two-year plus two-year curriculum structure could be harnessed to also expand access of adult and mature learners to higher education and consolidate linkages between higher education and further education and training institutions should be examined.

The CHE's Academic Policy Task Team has been conducting work around a new academic policy and qualification structure. The CHE is also convening an initiative to formulate a 'Joint Implementation Plan' between the South African Qualifications Authority and all the relevant stakeholders for the coherent implementation of a National Qualification Framework within the higher education and training band.

The Task Team proposes that the CHE Academic Policy Task Team and the Joint Implementation Plan committee should examine alternative degree structures,

education could be achieved over the next 10-15 years. These could result from:

— Better school throughput rates relative to the low levels of the last three years.

— Efficiency gains as a result of improvements in the overall management and administration of institutions.

— Improvements in the quality of learning and teaching at institutions that reduce high repetition and low retention rates

— Focused strategies to increase the participation of Africans and Coloureds generally, and women in particular, in areas of study.

— Increasing the incorporation of continuing education students to a greater degree than at present.

— Recognition of 'Prior Learning' initiatives with increased intake of adult learners.

— The proposed review of the degree structure.

— Reduced wastage through students in good academic standing dropping out for financial reasons. It is particularly the upper levels of the working class and the lower middle class that are hard hit by the present means test cut off at R70 000 per year family income. Both the coverage and the size of student loans need to be significantly increased.

Overall, improvements will necessitate the targeted allocation of resources in particular areas such as the provision of access for equity, academic support and development, and management and administrative capacity building. The adequate remuneration of academics is also a critical factor in obtaining sustainable improvement in the academic arena. In the long term, the solution lies in making dramatic and far-reaching improvements to the quality of educational outcomes throughout the educational system.

South Africa is not focusing sufficiently on promoting its higher education system internationally. There is immense potential to attract students from the Southern African region, other parts of Africa and elsewhere without reducing efforts to expand access to South African students. An appropriate framework and infrastructure that draws in various relevant government departments should be created for this purpose and internationalisation should be promoted. International students must be specially catered for to ensure that they enjoy rewarding social and educational experiences. Enrolling students from the rest of Africa would be a means of contributing to their human resource development and giving expression to our commitment to African development and the African renaissance. It would also be a source of revenue for institutions and the country.

The issue of the size of higher education also raises the question of the number of institutions that are appropriate to the needs of the country. The present number of institutions is inextricably bound up with South Africa's apartheid past. In the view of the Task Team, for reasons presented in the following chapter, it is not possible to sustain the current number of institutions. However, the current capacity of the system needs to be retained and the Task Team therefore proposes that there should be no closure of institutions, or that this should be avoided. However, in the interests of a sustainable higher education landscape there is a need to reduce the absolute number of higher education institutions through the mechanism of combination. This issue is dealt with in the following Chapter.

CHAPTER 4

NATIONAL STEERING AND PLANNING TOWARDS RECONFIGURING THE HIGHER EDUCATION SYSTEM

The current landscape and institutional configuration of higher education has its roots in an apartheid past, is inadequate to meet socio-economic needs and is no longer sustainable. South Africa does not have the human and financial resources to maintain the present institutional configuration. Senior and middle-level leadership, management and administrative capacities are absent or lacking in parts of the system. New patterns in student enrolments mean that a number of institutions are at risk. Some institutions also do not satisfy the specifications for 'bedrock' institutions to continue as independent institutions. The goal of reconfiguration is to build a rational, coherent and integrated higher education system that strives for excellence and is oriented towards equity and the production of knowledge and high quality graduates.

National steering and detailed attention to change management is critical for the successful reconfiguration of the higher education system and the achievement of a differentiated and diverse system. In this chapter, the Task Team sets out the pre-conditions and requirements for the successful reconfiguration of the higher education system and institutions, the processes that should be followed and the time-frames that should be established for the various activities and processes. It also advances a number of recommendations on the size of the system in relation to the number of institutions, closures, combination and funding. Finally, it provides examples of possible combinations that could create a more rational and coherent higher education landscape and calls on the Minister to investigate more fully these as well as other possible combinations.

Key requirements for reconfiguring the system

Key strategic interventions will be required to reconfigure the higher education system and institutions and build a new landscape. These include:

— Developing effective national steering, planning and implementation capabilities.

— Developing institutional missions and strategic planning in alignment with institutional mandates.

— Combining institutions and restructuring them in alignment with their institutional mandates and missions.

— Rationalisation and inter-institutional collaboration at regional level.

— Building inter-institutional collaboration in strategic areas.

— Developing strategic planning capacities and education management information systems.

— Building financial planning capacities and systems.

— Enhancing the quality of learning and teaching.

— Expanding the use of information and communication technologies in learning and teaching.

— Developing student equity in select areas, staff equity and redress and institutional redress.

— Addressing the personnel implications of reconfiguration.

— Developing leadership, management and administrative capacities at all levels of the system.

— Engaging in periodic reviews of national planning and of the achievement of policy and planning objectives.

Without attention to these key interventions, the success of reconfiguration and the creation of a new higher education landscape could be compromised.

National steering and national and institutional planning will be essential to achieve the desired reconfiguration of the higher education system and ensure that the system and institutions are aligned with national policy goals. The key steering mechanisms that are available are national planning, funding and quality assurance. For various reasons, to date these have not been highly effective in moving the higher education system in the direction of differentiation and diversity. The Task Team has had to consider alternative strategies for reconfiguring the system and ensuring a differentiated and diversified, as well as an integrated and co-ordinated, system.

The Task Team's investigation and reconfiguration proposals are part of national planning and related to the development of a national plan to which the Minister of Education has committed himself. The reconfiguration of the system and institutions will enable the funding and quality assurance mechanisms to operate in more focused and effective ways and ultimately also to ensure that future national planning is more focused and manageable.

The national plan, apart from incorporating the issues of size and shape of higher education, should also encompass agreed upon performance agreements and targets for the national system and for individual institutions related to the equity, quality, effectiveness and efficiency challenges identified in chapter one. Concerning equity, the targets could be around the increased representation of black and women students in the Science, Engineering and Technology (SET) areas of study and their distribution in various fields. They could also be concerned with increasing access for mature learners. In terms of effectiveness, the targets could be related to increasing absolute numbers of students achieving first diplomas and degrees and the extent of community and industry partnerships. Efficiency targets could be set around increasing the proportion of students that successfully qualify without failing, repeating or dropping out and the more extensive use of physical infrastructure and facilities.

In developing a national plan it is crucial to recognise that under apartheid, institutions designated for black South Africans and the technikons were disadvantaged. There was uneven application of policies to higher education institutions. For example, the present subsidy formula was applied to the historically white universities since 1983 and to historically black universities only later. Similarly, there was an uneven application of the subsidy formula to technikons. Provision for more significant levels of research funding for technikons was only introduced in 1994. Technikons were only given the right to award degrees in 1993 and to implement degree programmes only in 1995. As a result, they have not yet been able to establish any extensive postgraduate and research capabilities, though good potential exists at a few institutions.

It is also clear that higher education institutions have interpreted the White Paper in widely divergent and sometimes even contradictory ways. As a result, institutional responses have in some cases placed institutions on trajectories that are at considerable variance with what should be their mandates in a reconfigured differentiated and diverse higher education system.

For both the above reasons, the specifications that were used in chapter three for establishing the mandates of institutions must be applied to the present South African higher education institutional landscape with circumspection and flexibility. It is important to maintain the specifications as the minimum requirements for defining mandates. Concomitantly, in a context where specific institutions were disadvantaged, a measure of flexibility in the application of the specifications is necessary for social and educational reasons. This would permit developmental trajectories to be created for institutions to enable them to undertake different mandates. In this way, a particular historically black university could, within a negotiated period, be supported to pursue a different mandate. In the same way, a specific technikon could also be supported to develop a different mandate - for example that of a technological institution with strong links to industry and with extensive postgraduate programmes to a masters level and select doctoral programmes especially in the 'hard' technology fields. The capacities and capabilities of institutions are not fixed. Within the constraints of resources they can be developed and serve vital social needs. The Task Team strongly recommends that this consideration must inform the national planning process, the combinations that are agreed upon and the reconfiguring of the higher education landscape.

There must also be great sensitivity to the employment implications of reconfiguring the system and of institutional combination. A Social Plan should be developed within a six-month period to serve as a framework for addressing various issues. These include:

- The commitments and interactions that would be required from the different social partners to ensure the success of reconfiguration.
- The human resource implications of reconfiguration and combination.

— Legal obligations in terms of the Labour Relations Act.

— Possible new opportunities for staff as a result of a reconfigured system.

— Measures to reduce or avoid retrenchments and alternatives to retrenchments.

— Time-frames for resolution of issues and decision-making.

— Adequate resources to give effect to the Social Plan.

The Social Plan should involve the Department of Education, institutions and organised labour. Its development could draw on expertise in the Department of Labour and other state departments and on the experience of business and labour in developing social plans to manage restructuring and change. Detailed discussions and negotiations on implementation would take place at institutional level, guided by the national framework of the Social Plan.

Public and donor funds will have to be mobilised to undertake the reconfiguration of the higher education system and institutions. In the light of the inefficiencies in the system, there is little hope at present of additional public funding for higher education. Indeed, retaining the current level of public funds may be a challenge. The Task Team, however, strongly recommends that the Minister strive to ensure that funding is retained at its present level, despite the declines in student enrolments. These savings, supplemented with the mobilisation of donor funds, should be earmarked for the key strategic interventions that are required to ensure the reconfiguration of the system.

Human resources will also be required for effective steering and careful planning and implementation at national, regional and institutional levels. Without the mobilisation of such resources, reconfiguration of the system and the achievement of a new institutional landscape will not be possible. With the best will in the world, with its current staff complement the Higher Education Branch of the Department of Education will be hard pressed to steer the reconfiguration of the system. It is vital that the Higher Education Branch is provided the necessary finances to mobilise specialist personnel.

The building of a higher education system that produces graduates and knowledge of high quality has been a strong theme of this Report. The Higher Education Quality Committee (HEQC) of the CHE has been accorded the responsibility of accrediting, monitoring and developing the quality of academic programmes and academic aspects of institutional performance. The successful reconfiguration of the system depends on it being provided the resources to discharge these vital responsibilities effectively.

Over time, funding, national and institutional planning and quality assurance mechanisms must become effective instruments for sustaining a differentiated, diverse and co-ordinated and integrated system and for responding to changing social needs. An indispensable asset would be an effective management information system, which maximally utilises information and communication technologies for the collection and presentation of information and data and for enabling greater public accessibility to such data. There must be regular review of the efficacy of various strategies and policy instruments and the overall performance and state of higher education. For this purpose, the CHE's Annual Report, its annual consultative conference, the CHE Achievement of Policy Objectives Task Team and other mechanisms must be utilised effectively.

Processes for Reconfiguration

The Minister is advised to begin a process of consultations with key national stakeholders on the Task Team's proposals on the reconfiguration of the higher education system. An iterative process that involves the Department of Education and individual higher education institutions should follow these consultations. The purpose of the iterative process should be to establish the mandate of the institution and, where relevant, finalise institutional combination. The matter of institutional combination will, of course, also necessitate inter-institutional discussions. All these processes should inform the production of a national plan by the Department of Education.

Once the national plan is finalised and, in terms of the law, the CHE has advised the Minister on the plan, the process of combining institutions should be initiated and all institutions should be required to develop missions according to the new mandates defined out of the process of dialogue.

The approval of mandates and the development of institutional missions and strategic plans must be informed by high levels of realism. The goals and purposes of higher education, national and regional needs, as well as the specific histories, geographical location, key academic and other characteristics and capacities and potential capabilities of each institution must be taken into account. Collectively, the missions and strategies of institutions must strive to build public confidence and the credibility of the higher education system. They must also enable it to produce high quality educational outcomes and address the socio-economic needs of South Africa. Institutional combination must not be viewed as a threat but as an opportunity to re-orient and revitalise higher education in pursuit of important social and educational goals. However, the combination of institutions - whether through mergers or other mechanisms - will be demanding processes. Open and frank discussions and iterative planning involving institutional leaderships and the Department of Education, the commitment of institutions and purposeful action are key to success. In undertaking combinations, serious attention must be given to a number of issues. These include:

— Appropriate structures with the necessary financial resources and human resources to steer the combination.

— Institutional involvement in identifying the strengths and weaknesses and the advantages and disadvantages of combination, and in maximising the opportunities afforded by combination.

— Planning in an atmosphere of openness and integrity with the engagement of all the principal actors.

— Strategic planning processes and detailed action plans with clear and explicit goals and outcomes, planning phases and realistic time-frames.

— Sensitivity to human resource issues and careful attention to labour relations regulations and the rights and obligations of all parties.

— Using financial and other instruments as 'pulleys and levers'.

Time-Frames

A reconfigured system will not be realised overnight. Clear, explicit and realistic time-frames must be established for the processes and activities highlighted above. They are:

— Consultations around the reconfiguration proposals.

— An iterative process around institutional mandates and missions.

— The development of a national plan.

— Combinations and the development of institutional missions and concomitant strategic plans.

The first three activities are likely to require a minimum of six months. The final activity, especially where it involves combinations, could require between one and three years. It will not be possible to address every dimension of reconfiguration and pursue all the combinations at once. Implementation must be carefully planned and rolled out over a number of phases which combine goals, strategies and human and financial resources. Overall, a new higher education landscape with the qualities that are desired is likely to take a decade to achieve. Available human and financial resources will unavoidably shape the pace of reconfiguration.

Responsibilities

The implementation of the national plan is the responsibility of the Department of Education. It will require the full support and co-operation of institutions and key stakeholders. The implementation of institutional missions and plans is the responsibility of the council and management of an institution.

The Department of Education must effectively monitor progress towards achievement of the performance agreements and targets. As the Minister is required to consult with the CHE on the national plan, the CHE must also regularly assess progress around the national plan so that it is able to advise the Minister appropriately.

Funding

Once there is agreement on the reconfiguration of the system, it should be possible for the Department of Education without too much delay to produce a new funding dispensation and formula as proposed by the White Paper. Funding must enable the system and institutions to pursue the social and educational goals and targets that are defined in the White Paper and the national plan. It must ensure that institutions are provided adequate resources to effectively discharge their mandates and missions. It must also enable institutional redress that is appropriate to the mandates and missions of institutions.

The Task Team recommends to the Minister that there should no longer be a 'blind' research funding component but that research should be funded through earmarked funding. Such earmarked funds should make provision for dedicated research and development work related to curriculum, learning and teaching and provide incentives for research collaboration between academics based at institutions with different mandates. They should also support new academics for a set period and build capabilities at certain institutions placed on a developmental trajectory for reasons of social need and redress. The move towards earmarked research funding could result in shortfalls in public funds allocated to some institutions. In the short term, institutions would need to be cushioned from any dramatic reduction in their overall public funding.

Critical to providing access to greater numbers of black learners, to black and women learners in particular areas of study, and to learners from working class and rural poor backgrounds is expanding the coverage and level of student financial aid and making resources available for academic support and development initiatives. Such initiatives are central to creating equity of opportunity as well as improving the quality of graduate outputs. Efficiency gains that result from developing a more rational, coherent, co-ordinated and efficient system should be used to expand access and reinforce equity and quality.

Institutional combination

It is vital that a reconfigured higher education system be sustainable. This requires an effective regulatory framework. It also entails state funding of the public sector and the more efficient and effective use of scarce public resources. For this and other reasons indicated at the beginning of this chapter, the Task Team recommends reducing the absolute number of higher education institutions. This does not necessarily imply closing institutions and the concomitant sale or scrapping of buildings, facilities and plant, and retrenchment of staff, although Section 25 of the Higher Education Act makes provision for closure of institutions. The Task Team recommends that there should be no closures.

The Task Team instead recommends reducing the present number of institutions through combining institutions. Savings should result from an increase in size of the institutions with reduction of unit costs. Further benefits will accrue through the elimination of unnecessary duplication and rationalisation of programmes. The possibility of cross-subsidising programmes will be enhanced. Reducing the number of institutions should also realise cost benefits by reducing the numbers of councils and senior management and administrative teams that would be required

Combination is not an end in itself; it is a means towards the achievement of social and educational goals. In South Africa, these goals relate to:

— Overcoming apartheid fragmentation and the historical character and geography of institutions.

— Improving access for learners, particularly for blacks, women and learners from working class and rural poor backgrounds.

— Improvements in the quality of outputs of the higher education system and institutions.

— Improvements in student and staff equity overall, and in specific areas of the system.

— Increasing the effectiveness of the system and institutions with regard to mandates and missions.

— Increasing the efficiency (including administrative and financial) of the system and institutions.

— Ensuring a geographic distribution of institutions that best serves socio-economic needs.

— Ensuring greater levels of collaboration among higher education institutions, particularly on a regional basis.

— Ensuring a sustainable system and viable and sustainable institutions with capabilities to pursue their particular mandates and missions.

Legislative framework

The legislative basis for combination is provided for by the Higher Education Act of 1997. Section 23 of the Act states that

> ...the Minister may, after consulting the Council on Higher Education (CHE) and by notice in the

> Gazette, merge two or more public higher education institutions into a single public higher education institution [Section 23 (1)].

Section 23 also outlines the process that must be followed by the Minister to effect mergers. Section 24 provides for the 'merger of subdivisions of higher education institutions'. Section 38 of the Act makes provision for institutions to co-operate to enable the optimal use of resources in the performance of their functions, and to establish regional structures in the interest of such co-operation. It also refers to the possibility of financial incentives to encourage such co-operation. The White Paper states:

> ...emphasis will be placed on regional reviews of institutional plans as an integral part of the national planning process. This will be intended to promote regional co-ordination and collaboration as part of the national plan to enhance articulation of programmes, mobility of learners between institutions, the sharing of resources, including scarce academic staff, library and information facilities. It is also intended to reduce programme duplication and overlap. The Ministry will provide incentives to encourage and facilitate regional planning and co-ordination.

It also says:

> Incentive funding will be available on a selective basis to support the costs involved in regional collaboration among institutions which aim to consolidate, merge, share or otherwise collectively improve the efficient use of their facilities and resources for training, teaching, research or community service.

There must also be sensitivity to the historical contributions of institutions to the democratisation of South Africa, the identities and cultures of particular institutions and the language policies and medium of instruction of institutions. The characteristics (minimum student FTEs, distribution of enrolments across the three broad areas of study, staff qualifications and research outputs, etc.) that institutions should need to satisfy should be a further consideration when approaching combination. Finally, in considering combinations, the missions and orientations of institutions, their strengths and real capabilities, the existence of synergy and the prospects of creating robust new institutions should be taken into account.

Chapter three specified the key characteristics that should define institutions with different mandates. If these characteristics are employed in relation to the present 36 institutions, the following scenario prevails. Firstly, six institutions, all historically black universities and technikons, do not qualify as independent institutions. This is mainly a consequence of them having less than 4000 FTEs. For them to function as 'bedrock' institutions or to serve other mandates they would need to be combined with other institutions. The Medical University of Southern Africa also does not achieve the status of an independent institution because of its single-purpose function.

Secondly, the vast majority of institutions (19) have the characteristics that define 'bedrock' institutions. These are predominantly the technikons and historically black universities, though they include a few historically white universities. All the distance institutions, either because of their spread of students over the three broad study areas, or for other reasons also have the characteristics of 'bedrock' institutions.

Thirdly, a handful of institutions, all historically white universities, meet the characteristics of comprehensive postgraduate institutions. Fourthly, six institutions fulfil the characteristics of extensive postgraduate institutions with select doctoral level programmes. These include historically black and historically white universities.

Earlier in this chapter it was argued that the characteristics that should define the different mandates of institutions must be used in a manner that is sensitive to the distortions of apartheid planning and the nature of the responses of some institutions to the White Paper. It was also stated that the mandates of institutions should be the subject of an iterative planning process between the Minister and individual institutions.

The Task Team believes that combination offers the opportunity for different outcomes than the ones that are a legacy of apartheid, and the prospect of developing a new higher education landscape. Combination of institutions is also unavoidable and necessary for other reasons, which were advanced earlier. Appropriate combinations will significantly advance the reconstruction of the higher education system in South Africa and enhance the possibilities of achieving social goals. In particular regions, combination will ensure greater levels of collaboration among higher education institutions, reduce unnecessary duplication, promote greater efficiency in the use of resources, and respond to regional and local needs. Appropriate combinations would allow institutions to build on their strengths, help to develop new identities and cultures and contribute to the public legitimacy of higher education institutions as part of a new rational and coherent national system.

The Task Team had insufficient time to analyse in detail the institutional plans of every university and technikon and arrive at clear and explicit recommendations on combinations of institutions. However, drawing on some work around the institutional plans of universities and technikons and on various reports, the Task Team illustrates below some possible combinations for the purpose of demonstrating briefly the objectives that could be served by combination. The examples have a regional focus because of the emphasis of the White Paper on the promotion of 'regional co-ordination and collaboration' and on' regional reviews of institutional plans as an integral part of the national planning process'. The Minister may want to investigate in greater detail the possible combinations that are exemplified below. The Task Team, however, strongly recommends that the Minister should investigate the full range of possibilities for combinations, and should also be open to compelling combination possibilities that may emerge from the iterative national planning process.

The Task Team is united in the view that no public institution should believe that it is exempted from combination, from the need to change fundamentally and from contributing to the achievement of a new higher education landscape. The historically advantaged institutions, in particular, cannot assume that their track records with respect to equity, quality, social responsiveness and effectiveness and efficiency are beyond dispute and self-evident. Much remains to be achieved by all institutions to advance new social goals. There should be no room for complacency.

Bibliography

Billington, D. D. (1989, March). *The role of education in stimulating human development.* Paper presented at the annual conference of the Western College Reading and Learning Association, Seattle.

Billington, D. D. (1990). *Developmental aspects of adult education: A comparison of traditional and nontraditional self-directed learning programs.* Journal of Continuing Higher Education, 38(1), 31-38.

Brennan J., Kogan M. and Teichler U., (eds.), *Higher Education and Work,* Jessica Kingsley, London, 1996.

Brockett, R. (1983, April). *Self-directed learning and the hard-to-reach adult. Lifelong Learning*: The Adult Years, pp.16-17.

Brockett, R. G. & Hiemstra, R. (1985). *Bridging the theory-practice gap in self-directed learning.* In S. Brookfield (Ed.), Self-directed learning: From theory to practice (pp. 31-40). San Francisco: Jossey-Bass Publishers.

Brookfield, S. (1985). *Self-directed learning: A critical review of research.* In S. Brookfield (Ed.), Self-directed learning: From theory to practice (pp. 5-16). San Francisco: Jossey-Bass Publishers.

Carnevale, A. P. (1991). *America and the new economy: How new competitive standards are radically changing American workplaces,* (p. 134). San Francisco: Jossey-Bass.

Chong, Ng S.T., *Higher Education over the Internet : Dawn of the*

Virtual University, Tokyo, Regional Conference on Higher Education, 1997.

Cook, D. (1993). *Adult education* [class lecture]. Kent, OH: Kent State University.

Fisher, J. C. (1988). *Impact of anomia and life satisfaction on older adult learners*. Educational Gerontology, 14, 137.

Galbraith, M.W. (1994). *Connecting instructional principles to self-esteem. Adult Learning*, 5(3), 24.

Herbeson, E. (1991). *Self-directed learning and level of education*. Australian Journal of Adult and Community Education, 31(3), 196-201.

Higher Education: The Challenges of Change for Graduate Employment, Proceedings of the 5th UNESCO/NGO Consultation on Higher Education, Paris, February 1997.

Knowles, M. (1975). *Self-directed learning: A guide for learners and teachers*. New York: Association Press.

Knowles, M. (1990). *The adult learner: A neglected species* (rev. ed.). Houston: Gulf Publishing.

McCabe, D., Trevino, L. K., & Butterfield, K. D., *Academic integrity in honor code and non-honor code environments: A qualitative investigation*, Journal of Higher Education, 70, 2, 211-234, 1999.

Teichler, U., *Lifelong learning as challenge for higher education: The state of knowledge and future research tasks*. Higher Education Management, 11, 1, 37-53, 1999.

UNESCO, *Higher Education: Capacity-building for the 21st Century*, Proceedings of the 4th UNESCO-NGO Collective Consultation on Higher Education, Paris, 1994

UNESCO, *Declaration on Higher Education in Asia and the Pacific*, Tokyo, Japan, July 1997.

UNESCO, *Declaration on Higher Education in the Arab States for the XXIst Century*, Beirut, Lebanon, March 1998.

Index